THIS HOME WAS NEVER MINE

NIVELL RAYDA

LagimA
books

Nivell Rayda
This Home Was Never Mine

Nivell Rayda has been a journalist for 12 years, specializing in legal and human rights issues. His award-winning stories have appeared in The Jakarta Globe, Asia Sentinel, Global Integrity and various other local and international newspapers, magazines and literary anthologies. This is his first book.

FOREWORD

I remember feeling quite nervous when I set foot in Transito, a disused government complex at the edge of Lombok, Indonesia, converted to host about a hundred refugees, victims of one religiously charged attack after another, people who were driven from the land of their ancestors, all because they observed a different interpretation of Islam.

The reason for my nervousness was that I didn't have an outline. I wasn't sure that their stories were worth retelling. The voice recorder I was using was borrowed from a friend. I didn't have a lot of money to do my research. Had the plan failed I didn't know how I could finance another project.

When I arrived in August 2013, they have been living as outcasts for 11 years. They were quite used to having journalists around. But I wasn't interested in a spot news story or even a comprehensive news feature or analysis. I want to write a book about them. I need to know how they got there. To know what made them endured years of discrimination. What shaped their decisions to stay true to their religion. And to do that, I need to know their darkest secrets. Things they only shared with those closest to them. I wasn't sure how they would react.

I was planning to meet a woman named Faizah, a woman I'd interviewed very briefly two years before. I didn't make an appointment. I didn't keep her number. I wasn't sure she would remember me. I didn't even know whether she still lived in Transito or not.

The thing about Faizah that fascinated me was the fact that she was attacked three times. She had lost everything in each one. The first time I met her, she was sharing a three-by-four-meter space, partitioned from the rest with bamboo poles and old pieces of cloth, with her two boys, her mother, her father, her two brothers and a differently abled sister, whom I had mistaken two years earlier as her daughter.

I had planned to base my story on Faizah and her alone. As backup plans, I thought of doing a fiction loosely based on Faizah or interview each and everyone at Transito. But luck intervened. I discovered that Faizah had brothers and sisters with equally fascinating stories. Faizah was the third of nine children. They each had very different characters, and as I dug deeper, I realized their stories intertwined and shaped each other's lives.

So it is important for me to stay true, retell their stories as faithfully and as accurately as possible. I felt they deserved nothing less, for they have been vilified by those waging war against them, out to spill their blood, and the unsympathetic government that neglected them. Meanwhile, academics and human rights groups see them as statistics, as clients and victims in a narrow legal perspective.

The human perspective of the people of Transito is a narrative so few have heard. I felt no need to dissect these people in an academic and analytical perspective. I don't want to get trapped in a religious discussion of which faith is right and which is wrong. This is a story about a family whose lives are shaped by tragedies. Human beings with human needs and human wants. A story of selfishness and resentment, but also of sacrifice and love.

If I were to write a fiction, it would be impossible for readers to understand what happened, the reason behind their decisions and, above all, how they are not much different from the rest of us. It would also be impossible for readers to be able to visit Transito, see what remain of their homes in Ketapang.

Fact, as they say, is stranger than fiction. If I were to write a fiction, I don't think I could have come up with a better story. It wouldn't occur to me that a man would try to bribe his brother's wife into leaving her religion. That a timid son could emerge as a brave leader after a series of attacks. Or write about how a reckless man could risk his own life trying to reach Australia by sea in pursuit of a far-fetched dream, yet at the same time neglecting his own wife and children.

But I soon realize that it was no easy feat. Even after hundreds of hours of recording, dozens of people interviewed, thousands of photographs taken, piles of research materials and references gathered, retelling a story that happened years ago proved to be a monumental task. Everyone has their own version of the truth, often with slight modifications and subtle variations to impress, to hide embarrassing details or to compensate for the limitations of the human brain. Even when I tried asking the same person about the same event again and again. Some events were so traumatizing to some people that they had little recollection of what happened. Sometimes small details were lost in translation. The words were originally told in Sasak, retold to me in interviews in Bahasa Indonesia, and are finally presented in this book in English.

The limitations forced me to focus on what they might have said, might have done and what they might have thought, without sacrificing accuracy or allowing my imagination to run free without some basis in historical fact. In a way, they are my version of the truth, my own interpretation and analysis of what happened. Like paintings instead of photographs. Like biopics instead of documentaries. A book that is engaging and can accommodate the author's artistic expressions instead of a lifeless transcript of interviews.

THIS HOME WAS NEVER MINE

CHAPTER 1

The room was left quiet. The guests bewildered. Some thought he was talking in his sleep, delirious. No one was sure what he meant. They whispered to each other to confirm what they thought they heard. They assured each other that they heard the same thing.

'Aaaayyyy.... In three days there will be chaos,' the old man Nafsiah said just seconds before. His voice a high pitched growl, like a man dehydrated. The words were loud but all his missing teeth had turned the words borderline intelligible.

It was, as things unfolded, a prophecy. A warning that their lives would never be the same again.

Nafsiah sat with legs outstretched on a plastic mat. It covered just about half his living room, laid down to welcome the guests, old friends he had not seen in ages. The house was small just 6 by 6 meters with un-plastered, lime and sand brick walls. The floor was a solid concrete made to smooth using cement screed but wear and age had left it infested with holes, chips and cracks. The roof was a web of planks, beams and asbestos, still used in many peasant homes in villages across Indonesia, with no ceiling to keep the poisonous dust from falling.

The house sat on a 100 square meter property, just right at the edge of a small hill surrounded by farms and rice fields in a neighborhood named Montong Gamang. Overtime the fields in Montong Gamang were transformed into houses, offices and shops as the nearby town of Pancor grew. Pancor is a barren part of an already barren island of Lombok, an inverted egg-shaped volcanic island just east of Bali with the Sekotong peninsula protruding southwest into the Bali Sea.

Tobacco proved to be the perfect crop for the eastern part of Lombok, covered in volcanic ash with an elevation of 300 to 600 meter above sea level. Tobacco had become one of Pancor's biggest exports, second only to migrant workers who would become construction and plantation laborers and housemaids in more developed countries like Malaysia and Brunei. Nafsiah did not get his hands in the two lucrative industries. Working abroad would keep him away from his families. Tobacco, he believed, are poison. His first born, Sarapudin did not share his vision and worked as a tobacco farmer.

Nasipudin was Nafsiah's second son and the favorite of his seven children. A humble rice farmer like himself, Nasipudin was a hard working and honest man. Through years of backbreaking labor Nasipudin collected enough money to buy himself and his parents some land of their own. But the main reason why Nafsiah loved Nasipudin so much was because like him, he was an Ahmadiyya. It was Nasipudin who introduced him to Ahmadiyya, a faith he so dearly observed ever since. Nasipudin also asked his brothers and sisters to join. His eldest brother Sarapudin later went and married a non-Ahmadiyya woman and converted. Nafsiah's fourth son Slamet also left Ahmdiyya.

Earlier that morning, people had gathered for an Ijtima Anshar where Ahmadiyya men his age, some hailing from hundreds of kilometers away, get together every year for three days of sport matches, games, quizzes and religious discussions. Two of Nafsiah's seven children, Sarapudin and Slamet, who were not Ahmadis, did not join despite living just meters away.

Nafsiah had always looked forward to 2002, the year when the gathering was staged in his hometown Pancor. But when the year came, he was too ill to participate. He had been a diabetic for years and the condition had paved the way for peripheral edema where fluids collect in one's feet, ankles and legs.

Nafsiah was a skinny and petite man but his legs were the same size of an elephant trunk. His toes began to darken from infection and all over his soft, brown skin were black spots and marks which grew larger with each passing day. Standing up had been a struggle for Nafsiah, let alone to travel to the venue, two kilometers away in downtown Pancor.

Some friends had the idea of bringing the festivities to him. Nafsiah had always loved a good company and he was always hungry for stories and so they turned the ground in front of his home into a colorful jumble of shoes and sandals right after the sun had set.

Nafsiah was mostly quiet as the rest shared stories of the day and laughed. He was busy giving his legs a good rubbing. He was slipping in and out of his sleep, a change in his sugar level had made him drowsy. At one point he must have dreamt, perhaps of his wife who died giving birth to the couple's last child Maskanah. He had been raising his sons and daughters alone, until one by one they got married. And years later, it was their turn to care for their father.

It was the last thing anyone expected to hear. Nafsiah had been largely quiet throughout the night, giving very little response when people asked him questions and solicited opinions. They were chatting about other things and then came the very strange remarks for the elderly man. "In three days there will be chaos."

No one knew exactly how old Nafsiah really was but most agreed he was at least 70 years old. Education and access to healthcare were still luxuries when he was born and not many people knew how to read and write and so birthdates were mere guesses just like many rural families in Indonesia. From stories told by his parents, aunties and uncles, Nafsiah was circumcised around the time when the Japanese army first drove away their Dutch masters and landlords in 1942. Another story suggests he was in his teens and was able to pick up arms when Indonesia proclaimed independence in 1945.

Nafsiah grew up in a time when legends and mythologies are held as true, when fantastic and magical stories of men with the gift of foresight, flight, invincibility were believed to be more than tall tales. It was a time when Islam, despite being the religion of Lombok's majority, still intertwined with the supernatural, the shamanistic and the otherworldly.

He left behind the ways of the old when he became one of the first persons in Lombok to join Ahmadiyya in 1972. He followed in strict adherence to teachings of its founder, a man professed to be the promised Muslim Messiah, the Imam Mahdi, sent at the beginning of the end of days. A man accused of blasphemy by people practicing more mainstream forms of Islam. A man named Mirza Ghulam Ahmad.

Ahmadiyya taught its followers to be humble, to be compassionate, to entrust their fate in the hands of God, to persevere amidst oppression, to pray for those wishing them harm, to smile in the face of hardship, to detach themselves from earthly possessions. Nafsiah, who was a Muslim but never prayed, claimed to be upholding God's command but never bothered to study the Koran, emerged as a changed man. 'A source of vanity which will lead us astray ' Nafsiah would often say of the ancient magical skills.

But remnants of the old wisdoms remained. They were engrained to the back of his head. Now in his elderly, sick days they slowly returned like flashbacks of suppressed memories. He could sense an imminent threat was brewing, like a storm slowly gathering force. He could feel it at the back of his neck, at the pit of his stomach.

There were earthly signs too, somehow oblivious to his Ahmadi friends. Recent arrivals to Pancor included Ahmadiyya families violently driven from their homes in Sambielen village up north. Four homes and a mushalla (prayer house) had been ransacked and reduced to rubbles on June 22, 2001. A man named Hasan was fatally slashed, stabbed and beaten with his wife Ruqiah watching. Ruqiah tried to stop the murder but got stabbed herself in the process. She survived by pretending to faint. For more than a year, nine Ahmadiyya families from Sambielen had been living in limbo, driven from one village to the next.

Nafsiah must have thought about the atrocities in Sambielen often and felt that the persecution would spread and eventually reach here in Pancor. The conclusion was not without reason. Pancor and the adjoining town of Selong was once the center of Lombok's most powerful Islamic kingdom, Selaparang.

Centuries after Selaparang's reign ended a direct descendant of its kings, a small, skinny, elderly man with bushy, white eyebrows named Zainudin Abdul Majid founded the Nahdlatul Wathan. It became Lombok's biggest, most powerful and most influential Muslim organization with Pancor as its base. He would later assume the name Tuan Guru Bajang. He would build a thousand mosques and a thousand madrasahs (Islamic boarding school). He would have millions of followers, adhering without question to everything their religious leaders say.

Ahmadis in Lombok just numbered 3,000 in an island of 2.7 million. They were never a threat to Nahdlatul Wathan's enormous power of 2 million strong. But the presence of a few people following the teachings of a man accused of blasphemy, a self proclaimed Messiah from India, here in Pancor was a disgrace. It was unacceptable.

Since the time of the kings, centuries ago, religion was used by Selaparang as an excuse to fight its rival Hindu kingdom Cakranegara. And now, in the times of the Tuan Gurus and high clerics, religion would be used again to muster influence and control by instilling fear and hatred. It would break families apart, force Sasak people to kill another Sasak, Indonesians hating another Indonesian, humans feasting on the blood of another human all in the name of religion.

Tuan Guru Bajang died in 1997 but not his rhetoric. 'God commands the blood of the Ahmadiyya people to spill,' he would often say. In his living years he couldn't cry for an open attack. The country was still governed by a ruthless military regime at the time. It had a firm grip in all levels and aspects of civilian lives. Divisive issue such as religious intolerance was seen as a threat to stability and ultimately to the military's absolute rule. In 1998, this regime was toppled and a series of weak governments would lead to the rise of the hard-liners, the intolerants, the religious fanatics and the militants.

Five years after Tuan Guru Bajang's death, his followers had dominated Lombok's political landscape. They became politicians, administrative leaders and senior public officials. They took Tuan Guru Bajang's anti-Ahmadiyya rhetoric and amplified it. What started as harmless instances of taunting, name calling and friction soon became serious cases of discrimination, mistreatment, violence and killing.

Nafsiah sensed that Sambielen was only the beginning and an even bigger violence was upon them with Pancor its venue. The Nahdlatul Wathan had recently invited clerics from Pakistan, where Ahmadis were constantly massacred and systematically persecuted. They also invited religious leaders from Saudi Arabia which had outlawed and banished Ahmadiyya completely.

There were secret discussions and meetings about imposing the same tactics here. There were pamphlets spreading fear and suspicions towards the Ahmadis. Parents were told to keep their children from playing with their Ahmadi friends.

There were copies of a badly-written, poorly-researched, unbalanced article which ran on an ultra-conservative publication about how Ahmadiyya defied one of Islam's most fundamental tenants: Muhammad as the final Muslim prophet. The article detailed how Muslim caliphates destroyed and killed self proclaiming prophets and messiahs and how they butchered and persecuted their followers. Each copy had a later-added note: 'Will the people of Pancor do nothing?' A day after the publication spread, mosques across Pancor simultaneously chose Ahmadiyya and the obligation to wage war against the group as topics for their Friday sermons.

Nafsiah's warning was made a day after the sermons. Although the guests had heard about the sermons from friends and acquaintances, watched how people began treating them differently, they chose not to take them seriously.

Nafsiah could barely walk and never set foot outside. These facts would come to him as stories from friends and families. His son Nasipudin had his cattle stolen, his bathroom's water container drained. He heard stories of his young grandchildren, still in elementary school, were being pelted with cow manure by a fully grown man while passing his rice field.

After a long awkward pause the guests resumed their chatter, discussing about preparations for the following day, the last day of Ijtima Anshar. Nafsiah would never speak another word since.

The clock showed it was 9 p.m. The women were busy preparing food for the guests at tomorrow's farewell gathering. The food was to be repurposed for a funeral, Nafsiah's.

At 11 p.m. when the guests had left, when Nafsiah's son Nasipudin and his nine children had returned to their home, when Nasipudin's sisters and brothers were not looking, leaving Nafsiah alone in the living room unattended, Nafsiah took his last breath and died. Joining his long deceased wife.

CHAPTER 2

The sun slowly rose, illuminating Nasipudin's home. To the east was a housing complex, resting at the foot of the hill built by a property developer some 12 years back. The houses were basic, small and uniformed but with well manicured lawns, flowers and trees. They were professionally built with iron gates and a garage big enough to fit a single car, a luxury in a small town like Pancor.

Further east, the road joined a busy street, where public minivans and ojek (motorcycle taxis) would await passengers to take them to the town center where homes, markets, shops, hospitals, offices and banks were painted in fluorescent yellow, lime green and bubblegum pink as if they were colored using food dyes. More tasteful owners painted their buildings in deep blue, crimson red and indigo violet, the colors of gift wrappers.

A small road connected the housing complex to a neighborhood of peasants and underpaid laborers rising 15 meter high on top of a hill. There lies Montong Gamang. A place where Nasipudin, his children and their children called home.

Their houses were rustic and small, some made of concrete and bricks while others from bamboo and wood covered in dry straws and banana leaves. The houses were tightly spaced and separated by labyrinthine alleyways and dirt paths snaking haphazardly in all directions.

Nasipudin woke. A gentle breeze must have blown, sending a cool, refreshing air. Last night, he was a son. That morning, he was a 50 year-old Ahmadiyya leader in his neighborhood. The rice fields behind his home cast a yellow glow and the stream sparkled as the sunrise gently touched its surface.

Nasipudin and five of his children lived in a six by nine meter house surrounded by houses of his three oldest children and their families. The latest addition to the modest cluster of homes was a small house built for Faizah the third of Nasipudin's nine children. She moved there with her husband, Guntur when they got married a month ago.

Faizah was a bubbly woman of 22 who was full of life. She was smart, friendly and sociable while her husband was the complete opposite: quiet, reserved. Guntur came from Sumbawa, another island which along with Lombok would make up the West Nusa Tenggara province.

Guntur was born not as an Ahmadi but became interested in the group's spirituality and manner. He came to their mosque one day asking to be converted and marry an Ahmadi woman. An Ahmadi cleric played the role of a matchmaker. Nasipudin agreed to have Faizah wed to this recent convert he had never met, to his wife Zubaidah's objection.

Zubaidah was a loving and protective mother. She would often worry whenever her children got married and started their own family.

Khaerudin, the first child, was an exception. A mild-mannered, obedient son, he had successfully run his own shop for two years when he decided to marry in 1998 to an Ahmadi woman from Sambielen. The woman was just 18 at the time and called herself Suryani. She was shy and bashful. A year later they had a son named Hafidz.

Nurul, the second child, was the first to taste her mother's wrath. In 1997, she was the first of Nasipudin's nine children to marry to a childhood friend named Tohir. The marriage only lasted two years because despite their best effort they couldn't produce a child. She married again to a widower named Asmi in 2001.

Nurul was a beautiful woman with a sweet smile. A darling who had won many hearts. Men after men chased her, trying to woo her hands in marriage. But she was also headstrong. By then, with one marriage already down the drain, she was tired of young men her age. For days, Nurul had quarrels with her mother who disagreed that Nurul should marry an old man. Nurul allied herself with her father who also met Zubaidah's anger. Zubaidah had even threatened to leave the house from her strong rejection. But she relented when Nurul explained the reason for accepting Asmi's proposal.

'His children are all grown up. With him I feel no pressure to produce a child. He already has four children of his own. I feel he is a man of responsibility, commitment and wisdom. This is what I need. I don't want this marriage to end like my first.'

Zubaidah would do the same when Faizah was arranged to marry Guntur. She threatened not to come to her wedding if Nasipudin insisted. Nasipudin persisted. Zubaidah attended the wedding anyway.

But Zubaidah's biggest displeasure came when her fourth child Suhaidi asked to marry Khaerudin's sister-in-law. Khaerudin had been married for more than a year and his wife's sister came to live with them and babysat their newborn to escape her mean stepmother. Suhaidi had a crush on his sister-in-law. He would often visit his brother's home and made a move on the young girl. One day in 1999, Suhaidi asked his father's permission to marry the teenage girl. Suhaidi was just 17.

'Our son wants to get married, ' Nasipudin told his wife at the time.

'Who? Suhaidi? He's just a kid. '

'I already said yes. '

'Without consulting me? I'm his mother. '

'You disagree? '

'Of course, I am. What were you thinking? '

'It is better for them. They could otherwise elope or have sex out of wedlock and sin. '

'I carried him in my womb. I gave birth to him. Does my opinion mean nothing? '

Nasipudin tried to calm her down, which made Zubaidah all the more hysterical.

His three oldest children would live close to Nasipudin. He built them homes inside his land. They were basic. Each had a living room, a bedroom and a kitchen. They all shared one bathroom. They were temporary places before the children can afford their own.

Except Suhaidi. He was later told to build his own home near the family's rice field, two hundred meters away down the slope. For years, his mother could not forgive him for marrying so young and as consequence, never finished high school. Nasipudin thought for Suhaidi to live in a separate property was the best solution. It was separation that kept the family together. In 2001, Suhaidi had a daughter. He named her Yuni. Suhaidi was 19.

***

It was September 8, 2002, the day Nafsiah would be buried, two days from the foreseen chaos. People gathered at his home once more, this time to pay their last respect, chanting prayers for his safe passage to the afterlife. There were rice, vegetables and meat. Food originally prepared for Ijtima Anshar's farewell gathering. It was instead a farewell of another kind.

Nasipudin led the procession, giving his father his final bath before wrapping him in a white burial shroud. Gently, the men assisted Nasipudin to place Nafsiah's body on a stretcher. Nafsiah's body felt light, as if all of the fluids inside his legs had disappeared. No one spoke of Nafisah's prophecy. No one spoke of the telling signs of impeding chaos.

Facing the direction of Mecca a rectangular hole was dug four meters deep in a family burial site just behind Nasipudin's home. Khaerudin just stood in silence. He watched from a distance as they lowered his grandfather's body into his final resting place. Suhaidi was standing in the front row, reaching out to help and taking initiatives. The two brothers were very different, one very shy and timid the other brave and reckless.

The women would have done little but cried, hiding their faces with the edge of their headscarves. Masitah, the fifth child, was probably holding her mother's shoulder all the time, hugging her from behind. On his father's arm was perhaps Nisa, the sixth child. She had lost the proper use of her legs from muscular dystrophy. She was normal up until she was 15 months old. As a toddler she would often had high fever, and would often fall. The muscular dystrophy had slowed her growth, both physically and mentally and made her muscles become weak and floppy. At 15, just three years younger than Masitah, she had the body of an 8-year-old.

Banding together, traveling like a pack were Nasipudin's three youngest sons: Malik aged 11, his brother Safir, 8 and the last child Kasafuloh, 6. They observed the funeral with curiosity for several minutes before deciding that playing was a more fun thing to do.

'Behave!' Faizah must have told his smaller brothers. 'Go play in the fields.'

Faizah had the luster of a newlywed, her new husband less so. Old friends and distant relatives constantly asked her if she was pregnant, a common question for a newlywed. She would just giggle, hiding her discomfort and embarrassment. Out of politeness she would respond, telling them 'no' and they would look at her in pity, hugging her as if telling her 'it's alright.' Society dictated that it was not. Here in rural Indonesia and some parts of the city, producing a child is the single most important duty of a wedded couple.

Faizah just gazed at her husband whom she barely knew. He was tall and chubby with a handsome round face and dark curly hair. His skin was fair, unlike the weather-beaten skins of other people in this neighborhood of farmers.

Guntur was still a newcomer. People would come up to him for small talks but he would only give short answers. They were either a 'yes,' a 'no,' or an 'I don't know.' Throughout the funeral he just stared emptily into the ground beneath his feet, or looked up to the movements of the bamboo trees shading the burial ground. He tried avoiding eye-contact as much as he can. Occasionally, he walked away from the crowd to be alone or retreated to his house.

From down the road someone must have called Faizah by her nickname. 'Ijah!' It was Mrs. Atun, a woman in her 40s hailing from the middle-class housing complex below. Shortly before she was married, Faizah worked for Mrs. Atun as a housemaid. When Faizah first came to work for her , Mrs. Atun would deliberately left paper notes in the pockets of her laundry. Faizah always returned what little money she found while washing her clothes. Mrs. Atun was so impressed by her honesty and her hard work. She was also impressed at how well she got along with her children.

Mrs. Atun was not a Sasak ethnic group, she was not an Ahmadi, but she loved Faizah like a sister. She missed having her in the house. She missed her smile, a wide grin on a dark round face. Her small eyes which disappeared whenever she smiled or laughed. Faizah used to get scared of everything, ghost stories, creepy crawlies, making her an easy target for picking. She missed her loud screech of a voice, her lively, childlike demeanor which always made Mrs. Atun laughed.

'I miss you,' Mrs. Atun would have said while hugging Faizah tightly. The hug was probably so tight that Faizah had to reposition her headscarf.

'How is your husband?'

'He's ok.'

'He's treating you ok? What are you up to these days?'

'He's nice. I'm just helping at my brother Khaer's shop.'

'Are you? That's wonderful. How do you like it so far?'

'I'm still learning.'

'The kids miss you.'

Faizah just smiled, unsure how to respond.

'We're moving away. My husband just got transferred to Java.'

'That's great. Oh… but then I will never see you again.'

'I want you to come and work with me again. Come with us to Java. You can go with your husband. We'll find him work.'

'That's nice of you. I'd love to go with you. But I can't leave my parents and I promised my brother I will help him at the shop.'

'I understand.'

The two hugged for one last time before saying their last goodbye.

CHAPTER 3

The prophesied violence was one day away. It was Monday, September 9, 2002 and the children were back at school. Offices and shops were starting another week.

But the Ahmadis noticed there was something different about the way people looked at them. Faizah was no exception. On her way to the market people stared at her. Their expressions showed contempt, some curiosity. There were also sympathetic faces like those shown to a parting friend or someone who had a misfortune.

The market was full of people, abuzz with vendors shouting, trying to attract shoppers and onlookers to their collection of meat, fishes, vegetables and fruits. The vendors were mostly women armed with an oversized bamboo basket and a sheet of tarpaulin mat laid flat on the ground where the food was displayed. The damp ground and dirty cement pathways were drenched in foul and nauseating smell of rotten vegetables and blood.

Behind the food vendors were more permanent stalls selling shirts, trousers, footwear and caps, with blue and orange tarpaulin tents to shade collapsible, wooden tables and makeshift clothing hangers.

Behind the stalls were kiosks, like those occupied by Khaerudin and his new assistant Faizah. The kiosks sold things of value or requiring proper storage. Khaerudin's shop was selling cooking oils, canned food, rice, packaged snacks and treats. It was big and strategic, taking up two units in one of the market's busiest section.

The market has always been the family's second home. Since they were small, their father Nasipudin had worked as a plantation laborer at his distant uncle's rice field and was granted permission to grow other crops and vegetables on an empty, small stretch of land. Their father would come home in the afternoon with vegetables for their mother to sell the following morning. As kids, Nurul and Faizah followed their father to field. As teenagers, they followed their mothers to the market.

Nasipudin was an honest man. He would divide what little profit he had with his uncle, even though his uncle never asked, even though his uncle was not an Ahmadi, even though he was just a distant relative.

'What is this for?' his uncle would say when Nasipudin showed up at his house with a stack of crumpled, dirty, old small notes.

'This is for you. Your cut of the profit for letting me grow food on your land. '

His uncle would just smile and tell him to save it for his family. But Nasipudin would return again and again with similar stack of dirty, old notes. Nasipudin made such a big impression on the man he put Nasipudin's name on his will.

For once in his life, Nasipudin had his own land. It was small, sitting right at the edge of a small road. The land was bought by a childless couple from Java. Nasipudin never knew their full name. He and his children simply referred to them as Mr. and Mrs. Marwan. The Marwans were looking to build a house of their own, having lived their entire life on homes rented by their offices. The money Nasipudin got from the Marwans would be used to buy himself and his father a nice property on the top of a small hill called Montong Gamang.

There was an added bonus to the purchase.

'I'm not planning to build my house right away. So you can still work your land before construction starts,' the Marwans said.

As he did with his uncle, Nasipudin split whatever profit he would make from the market with the Marwans. The Marwans tried to refuse but Nasipudin insisted.

'It wouldn't be right for me to keep the money I get from selling food grown on your land,' Nasipudin told the Marwans.

The Marwans reluctantly accepted and showered the family with gifts. Nasipudin and Zubaidah came to the Marwans with a stack of crumpled, old notes and returned with heavy sacks of rice, cooking oils, sugars and clothes.

Khaerudin never showed an interest in market life as a boy. He never dreamed of becoming a vendor like his mother. Becoming a vendor means talking to potential buyers, negotiating on a price, lobbying market officials and supervisors. Khaerudin never liked talking to people, hanging out, socializing. He was a shy boy who liked to carve wood at the privacy of his room.

It was the Marwans who took him out of his shell. Nasipudin and Zubaidah would often go to their homes and bring 'gifts' from their oldest son: decoration pieces which Khaerudin had hand-carved.

'Your son has a real gift in carpentry,' Mrs. Marwan said.

It was right around the time when they decided to start building their home on the land where Nasipudin worked. Mrs. Marwan did not want the family to lose their source of income so she gave Nasipudin a horse and a carriage which he could rent to paying customers. She also asked if Khaerudin would consider coming to the construction site of her home and build the pair a cabinet.

Khaerudin would build more than a cabinet. He went on and did all of the furniture at the Marwans' new home. Khaerudin was generously paid but his parents would not accept his money.

'You earned it. This is your money. So you go and spend it,' his father said.

The Marwans had their house completed by the time Khaerudin was 21. With their house completed, they offered him a change of profession.

'Do you want to try your hands at becoming a vendor like your mother?' Mrs. Marwan told Khaerudin. 'I have a vacant kiosk at the market. It is quite strategic but the tenant couldn't pay his rent. You can use it if you like.'

Mrs. Marwan lent Khaerudin the kiosk and enough money to start his own business.

***

Nasipudin's family had been selling vegetables in the market for twenty years. They knew everyone by name, every vendor, every regular buyer, every middleman, every management official, every busker, every beggar, every scavenger, every parking attendant, every motorcycle taxi driver, every sanitation worker, every porter and laborer. But that day, people stared at Faizah and Khaerudin like villainous strangers. The two siblings just ignored them and kept their distance.

Khaerudin and Faizah opened the padlock securing their store and slid open the folding metal gates. They readied the scale, pushed the wooden display boxes outside, suspending the children snacks up to a metal hook near the ceiling. The snacks were held together with wires, skewering the edge of their colorful wrappers.

The siblings then arranged plastic jars containing more snacks up on the counter. Faizah divided a drum full of cooking oil. Placing it into clear plastic bags each one liter in size. Faizah measured the oil carefully to make sure they contain the exact same quantity before sealing the bags with a rubber band. They took the broom and swept the floor, keeping it clean to welcome shoppers.

***

Buyers came and went, bringing along with them gossips and whispers. The same stories came from people passing by.

'Did you hear? They're going to drive away these Ahmadiyya people out of here,' one passerby must have said.

'Ahmadiyya? The blasphemers? Great,' said another.

'Did you hear the sermons last Friday? I heard they prayed differently,' another shopper would have told his friend.

'Yeah... yeah... I heard. They renounced Muhammad as the final prophet right? Good thing people finally standing up against them. People committing such blasphemy deserved to be killed.'

As the day passed by, they were more whispers, more accusations, more words of hatred.

'I heard they get paid for joining Ahmadiyya.'

'I heard their Koran is not really the Koran. Something else.'
'Tazkirah!' 'Yeah... that's it... Tazkirah.'

'If I met an Ahmadiyya guy, I'd kill him, right here, right now.'

'My cleric said it's OK to kill an Ahmadiyya person. It's OK to steal from them.'

Khaerudin and Faizah just remained silent, too afraid to talk back and say they were wrong. They didn't want to reveal their identity. They were not sure how people would react if they did. There were people at the market who expressed hostility towards Ahmadi vendors. Their mother Zubaidah had her basket knocked down spilling its content to the dirty, muddy ground. Her vegetables and meat were deliberately stomped, spat at. This would happen to virtually all Ahmadi vendors, the culprits: other vendors, people they knew, people they once lent money to, people calling the same neighborhood their home, people of the same Sasak ethnic group, people who were somehow connected through blood or marriage.

Sulaeman, an Ahmadi from the Sawing area of Pancor, was brave enough to talk back at a group of young men when they knocked down his display box filled with sandals.

'Why did you do that?'

'Hey you Ahmadiyya dog. You offended our religion.'

'How?'

'You call yourself a Muslim but you have a different Shahada,' one of the youths said referring to an Islamic creed, a declaration of belief to the oneness of God and the acceptance of Muhammad as God's prophet.

'My shahada is the same. I say this five times a day whenever I pray.'

'Liar.'

'Who said I'm a liar. Where do you hear these things?'

'The clerics.'

'Your clerics are lying.'

Sulaeman was cornered and almost beaten before a security guard shouted at them. His life was spared.

***

Echoing in the buildings and houses was the call to prayer, blaring from the speakers of mosques and prayer houses. The sun had just set, leaving a colorful spectacle in the sky. Pancor seemed to lose its vibrancy. The frantic market had become the darkest and most deserted part of town. Everyone was home, Nasipudin's family included. Beyond the chirping sound of the crickets and the echoes of the call to prayer everything was quiet.

But this was not a time of peace for Faizah. The foul words she had heard earlier in the market still rang inside her head. To ease her troubled mind she sought peace in the form of prayers. She grabbed her mukena, a long, two-piece, white garb women used for praying, and took her husband to the community's mushalla. She wished she could just pray at home but her husband Guntur was still learning how to perform the daily prayers.

Guntur was born a Muslim. His whole family had been a Muslim. But he never prayed. His family never taught him how to and never cared much about religion. Guntur only knew that it begins in a standing position, hands up in the air parallel to his ears and the word 'Allah hu Akbar' (God is great). Guntur knew that a prayer ends in a seated position, eyes turning to his right and left shoulders while saying 'Assallamu alaykum' (peace be upon you). He didn't know that he was greeting the two angels each man is accompanied by, keeping records of each deed, good or bad. Guntur was never taught how to read the Koran. He just raised his arms in the air, hands close together to form a cup and said 'amen' to every Arabic word he would hear, thinking they were prayers.

Faizah had to teach him everything about Islam. She taught him what to recite during prayers. She taught him to read Arabic alphabets so that he could read the Koran. She bought him guide books on how to read the Koran, the same used by Muslim children when they started to learn.

Faizah was a Koran teacher. She was the best reciter in the neighborhood. After the dusk prayer, Maghrib, Ahmadi and non-Ahmadi parents would send their children to the mushalla where Faizah taught them to read the Koran. She missed teaching them. She had to stop so that she could teach her shy husband at the privacy of their home.

Her father Nasipudin took her place, sometimes Masitah, sometimes Nurul. Ahmadis were taught how to read the Koran at an early age. Ahmadi children, before reaching their teen, could memorize the first and last chapters of the Koran. They were taught its literal and symbolic meanings. They were told to memorize the Hadiths, the sayings of the Prophet Muhammad.

Spirituality was a deep part of Ahmadis' lives, not like observers of the mainstream Islam here in Lombok. Like Guntur, there are many who never opened the Holy Book their whole life. Like Guntur, they would think every Arabic word coming out of their clerics' mouth to be prayers and say 'amen.' They would follow the clerics' every word, without question, even when they were instructions to kill their neighbors.

The clerics and the Tuan Gurus never cared if their followers can read the Koran. They never cared if people prayed five times a day. In Indonesia, clerics only appear on television, in huge sermons and lavish gatherings, brushing shoulder with the top brasses of government offices and agencies. Clerics in Indonesia don't go to small neighborhoods, visit poor people's homes and pay attention to their spiritualities unless people pay them to deliver sermons, to bless new houses and newborns. Being a cleric was a profession. It was never about dedication, not a calling, not servitude to God, not propagation of His words.

The clerics were feared. They were famous. They had billboards bearing their faces. They had influence and powerful friends. They lived in marble-clad mansions while their followers lived in poverty, struggling to put food at the table. They would give alms every year during the holy month of Ramadan to poor, sick, old people who would risk stampede. They would invite television crews when they do.

The clerics and the Tuan Gurus never cared if their followers can read the Koran. But Nasipudin and his children did, even to non-Ahmadis.

It was to be the last time Ahmadi children can sit side by side with non-Ahmadi children together in one mushalla. Words from the Holy Koran were recited soothing Faizah's troubled mind. She sidelined her fear, her worries, the thought of the horrible words she heard at the market, Sulaeman's near brush with death, her mother's mistreatment, the countless malicious stares.

She thought the worst was behind her. She was wrong. Chaos was still one day away.

CHAPTER 4

The moon was a thin crescent with dark orange glow, its luster too faint to illuminate the earth below. It was a dark night, the day of the prophesied mayhem. The air was still, not a breeze strong enough to blow the leaves in the tall trees above. The men and boys in Nasipudin's family were sleeping in their checkered sarongs and sleeveless white undershirts while the women in cotton nightgowns with floral prints.

There was a knock on Nasipudin's door. It was Khaerudin, still awake to sort out receipts from his kiosk, staying up late to do some bookkeeping. Khaerudin's mother Zubaidah answered.

'Mother, please turn all of the lights on our front porch!'

'What's going on?'

'I'm not sure. Uncle Arifin just came to my house. He said there's been an attack on some Ahmadis'

'What? Where? Was anyone hurt?'

'I don't know… Uncle just said our mosque was attacked. Uncle wants us to turn off all the porch lights so we don't attract attention'

'Alright then, go fetch your brother!'

Khaerudin probably went to Suhaidi's house in the middle of the rice field. Working his way down the muddy path on top of embankments used to keep the rice fields drenched in water. The pathways were small, wide enough for a single person to cross. It was slippery. It was dark.

Suhaidi was probably asleep, as was his wife Sri and their daughter Yuni who was still learning to walk. Khaerudin told him what happened. Suhaidi most likely must have wanted to see it for himself. There was an argument between the brave and hasty Suhaidi and his cautious big brother. Khaerudin told him he should stay in the neighborhood and look after their mother, brothers and sisters as well as his own wife and daughter. Suhaidi argued that Khaerudin can take that role and he would be of more use if he were to go the mosque and drive away the attackers. Khaerudin said there was nothing he could do there. But there was no stopping Suhaidi when his mind is set. So they parted ways. Leaving Suhadi's wife and daughter in Khaerudin's care.

***

Inside Nasipudin's house, Zubaidah woke everyone, first her husband, then Masitah, the oldest daughter still living in the same house, Nurul whose house was next door, then Faizah. Her voice was a whisper. She wanted none of her non-Ahmadiyya neighbor to hear. She didn't want to disturb the boys. They were too young to understand.

'Aaayyyy… Tahajud! Tahajud!' Zubaidah told them. She was referring to the optional midnight prayer traditionally performed when one wishes for guidance, good fortune and protection from God.

'There is an attack. Don't turn on the lights! Pray! Pray! Perform the Tahajud!'

Nurul and Faizah were puzzled. They were curious to know more.

'Later, I will tell you. Just do as I say!'

They complied.

***

Khaerudin went inside his father's home along with his niece and sister in-law. His wife was already there. Nurul and her husband Asmi stayed at their room. So were Faizah and her husband Guntur.

Faizah cried, thinking why anyone would want to ransack their mosque. She was careful not to show it to her new husband whom she barely knew. 'Love will eventually come,' said those forcing their children to marry those they do not love. For Faizah love has yet to come. A month ago they were strangers. His quietness would make him a stranger still to Faizah.

One by one, the tahajud was individually performed. A tahajud was never meant to be performed collectively, unlike the five compulsory prayers. Praying as a group also meant that one has to be an imam, the prayer's principal and he would have to recite verses from the Koran loudly for his followers to hear, bringing unwanted attention.

After everyone had prayed, Nasipudin noticed one of his sons was missing.

'Where is Suhaidi?'

Khaerudin explained that against his wishes, Suhaidi chose to go and see the attack first hand.

'That kid!' Nasipudin said.

His attention turned to the family members who were at his house. Nasipudin told his children that himself, Khaerudin, and his son in laws would try to stand guard and that they would alert them the first sight of trouble.

'If anything happens I want you to all run to the back of the house. Remember not all people in this neighborhood are sympathetic towards us. But we can trust our family Sarapudin. We will be safe there. He's a well respected man in this community. They wouldn't touch him. But be careful! We don't know who maybe watching. So try to stay out of sight!'

The women nodded.

'Now go and try to get some rest.'

They tried to sleep but failed. Their grandfather's last words came to mind. For Faizah, lingering in her thoughts was Mrs. Atun's offer to come to Java. Had she thought only of herself she might have taken the offer. She was glad that she didn't. Her family meant the world to her. Had she taken the job she would die in remorse for being unable to be with her family in a tough, uncertain time like this.

She must have lost sleep thinking of death. She was fearful but the promised afterlife was also appealing. She worried of her husband whom she barely knew. He still struggled to read the Koran, still learning how to pray. 'Is there a place for him in heaven?' she probably wondered. She thought about her own devotion to God, to His command, to her own religion, to the prophet, to the messiah. She wondered whether she prayed enough to ensure her place in the afterlife. She thought whether she would be reunited with her family in heaven.

She looked over to his father as she lied in the floor of her father's living room, pretending to sleep. Her father was small but muscular. His face almost a perfect square with a sturdy jaw line. His dark eyes were small, hiding behind a row of long eyelashes sitting below bushy eyebrows. His short cut, thick hair was turning grey.

There was an air of calm around him, one that for Faizah at least, was infectious. She was at peace watching him. He seemed to embrace whatever fate lies ahead. He accepted it as God's plan. Faizah felt at peace watching her father. Finally, for a brief moment, she was able to sleep.

***

Faizah was awakened by a knock at the door. It was Suhaidi. All the men of her family were finally together. Her mother quickly got up and hugged him, her grudge, her anger, her disapproval for Suhaidi's marriage suddenly vanished. Nasipudin was less emotional. He wanted to hear whatever news his stubborn son was carrying.

'So... What did you see?'
'Our mosque... It's gone.'

***

The family did not get much sleep that night and sunrise had brought a day of uncertainty. Nasipudin was lost for words when his sons Malik and Safir asked him if they should go to school that day.

Malik was a smart boy and Nasipudin had always dreamed of him going to college one day. Khaerudin was a vocational school graduate, Nurul only made it to sixth grade, Faizah didn't go to high school, Suhaidi dropped out of tenth grade, Masitah only had a junior high school diploma.

Nasipudin had high hopes for Malik and his younger brothers. Malik was not at the top of his class but he had a passion for learning. He was critical. He was curious. But above all he was determined. So when Malik and Safir asked if he could go to school he said 'yes.'

Malik and Safir never knew that their mosque was attacked the night before and Nasipudin thought it was best they shouldn't. Malik's school was right across the street from the East Lombok District Police Headquarters, about a kilometer north from where they lived while Safir's was slightly further away. But with an attack so fresh Nasipudin felt they shouldn't travel alone. Their older brother Suhaidi went with them to school.

Faizah was also unsure whether she should go to the market but she was curious to hear from other Ahmadi vendors what had happened. Faizah convinced Khaerudin to take her to the market after promising they would head back if there was any indication of another attack.

The market was a short drive northeast but the two agreed to make a detour west and see how badly the mosque was damaged. It was carnage. Sitting on a busy street was the skeleton of what used to be their house of worship. The outer walls were obliterated, reduced to piles of brick and concrete fragments. The roof had collapsed altogether, sending its tile roof to the ground and shattered, littering the floor. Dotting the property were rocks and bamboo poles which the attackers must have used to tear down the walls and roof. The mosque's contents were either looted or burned.

The mosque sat right across the home of Syahdan, the chief of the East Lombok district. He had seen that the mosque was being renovated. The Ahmadis planned on refurbishing the mosque and make it a two-story structure, big enough to host 500 congregation members. Syahdan must have felt like it was a sign that the Ahmadis were growing in size and slowly becoming a threat or at least de-legitimizing his rule. A group of blasphemers left to blossom right here in the birthplace of Lombok's biggest Muslim organization? Under his rule? Signs of which sat before his eyes? Right across the street from where he lived? It must have been unacceptable for Syahdan.

***

By chance Faizah ran into Khadijah, the wife of the mosque's main cleric, Raehanudin. She was pacing up and down the street barefooted in her nightgown, her hair fully exposed without a headscarf. Faizah told Khaerudin to stop.

'Mam, what happened here?'

'It was chaos. My husband and some committee members were having a meeting at the mosque. Next thing you know there were shouting and pelting. Just a few dozens at first. My husband and the others fled to safety. But the attackers went after my husband. They shouted something about killing him. He managed to leap over the back wall and escaped through the alleyways. I just hid with the kids. They went inside my house but before they could find me they left.'

Faizah just stood in silence, imagining the horrors she must had faced.

'The attack stopped for a while. We took that opportunity to escape. But then they came again and finished what they had started. The mosque, our house, some Ahmadis' homes nearby… all of them ransacked, destroyed. There's nothing left.'

'Where's your husband now?'

'At the police headquarter. I will join him there. I just came to see if I can salvage something. But they're all gone, looted.'

Their conversation attracted attention. It was a busy street and they were well exposed.

'We must go. It's not safe to stay for long,' Khaerudin said.

Faizah nodded and the siblings were back on their way.

***

The market was unusually quiet. Ahmadis made up almost half the vendors at the market and most chose to stay inside the safety of their homes. Those who came found their shops vandalized with graffiti saying 'infidels' or 'blasphemers' like markers guiding future attackers on where to target next.

The siblings met Sulaeman who was just as curious as to learn what had happened. He was much better informed than the siblings.

'But I thought you were also at the mosque last night,' Faizah said.

Sulaeman said he was. He was among the ten members of the local Ahmadiyya committee who had gathered for their monthly meeting. They were about to discuss how much money the mosque had gathered from the congregation members' regular contributions. They were about to talk about earmarking some money to send underprivileged kids to study at an Ahmadiyya boarding school in Java. They were to have this meeting after their dusk prayers.

'Next thing you know a rock flew through the window, sending everyone to a panic. The men hurled them away and arming themselves with rocks. We saw at the end of an alley were dozens of people running towards the mosque.' Sulaeman said, being the great story teller that he was.

He spoke with enthusiasm that the men eventually chased the attackers away, mimicking the sound of rocks hitting the ground, hands simulating every action, every swoosh of the attackers' bamboo poles, his body reenacting the dodging movement the Ahmadis made when rocks were being hurled at them.

'They fled. I pretended I was going to chase them away and seeing me they ran. Actually I was also scared to chase after them. One of the guys told me: 'Don't go after them! Just call the cops!' And so I did.'

Sulaeman said when he got back from the police station there were already hundreds of people, surrounding the mosque. His friends were hiding in Azhar's home 200 meters behind the mosque deep down the alleyways where people's houses nearly bordered rice fields.

'Police came, one (officer) and then two, minutes later three. I couldn't find my friends. I just watched, trying to blend in with the crowds careful not to reveal my identity. Rocks were flying. I met the committee chairman Azhar. He said 'Man, just go home.' Before long there were thousands. Police could no longer contain the crowd, it's not like they tried anyway.'

Sulaeman continued to tell his story, leaving Faizah and Khaerudin bewildered at how casual he did this. Sulaeman was a tall, skinny man in his early 40s. His family hailed from Sumatra but he moved to Pancor some 10 years back. He always had a way with stories, retelling every detail like it happened minutes ago.

Eventually he shared some information which he did hear minutes before.

'We have bigger things to worry now. I heard more attacks will come tonight.'

CHAPTER 5

From the words of his friends, Nasipudin learned what happened the night before. He learned that no one was hurt. He also learned that after attacking the mosque the attackers went to a neighborhood called Bermi where five Ahmadiyya families lived. The attackers went into every Ahmadi's home. A man named Parmono was captured and had a machete pressed against his throat. The attackers said they were ready to cut off his head. They were only trying to scare him away. Parmono and the rest of the Ahmadis from Bermi were taken to the East Lombok District Police headquarter as did the Ahmadiyya cleric Raehanudin and the group of Ahmadis living behind the ransacked mosque.

Nasipudin also learned that more attack was expected. The attackers had a network of informants, telling them where each Ahmadiyya family lived. The attackers knew where they worked, where their shops and fields were. There were Ahmadis who were stalked. There were Ahmadis who had their homes watched.

There were sermons. There were secret meetings. They had one goal 'driving Ahmadiyya people out of the island.' To do this they would use the hands of their neighbors, families, friends while the masterminds stayed in the shadows. There were promises made, to Muslims who never bothered to study their religion, let alone followed God's command or stayed away from sinful acts. They were told their sins would be wiped away if they helped with the cause.

In the land of their ancestors, the Ahmadis in Lombok would be treated as outsiders, they were outcasts. From the hands of their relatives their blood would shed, their homes reduced to rubles, persecuted and driven away.

Nasipudin just smiled when he heard this. Through Ahmadiyya he head learned how to detach himself from earthly desires. He had learned to fear nothing but God's wrath.

'Whatever plan God has for me, I will gladly accept. I can only pray so that my family will have the strength to carry out His plan.'

***

Back at the market Khaerudin whispered to Faizah:

'Let's just get all our stuff from here.'

'Where will we put them?'

There was a long pause. Khaerudin thought hard. The stuff needed to be put in a place not only big enough but also where the attackers wouldn't dare attacking. They needed someone they can trust.

'The Marwans,' Khaerudin said.

Khaerudin went to talk to the Marwans while Faizah got everything ready to be transported. The Marwans agreed to store their belongings for safekeeping. Khaerudin also went in search of a pickup truck they could rent. There were pickup trucks for rent at the market but that put them at risk of being seen by people who hated them. Renting a pickup truck from another neighborhood was the safer option.

Khaerudin eventually found a pickup truck for hire. The pair loaded everything they had at the store and rushed over to the Marwans.

'Is it ok if I leave you with some documents too?' Khaerudin told Mrs. Marwan.

'Of course!'

Khaerudin left Mrs. Marwan his father's land deeds, certificates, school diplomas, their brothers' report card and a Koran.

'Khaer, what's this? I can't take this,' Mrs. Marwan said while picking up the Koran Khaerudin had given, her arm extended ready to give back the Koran.

'It's the same Koran. We use the same Koran as anyone else. Believe me!'

Mrs. Marwan reluctantly agreed to take the Koran.

***

At school, Malik noticed all his Ahmadi friends were missing. Malik was in the fifth grade and there were other Ahmadi kids at other grades too. He noticed that he was the only Ahmadi boy in the whole school. Malik's teachers would never look at Malik in the eyes as if they were mourning the boy's impending fate, as if they tried giving him a warning but couldn't out of fear of being caught helping the blasphemers.

All day, Malik's friends did not talk to him. Malik tried to approach them but they did not want to speak a word to Malik. When they played marbles, they would not let Malik join.

'Here comes a dingkong. Run…!!!' They all disbanded. This would happen every time Malik tried to strike a conversation or ask if he could play with them.

Malik never understood what 'dingkong' meant but they way his friends used that word, he knew it was derogatory.

**

There was uncertainty which came with darkness and the anticipation of peril brewed from the warnings of a repeated attack. The two permeated through the minds of Nasipudin and his family, each lying on their beds with wakeful eyes. They were alert, vigilant, restless. But a long day it had been. 'If God is willing nothing will happen tonight,' they told themselves, reciting prayers to keep them out of harms way.

With their prayers sent the women went to sleep. The men stayed close to the doors, keeping one eye on their family and another on the look out for signs of danger. But as the night went they too fell asleep. They prayed that God keep them safe from harm but God had another plan.

'Attack! Attack! Kill the Ahmadiyya!'

A mob was heard, their voice grew stronger as they inched closer. Faizah looked out the window and saw a group of men, at least one hundred strong, walking past the rice field below heading north towards them. She jumped off her bed, waking her husband as a result and cried 'Mooooommmm!'

The family scrambled, hurriedly making their way to the back of the house without finding time to put on their headscarves or locating their shoes and sandals. There were 10 Ahmadiyya families in Montong Gamang, including Nasipudin's brothers and sisters and aunty and all rushed to safety.

They passed a field filled with tall, thorny shrubs and broken glass. The field was dotted with tall trees with saps known to cause painful inflammation. Panic had replaced all senses and reason. For some reason Nisa weighed nothing at all, Nasipudin's 65 year-old aunty Nafsilah from next door ran like a teenage girl. They headed for the home of their uncle Sarapudin. The journey only took minutes but it seemed like eternity.

Sarapudin had many children and grandkids of his own and that night he had to open his door for dozens more. The living room was soon crowded with women still in their nightgowns, trying to catch their breath. The men stayed at the front porch and alleyways on the look out for signs of attack.

On his mother's arm was Khaerudin's three-year-old son Hafiz, who had just learn a new word: 'attack.' He would say this word repeatedly even in his sleep. Suhaidi's daughter Yuni, barely a year old, was crying constantly and had to be silenced using her mother's finger. They had left Yuni's pacifier at home. Nasipudin's last child Kasafuloh, still six-years-old was shaken, tearing up but not making a sound. Staring emptily at the walls were his brothers Malik and Safir.

There were Masitah, the teenage girl, looking after Nisa who could barely walk from her muscular dystrophy. There were Faizah and his shy husband Guntur. There were Nurul and her elderly husband Asmi.

There was no Suhaidi. Unknown to the others, he stayed at the field while the others fled. Curious, he watched the mob from a distance behind the cover of darkness, tall trees and shrubs. He saw them working their way across the rice field below the hill, slowly marching in one row with torches in their hands. The attackers were like a giant snake made of fire.

With just meters from their home, as Suhaidi prepared to make a run for his life, the mob continued their way north to Sawing, where five Ahmadiyya families lived including a man from Sumatra named Sulaeman.

Sawing was less than a kilometer away from Nasipudin's home. The sounds of pelted rocks smashing people's brick homes were loud and clear. The shouts of the assailants were like a distant buzz, their exact words incomprehensible. There were sounds of a police siren approaching and minutes later the sound of shots being fired. Afterwards there was more shouting followed by silence and finally the sound of the door being opened. It was Suhaidi.

This time Nasipudin probably did not quiz him as to what he saw. He just looked at his son with a stare as if showing his disappointment.

In another circumstance, he would ask Suhaidi to follow him where he would scold his son in private. It was no time for wise words of a father. But he made sure, from his stare, from his silence, from his pronounced breathing, that Suhaidi knew his father was angry.

He was angry that Suhaidi had abandoned his wife and child, that he had made everyone worry. He was particularly upset that Suhaidi had shown disrespect for the host, Nasipudin's brother Sarapudin. Sarapudin had offered the family protection and Suhaidi took that for granted by risking his life for no worthy cause.

Nasipudin's anger was apparent and everyone in the room didn't dare to say anything to neither Suhaidi nor Nasipudin. Suhaidi just kept his head down out of shame and regret and didn't say a word. But it was Nasipudin who broke the silence.

'Let us pray…. for our safety, the safety of our family and the safety of our friends who were attacked tonight. Let us pray that God forgive the attackers and show them the path to righteousness.'

Nasipudin's prayer provided the family some much needed comfort. The prayer, as simple as it was, erased the troubles in their mind, the worries of losing their possessions, the grudges they held against the attackers, the feeling that somehow they have done something wrong by practicing their belief. One by one they closed their eyes.

***

36 hours had past since the mosque was attacked, 31 since the attack on Bermi neighborhood, 7 since the attack on Sawing. Malik had gone to school, accompanied by his two bigger brothers.

From the middle-class neighborhood came a government official sporting a tight-fitted, light brown, safari shirt and matching trousers. He came in search of Ahmadiyya families. Who told him where to find these Ahmadiyya families was a mystery.

Nasipudin and his family had returned to their home that morning. The official knocked on their doors and was told to come inside the house. The official took off his shiny leather shoes revealing a pair of socks. Without spending much time on small talks he revealed the purpose of his visit.

'If you leave Ahmadiyya now, you can stay at your home and no one will bother you ever again. If you don't want to leave then we won't be held responsible for your safety. But for the time being, let us all go to a safer place. We have a car waiting to take all of you.'

Nasipudin politely replied. 'We have chosen a belief which we hold as true. They can have everything… my house, my land, my livestock, my life. But we will leave and follow you wherever you will take us to.'

Nasipudin told his family to go with the official. 'I will stay here and wait for your brother [Malik]. Go with this nice man.'

Zubaidah chose to stay with her husband. The pair felt it was better that Nisa should stay too. They worry that no one will take care of her where they were going.

'I will come back for you, later in the afternoon,' the official said.

Nasipudin gave the official a nod.

There were two cars waiting at the foot of the hill, each was crammed to fit 11 adults and children. Nasipudin watched them drove off. They were heading to the East Lombok District Police headquarter.

Nasipudin returned back to his home after bidding the others goodbye, walking slowly through the tight neighborhood road. He gave his house a good look as if to bid it farewell. He remembered when it was still an empty plot of land. It was the first land he had ever owned, bought from the money given by the Marwans. From where he stood, he built a makeshift home out of wood and bamboo. After returning from the fields he would collect sands from a nearby stream and put them in goony sacks. He would collect clay which he pressed into a mold and baked using makeshift ovens to make bricks.

It took him years to produce enough bricks to build his home. He would do this everyday until the walls were standing. He struggled to muster enough money to buy wood and pay for labor for the roof, until his brother-in-law came and gave the family money. His brother-in-law felt sorry to see his sister living in a bamboo hut with nine children.

He had many fond memories with the house but now he must leave it in the hands of the people who were out to destroy it.

'This home was never mine ' he thought, assuring himself that it was the Almighty God who had bestowed him with wealth and fortune and whenever He pleases can take everything away.

He went inside and fetched a wooden money box filled with small change and crumpled bank notes, money he had painstakingly saved every time he made a little extra cash. He picked up a shovel, made sure no one was looking and started to dig his backyard, burying the box for safekeeping.

***

At noon, Malik returned from school and immediately went to his house. Before he went to school his parents took him back to the house where he took a bath and changed into his white top and red shorts school uniform. His mother combed his hair. He expected his parents to be home. There was no one there. His parents were at his uncle's home.

Malik was exhausted. He was thirsty and hadn't had anything to drink from his one kilometer walk from school. He was tired from all the taunting at school, from the stares he had received. He was mortified when some grown men called him names. He was puzzled how adults were capable at such an infantile act.

He was confused why his brothers didn't pick him up after school like they said they would. Finally he decided to head over to his uncle's home. He saw his mother, his father and his crippled older sister. He asked where his other brothers and sisters were. His mother explained what happened and assured him that they were safe.

'When will join them?'

'Later, in the afternoon. Stay close to me. Don't go too far.'

Zubaidah went back to their house. She wanted to search for Malik and Safir's school report books, oblivious to the fact that the day before Khaerudin had taken them and gave them to the Marwans for safekeeping along with other important documents. They were the two most important things in the world, she thought. Without them, in her mind, Malik and Safir would not be able to continue their education, particularly with people forcing them to leave Pancor.

Zubaidah searched everywhere. She opened every drawer, every cupboard, looked under every bed and found no trace of the report books. After hours of searching she started to become frustrated.

Looking at his mother's frustration Malik held her hands.

'Are you upset about leaving our house behind? Don't be! God didn't do this to us. It was those bad people that did this to us.'

It was as if God had spoken through the mouth of his 11-year-old boy. The words had lifted a huge burden off her shoulder and pressing her chest. She gave Malik a good hug.

Nasipudin came into the house. 'I don't think that official is coming to pick us up. It's getting dark. We have to go. It's not safe here.'

CHAPTER 6

The hall was vast, thirty meters wide on each side, with tall wooden ceilings and glistering white tile floor. Police often used the hall for gatherings and ceremonies but this time it was a makeshift shelter. Nasipudin, his wife and their two children arrived at the Police headquarters as it was getting dark. They were among the last people to be placed in the hall, which had turned into home to more than 350 Ahmadis from all corners of East Lombok district. That number eventually grew to 383.

There were people that the family had known all their lives. In one corner sat their spiritual leader, the Ahmadi cleric Raehanudin, whose house was among the first to be destroyed, sporting the same batik shirt as when he was first brought to the headquarter more than 24 hours before. In another was Azhar, the chairman of Pancor chapter of the Ahmadiyya congregation. He was in charge of the Ahmadis' civic affairs while Raehanudin look after people's spirituality.

There was Sulaeman and his father-in-law Mahmuludin, who was said to be the richest Ahmadi in Pancor. Mahmuludin was a hajji, one of the few Ahmadis who were wealthy enough to have performed the hajj pilgrimage. Over time the number of Ahmadis performing the hajj dwindled as Saudi Arabia banned all Ahmadis from entering the holy cities of Mecca and Medina. The Indonesian government had also refused to accommodate Ahmadi pilgrims and eventually refused to acknowledge them as Muslims altogether.

There were people from Bermi. There were people from Sawing. There were people from Kelayu. There were even people from other East Lombok towns like Keruak, Pringgabaya, Medas and Sembalun.

There were elderly people with pearly white hair and no teeth like Nasipudin's aunty Nafsilah. There were aging men and women who were losing their eyesight from cataract like Nasipudin's uncle Sadarudin. There were month-old babies who cried continuously like Suhaidi's daughter Yuni. There were differently abled people like Nisa. There were newly weds like Faizah. There were restless youths like Suhaidi.

There were relatives who had moved out of Pancor, by then reunited under one roof. There were close friends from the market. There were strangers they had never seen. There were people they met only once or twice at Ahmadiyya gatherings.

There was Nasipudin's sister Fahriah who had just bought a place in downtown Selong. There was his other sister Fatimah, who along with his brothers Maskanah and Kamarudin was living with their late father.

There were plastic mats on a cold floor, their beds for the night. There were social workers roaming around, interviewing people and taking notes. There were heavily armed guards, young police officers fresh out of the academy, waiting outside the hall, sitting and smoking their cigarettes on the pavements and halls and asphalt driveways. Some were sitting on police personnel carrier trucks with dark tarpaulin roofs enclosing the truck beds.

The police officers were having their dinners, rice packets with brown wrapping papers serving as makeshift plates. It was basic but it was a proper meal.

The Ahmadis were given cardboards full of instant noodles, laden with preservatives, just as dictated by the government's official refugee handling or disaster mitigation guidelines. The noodles required boiling water before they were ready to be eaten. There was no fresh, drinkable water to cook them with. There was no stove. There was no pan or cooking pot.

There were people who were so hungry they ate the noodle straight out of its colorful wrappers, uncooked. They would have diarrhea and stomachache as results. But they had no choice. It was either going to bed hungry or going to bed with a stomach pain and feeling sorry for not staying hungry.

The presence of 383 men, women and children made the vast hall seemed small. The heat, sweat and moisture generated from the crowd were suffocating. The buzzing noise of people's chatter was unnerving, masked only by crying children and the sickly coughing of the elderly. Occasionally, babies wet their diapers, sending a foul stench across the room half-drenched in baby's urine.

Nisa tried to get up and stand but her family wouldn't let her walk. They were afraid that she would disturb others or fell into a pool of baby's urine nearby. Her muscular dystrophy began to worsen. Her muscle was so weak she was virtually a breathing skeleton.

The condition also took a toll on her mentally. Imprisoned by her illness, her mind was the only part of her body which is able to wander. Her family, who never consulted to any physician about Nisa's illness, wondered if she had any thoughts at all. But even if they had, Nisa was beyond saving. Children her age with the same condition were all bound to a wheelchair and were lucky to live pass 25. She faired better and at 15 could stand on her own for a little over a minute. But she was heading towards the same fate.

During her time at the hall, all she could do was lie down and sit, occasionally moving and playing with her arms and legs. From time to time, her family would try to talk to her but got no response. With muscles in her lower arms grew weaker, her hands began to twist inwards and calcium piled on her wrists locking her hands. Her legs began to deform, curving outwards. Over time she would never walk again.

As the refugees tried to get some rest, a gun shot was heard. Everyone ran to see what had happened. A mob had gathered at the back of the police headquarter, young men with bamboo poles and wooden plank shouting and screaming.

The Ahmadis could do nothing but watch, as police officers formed a barricade to stop them from going beyond the police headquarters' metal gates. The mob marched passed by the compound, slowly making its way north. More shouting was heard and moments later the sound of pelted rocks. Police did nothing to stop the mayhem even though the mob was only meters away. Suddenly there were towering flames illuminating the night sky with thick black smoke snaking up into the air. The mob had attacked a shop sitting just 500 meter from the police headquarter. The shop's owner was an Ahmadi man. His name was Awaludin.

***

The attack on Awaludin's shop had left everyone restless. Nasipudin who used to stay calm and submissive to God's will, started to see that a murky future was upon him. Earlier he thought they would stay at the police headquarter for a couple of days. He thought the attack would recede and things would slowly return to normal. He never thought that the Ahmadis would be constantly harassed until they were driven from their hometown. He never thought it was going to be a persecution.

He began to regret his decision to bury his savings. With no proper food, no apparent action from the people who were sworn to uphold the law, no certainty of what their future may be, he began to look for ways to return home and unearth his buried wooden money box.

***

When morning came, Nasipudin began to talk to every officer he could find. The younger officers told him he should talk to their commanding officers. The commanding officers told him they were only there to protect the refugees within the confines of the hall and that he should speak to those in charge of public security. Those in charge of public security replied by telling Nasipudin it was impossible to take him back to his home without first seeking clearance from officers in charge of intelligence. Those in charge of intelligence told him it was not safe.

Finally he met an officer who was willing to help him. He was a mid-ranking officer in his 30s. His brown uniform had colorful insignias and ribbons. He wore his rank on his shoulder in the shape of golden flowers. Nasipudin recognized him as a police neighbor who lived down the hill in the middle-class housing complex. In a soft spoken voice Nasipudin explained to him his situation.

'I will see what I can do. You just wait here.'

Nasipudin waited for hours as the officer walked inside the complex's main building. As he waited, Nasipudin watched his town slowly coming to life. People were out to the market, to their offices, to their tobacco farms, casually riding their motorcycles or walking together with their neighbors. They made jokes and laughed together as though nothing had happened.

By the gate, Malik watched his friends from school walking merrily with their well-combed hair hidden underneath oversized caps. They wore spotless white uniform top and red shorts and skirts. They were carrying colorful backpacks, with cartoon characters printed on them. They wore black sneakers and white socks all the way to their knees. They had smiles on their faces, unaware or unfazed that their friends were being evacuated to the police headquarters and had to live in harrowing conditions without access to proper food or rest as men destroyed their homes and looting their possessions.

Suddenly the officer returned, bringing with him two of his men. 'Follow these officers!'

Nasipudin's face changed into that of relief. He repeatedly thanked his police neighbor and followed the two officers into a police truck. It was painted in dull grey with a bulletproofed metal box replacing its truck bed, used to house and transport criminals. The box had two rows of wooden bench and three small windows reinforced with iron bars. Nasipudin was told to sit inside it as they drove to his neighborhood some 10 minutes drive away.

The police trucks presence at Nasipudin's neighborhood would bring commotion, a weird blend of confusion, anguish and jubilation. Oblivious to Nasipudin's true intention, the neighbors taught that Nasipudin had been arrested.

'Look, it's that Ahmadiyya man!' said one neighbor.

Children ran towards him and called him names 'Dingkong! Dingkong!'

Nasipudin ignored them as the two officers walked with him up the slopes of the tiny hill, grabbing him by the arm right under his armpits. Nasipudin, who had never committed any crime all his life, was treated like a criminal.

The series of attacks had fueled mistrust, some say madness. Everyone was trying hard to look as if they side with the majority, to root the 'righteous' assailants, to defend their final prophet who died centuries ago. Nobody dared to openly express sympathy and compassion for their Ahmadi neighbor, their kin.

They did this out of fear of being attacked, out of fear of not conforming to what others hold as true: that the Ahmadis don't believe Muhammad to be the final prophet, that the Ahmadis had defiled Islam, that it is their obligation to destroy the Ahmadis. Even though they are neighbors, even to those who are related by blood and marriage, even to people who taught their children how to read the Koran and asked nothing in return.

Nasipudin just looked down on the ground as people circled him, calling him names and pushing him around.

'Hey, Ahmadiyya man... Where's your prophet now, Ahmadiyya man?' one person said.

'Infidel!' the other shouted

'Blasphemer!'

The officers tried hard to keep the crowd away. They were ready to evacuate Nasipudin the second the crowd was to go out of control. It never did.

In front of his house, Nasipudin stopped as the taunting grew louder. He paused for a second and reached out a shovel from inside his home. For some reason the crowd cheered when he started to dig his backyard.

Nasipudin's brother Sarapudin was not in sight, he stayed inside his home just meters away, afraid he would burst into tears when he saw how his brother was humiliated by the people they knew. He must have cried anyway, sobbing uncontrollably in remorse for his inability to stop the madness.

Nasipudin found what he came for, a wooden money box by then covered in dirt. The crowd went wild with more taunting.

'Look! Ahmadiyya man collecting his pay,' one yelled.

'Hey... Ahmadiyya man... Did your prophet give you that?'

Nasipudin stayed strong, never lost his patience or broke into tears. In his heart he sent a prayer.

'God... forgive these people!'

He took the wooden box, gave the dirty surface a wipe and drove off with the officers. It was the last time he saw his house.

CHAPTER 7

With money in their hands, Malik, Safir and Kasafuloh were
ecstatic, running directly towards a food stall at one corner of the
police compound. They thought of all their favorite treats and snacks
they could by then buy: candies, lollipops, wafers, biscuits, cornmeal
snacks, steamed bananas with palm sugar caramel, sugar coated
flour balls, popsicles or perhaps some refreshing fruity drinks.

'We're out,' said the lady shopkeeper, standing in front of
hoards of snacks and their colorful plastic wrappers. Oblivious to the
boys the shopkeeper had been told by her clerics that it was sinful to
do business with the Ahmadis.

'We're closed,' she yelled. 'Go shop somewhere else!'

The boys were stunned. Malik probably wrapped his arms
around his brothers' shoulders and swiftly turned their bodies and
walked out of the shop. They would say nothing to the shopkeeper,
even though they could see that the snacks they had came to buy
were sitting right in front of their eyes. They were kids but old
enough to understand that they were not welcomed.

They head to the food stall by the police headquarters' gates.
Sticking their heads in between the metal bars they called out to the
man keeping the food stall.

'Sir… Sir… We want to buy your snacks.'

The man pretended he couldn't hear the boys, lounging on a
wooden bench with his back reclining against his stall, staring
emptily across the street. After minutes of trying, the boys gave up
and slowly walked to the hall. They returned their money to their
father with their heads down.

Nasipudin's older children were treated the same. They tried
buying some food but no shop in and around the police compound
would take their money. But there was one who did, a woman
carrying a big bamboo basket wrapped to her body with a piece of
long old scarf, selling rice packets at an inflated price.

Nasipudin had to spend nearly a fifth of the money he had retrieved to feed his children and their families. It was that or another go at some uncooked instant noodle.

Nasipudin shared one packet with his wife. He would eat only the rice and some chili paste, leaving the tastier vegetables, roasted peanuts and chicken for his wife and small children. Nisa had to be fed. Her weak arms could barely lift a spoon. Her hands were too crooked to grip anything.

With their stomachs half full some went for a nap. There was not much they could do at the police headquarters. People just sit and did nothing, dozed off and prayed at a mosque inside the compound, located just meters away from the hall.

The Ahmadis observed their religion faithfully. Every time they heard a call to prayer they immediately went to the mosque and prayed together, even though Muslims have the option to pray privately at the comforts of their homes. Many Muslims prefer the latter. Some care little about praying at all, leaving their lavishly-built mosques largely deserted except during Friday prayers. The Non-Ahmadi mosques in Lombok were in the thousands. So many were the mosques and so few those frequenting them, mosques in Lombok had to take turns staging Friday prayers. The Ahmadis were the complete opposite. They build simple mosques which are always filled with activities and life and prayers.

Suddenly Nasipudin was summoned by a police officer. Some neighbors he had met that morning came to see him. They were people who were never sympathetic towards Ahmadiyya. Nasipudin greeted them with a smile and asked why they had come.

'There will be an attack later tonight and your house is the primary target. Just repent! Confess that you have committed blasphemy! Leave Ahmadiyya and your house shall be spared. Go back home! Go back to our village and we will live once again as neighbors.'

'What for? For a house? For some bricks and mortars we won't carry with us to our grave? That house was never mine. They can take away my house. My possession. My everything. It doesn't matter. In God's eye only our deeds matter. This is our faith. We will die sooner or later and we will die as Ahmadis.'

The neighbors were shocked. They weren't expecting such an answer from Nasipudin. After giving Nasipudin one final warning: 'leave Ahmadiyya and your house shall be spared.'

***

The day grew old and nightfall was mere hours away. The lady selling rice packets was nowhere to be seen. Even if she was around, Nasipudin only had enough money to buy his big family four more descent meals. Nasipudin had no idea what to do.

His options were slowly becoming limited. The family was not allowed to leave the compound. He couldn't fetch some rice at his barn or pick vegetables from his garden for the family to eat. His family had been drinking uncooked, unfiltered, ground water and eating raw noodles would make his family terribly sick.

He sent a prayer asking for God to show him a way. Just when he thought all hopes were lost in came some familiar faces, a sight for sore eyes, the Marwans. On their hands were some of the things Khaerudin had left two days earlier: rice, meat, vegetables, seasonings, chili sauce. The Marwans had also brought a few things of their own: blankets, pillows, clean clothes, toiletries.

Mrs. Marwan called out for Khaerudin. As he approached her, Mrs. Marwan took out from her purse something which Khaerudin and his family had never seen.

'This is a cellular phone. I have saved my number. If there is anything you need, anything at all, I want you to call me.'

Khaerudin nodded. Suhaidi saw what happened and was envious. In 2002, there were not many cellular phones around, particularly in a small town like Pancor. Suhaidi had only seen cellular phones in the hands of rich tobacco farm owners. Khaerudin never saw one in his life.

'You know how to use this don't you?'

Khaerudin just stood in silence. He had never used a cellphone in his life but was too embarrassed to say it.

'Here… let me show you!'

The two looked carefully as Mrs. Marwan showed the brothers the functions of each dial. She taught the brothers new vocabularies like 'miscall' and 'text messages.'

'This is a charger. You plug this end to your phone and the other end to a power plug. Whenever you're low on battery, always charge this phone.'

Nasipudin was almost in tears. His wife Zubaidah hugged Mrs. Marwan tightly while sobbing in her shoulder. The Marwans were not Ahmadis. They were not neighbors. They were not related by blood. They were not even from Lombok. But they were so nice, so caring and so giving. As people around them were out to harm them, the Marwans reached out to them, helping them at a time of need.

When night came the Marwans left. Nasipudin felt at ease, at least one huge burden had been lifted, one problem solved. But just when he thought his fortune had changed the police neighbor came to Nasipudin with ill news.

'Mr. Nasipudin… Your house is under attack.'

Smiling casually, Nasipudin replied, 'Good. Thank Goodness. Through His grace our house was built. We are mere occupiers. The Lord has reclaimed what has always been His.'

***

The Ahmadis had lost track how many days they have spent at the police headquarters, some said five some said more. With each passing day came another wave of uncertainty. At nights there were sounds of angry mob, gunfire and police sirens. During the day, everything went back to normal like it was all a bad dream. Neighbors, government officials and family members would all came as bearers of bad news, bringing words that their possessions had been looted, their houses had been smashed to bits. Rubbles and metal skeletons were all that was left.

Some people acted as carriers of warnings, threatening those whose houses were still standing that they shall too meet the same ill fate if they refused to leave Ahmadiyya.

The brave Nurul and Suhaidi were never satisfied with hearsays. They made an escape from the precinct while the guards were busy eating dinner. They leapt the metal gates, quietly making their way away from the illuminated main street and took cover in the shadow of dark alleyways and back roads. They were careful to remain invisible. Taking the long way round to avoid people they deemed 'unsympathetic.'

The moon was almost full, bright enough to shed light on where they were going. The plants in the fields were glowing. The neighborhood was colored in shades of grey. True colors were only brought from the houses' interior lights and television sets. There were laughter and chatters as if no malice had happened.

In the shadows they waited for everyone to sleep. Carefully watching from a distance, the rubbles of their former homes. It soon became apparent that their attempt to save whatever they could would prove to be futile.

Their fear was confirmed as they inched closer. Suhaidi's home was no more than a flat slab of concrete. Every brick, every wood beam, every door frame and all of the things inside were gone. Looted.

What remained of his father's home was the concrete rim of their well. There were a few bricks left standing, charred and blackened by fire. Nothing of worth was salvageable. Not even a few plates and pots and pans. Not even old clothes to change the ones they haven't washed for days. The barn was empty. Their father's buffalos were stolen, as was the horse the Marwans had lent so that Nasipudin can operate his cart.

The siblings returned to the police headquarters, confirming what their family had always heard.

'Is it true that our house had been destroyed mom?' Kasafuloh asked his mother Zubaidah while sitting on her lap, heads resting on her chest.

'Don't you worry! When we collect enough money we will build an even bigger house than the one before.'

***

Days of uncertainty would have its toll on the hundreds of refugees who were there. Some grew sick, others delusional. Some Ahmadiyya members would have nightmares and others utter mental breakdowns. Some had been suffering insomnia others hypersomnia. By then, the vast hall would have appeared to have grown smaller, more and more depressing. The smell of urine and unwashed bodies were becoming stronger, more nauseating.

The Ahmadis were not the only ones suffering. Zubaidah's non-Ahmadi brother Ridwan came and was immediately in tears, vomiting blood continuously until he decided he could no longer stomach what had happened to his sister and her family. Other families did not fare much better. Some visiting family members fainted. Others went hysterical, some outraged.

To break away from the harrowing conditions, the solution seemed deceptively simple: leave Ahmadiyya and all shall return to normal. But the Ahmadis wouldn't do it. The persecutors and their use of violence and intimidations had failed. The persecutors tried to use another tactics.

The Ahmadis one morning woke to discover that their leaders were gone. It would be much later that they knew that Raehanudin, Azhar, Sulaeman, Musifudin, Syapi'in, Mahmuludin, Arifin Faruk, Awaludin and Amin Agus, all local Ahmadiyya committee members were taken to the local Military Command headquarters while everyone else was sleeping. This confused the Ahmadiyya members. They have observed strict adherence to their spiritual leaders and by then they were a herd without a shepherd.

By day there were rumors that one of their leaders had left Ahmadiyya. No one was sure where the words originated but they spread like wildfire. In the afternoon they were pamphlets being pasted on the walls of the police compound's mosque reinforcing that belief.

To the Ahmadiyya leaders evacuated to the military headquarter, there were words that a huge sum of their followers had converted to mainstream Islam. By night, people were individually asked if they wished to leave Ahmadiyya knowing that their leaders had forsaken them, to which they replied: 'You can put a bullet to each of our head and we won't waver.'

There were rumors: the Ahmadis shall be driven out of Lombok, forced to migrate to Qadian, the birthplace of their Indian Messiah. This would make the Ahmadiyya followers confused. They were mostly peasants and humble shop owners who never traveled out of Lombok, let alone to another country. How would they survive in a foreign land where people don't speak their language?

Everyone was panicking. Some cried at the prospect of leaving the land they called home. Suhaidi was an exception. He was excited by the thought of going to another country. To him, going to India would be an adventure, a break from his benign existence as a poor peasant and market laborer. He wondered of the things he would see, the places he would go once they moved to India.

It was a bluff, false information meant to create more uncertainty in the minds of the Ahmadis. But this would send their non-Ahmadi friends and families into a panic.

'Leave this religion of yours! Leave it!' Zubaidah's sister Ramlah said, yelling hysterically, sobbing uncontrollably.

'You're not going to India! I won't let you!' she yelled, screaming at the top of her lungs as people struggled to calm her down. She resisted. Kicking and screaming as people began to stare.

'I won't let you! Please... How could you do this me? I'm your sister. Curse your prophet and his religion. Just leave Ahmadiyya! Leave!' she yelled some more. As her emotion peaked, she went into a shock. She fainted. Zubaidah was crying as did her daughters. Faizah's eyes reddened, flooded with tears which soaked her cheeks and nose.

**

It was hard to believe that the attempts to drive away the Ahmadis were not systematic. The rumors spread like wildfire, beyond the walls of the vast hall, beyond the compound. Who spread them and how, remained a mystery. Even how the rumors originated was never answered.

For days the attack on Ahmadis' homes continued. Khaerudin learned about the assailant's movement from calls made by Mrs. Marwan. Others learned from visiting families and friends. Who decided which neighborhood to attack, who the attackers were and how the attackers knew which house to destroy and which to be left alone were unknown.

One night the assailants targeted an Ahmadiyya burial ground, destroying a wall dividing it with a Christian cemetery. The message was: Ahmadis should be treated as non-Muslims. But such act must have been coordinated, the Ahmadis thought. People just don't go attacking an unassuming wall out of spontaneity as everyone seemed to claim. Eventually 81 homes and 8 shops were destroyed.

Faizah wondered whether her husband would crack under pressure. A month ago he was a stranger who didn't know how to pray and read the Koran. The other Ahmadis had years of indoctrination allowing them to be able to resist the systematic pressures for them to leave Ahmadiyya. She was unsure if he would remain head strong about his decision to join Ahmadiyya. She was also uncertain if he didn't regret his decision to marry her. He was after all a tall, handsome man while she an unattractive, short, chubby woman with weather-beaten skin. The fact that he hadn't left, was not enough to convince her that he was here to stay.

The test of his faith came on the seventh day in the form of Guntur's cousin who had traveled all the way from Sumbawa with two other relatives. The three asked to meet Guntur and told Faizah that they wanted some privacy.

'Your family is worried about you. They want you to return back to Sumbawa. Besides… why are you here anyway? What are you doing joining Ahmadiyya? Are you trying to be a saint?'

'I don't want to be anything. I just see Ahmadiyya as good.'

Faizah ran and grabbed her husband by the arm. The family tried to stop her. Before long, it turned into a tug of war.

'This is my husband. Let go!'

'You let go! My family is worried sick about him.'

'No way you are taking my husband. Go and ask permission from the police who put us here.'

The pair let go of Guntur. Without much thought, Faizah grabbed her husband and the pair ran into the hall.

***

That night Faizah took her husband for a private conversation. She asked him to follow her to the backyard of the compound behind the hall.

Softly she spoke: 'So how do you really feel? You don't have to go through all this hardship just because of me. My place is here with my family, with the religion I chose to believe. But you… you have the right to be happy. You have the right to be with whom you choose to live, away from fear, away from persecution.'

Guntur just stood quietly not saying a word.

'It's not that I'm asking for a divorce or anything. I know divorcing is a sin. But we are both trying to find a solution. If you want to join your family, it's ok. We can separate for a while.'

'No. I'll follow you no matter what.'

Faizah was tearing up. She grabbed Guntur, locking her arms in his. She gave Guntur a good look. She felt at ease. She felt she could trust this man she hardly knew. She felt that from that moment on she could truly consider Guntur as her husband, the leader of a family she could call her own.

People said 'love will come eventually over time' to daughters they force to wed. For Faizah it took one month and a week filled with chaos, violence, destruction and the presence of three unexpected guests. Her love for Guntur had finally come.

***

Their days at the precinct were entering its third week. People had lost track of time, lost all sense of personal wellbeing.

On the sixteenth day, when everyone was fast asleep, the Ahmadiyya men were awaken and told to head down the police compound's mosque. The Ahmadis were all feeling drowsy from the few hours of sleep they had. One by one they picked up their sandals and headed to the mosque where they were told to sit down.

An official was waiting. He must have been high in rank. Other officers saluted him. He had many ribbons and badges on his light brown uniform. A cap sat on his thinly shaven head, hiding his eyes in the shadows. He gave a good look of everyone in the room.

'Can I have everyone's attention?'

He waited for everyone to quiet down. With a loud, piercing voice he didn't have to wait for long.

'This police headquarter is no place for Ahmadiyya refugees. We have more important duties than to feed and house you people. Now we ask for your cooperation. For those of you who choose to stay in Ahmadiyya we will escort them out of this island, Lombok. If you choose to leave Ahmadiyya we will compensate your losses. We will even multiply them.'

Everyone gasp.

'If you want to go west, I will take you to Lembar port. If you want to head east I will take you to Kayangan port. Board a ferry and you will no longer be my responsibility.'

Everyone looked at each other.

'Now I ask you, who here wishes to stay in Ahmadiyya please rise and stand up!'

People were confused, looking at each other without saying a word. They had just woken up but they were asked to make such tough decision.

Amid the confusion, one suddenly stood up. It was a blind Ahmadiyya man. Seeing this, the rest of the congregation: men, women and children followed suit. The high ranking officer was stunned. He couldn't believe what was happening.

The crowd came alive, whispering to each other with a sigh of relief.

'You're a very brave man,' one person said to the blind man.

'Why? What happened?'

'Well… you were the first to stand up?'

'I was the first to stand up? Were you following me? I couldn't see. I'm blind. I thought you all have stood up. I thought I was following you guys'

***

The next morning, dozens of minivans were waiting, parked in front of the police headquarters' main building. The Ahmadis were told to pack up their things and sit in the vans. No one was sure where they were taken. Suhaidi was preparing himself for India. The rest of the family cried, thinking they would never see their friends and families ever again. They were leaving the homes of their ancestor, their birthplace, the town that they loved, the fields and market where they worked.

Nasipudin told the family to gather one last time before they got into the waiting van.

'Wherever we shall end up we will stick together. Wherever we are taken, there God has prepared for us His blessings. Wherever we will head to, we shall rebuild our lives.'

With the minivans packed with people and their belongings, they began to move, slowly moving its way out of the police compound. The vans began to pick up speed as they drove along the open road. Some children began to cheer.

'Mom... Mom... This is the way to our mosque isn't it? Will we pass our mosque?'

The mood of the children changed when they did pass their mosque. For the first time they learned that it had been destroyed, reduced to rubbles. Looters had stolen everything inside. Scavengers had stripped the fallen structure out of its tile roof, iron rods and wooden beams. They cried, unable to comprehend the atrocity, the maliciousness of men.

The passed a sign telling them that they had left Pancor. The minivans moved past big two story homes encircled by rustic, small dwellings. Past a grand mosque with towering minarets. Past small patches of rice fields. They continued their journey west, past rows of stores colorfully painted in bright yellow, green and orange, selling electronics and household goods, the things they used to have. They passed hundreds of motorcycle taxis offering service to thousands of shoppers.

At an intersection was an even bigger mosque with taller minarets. The minivans made a left turn, past women sweeping their porches, dirtied by the blinding dust swooped up by passing motorists. They drove past curious onlookers, past children returning home from soccer match, past a decaying mushalla, roof covered in dry leaves. Past a chicken slaughter house, past a small market, this time rustic and colorless. Past giant banners bearing the face of some politicians, past a well-preserved colonial building which had been converted into the headquarter of a government agency.

Minutes into their drive, they passed endless stretch of tobacco fields, dotted by tobacco collecting houses and processing plants. A small hill where the dead are buried, under the shade of frangipani trees greeted them as they approached a dam. They drove past empty brick structures used to cultivate bird's nest. Minutes away was a big gate saying that they were leaving East Lombok.

There were more big mosques, more markets, more rows of colorful houses and rustic homes. They drove past another sign, this time welcoming them to West Lombok. At a statue of two women holding water jugs they made a right, past a small back road shaded by tall trees. They passed countless of unmanned intersections, Hindu temples, mosques and homes which littered the snaking narrow road.

The vehicles slowed, making a right turn to a complex with four decaying buildings. It was their destination, their home for then after. It was a place called Transito.

CHAPTER 8

Transito was a complex owned by the Indonesian Ministry of Manpower and Transmigration used to temporarily host transmigrants on their way to less populated Borneo or Sulawesi. Lombok was a major producer of transmigrants.

The island was small, just a two hour drive will get you from end to end. It was barren with farms slowly encroached by housing areas and hotels as the island shifted its economy from agriculture to tourism. It was dangerously overpopulated and friction was rife. In 2000, Lombok was the scene of a religious conflict between Muslims and Christians, then came the persecution against Ahmadiyya, there would be occasional riots and clashes between Muslims and Hindus.

It was hard to break away from poverty in Lombok, particularly if you were not a landowner and get your hands at growing tobacco. With its specific need for special care, tobacco too proved to be a gamble. Half of Lombok's transmigrants lost their money to tobacco. Transmigration provided an escape, a fresh start, a hiding place from the debt collectors pounding their doors.

Transito, as the name suggest, provides the transmigrants a place of transit, a temporary shelter before the government finds them a new place. They come from Central, East and West Lombok and Sumbawa Island with their dreams to Transito, located in the northern part of the provincial capital Mataram, With the transmigrants coming just once or twice a year, it too became the ideal place as a temporary stop for the displaced Ahmadis.

The complex was at least sixty meters long and fifty meters wide. There were four main buildings in Transito, each ten by thirty meters and each in various stages of decay. The buildings were separated by narrow passage ways made from concrete blocks covered in sands with a gutter running on each side. Its front yard was made of one giant concrete slab. Sitting on opposite ends of the slab were what should have been a garden, left unattended, infested with weed, augmenting the sorry state of the entire complex.

The roofs were made of asbestos, some parts cracked and leaking. Only run-down, mold infested plaster ceilings were stopping the roof from sending blinding, choking dusts to the inhabitants below. In some parts, the ceilings were missing, holed, fallen off, revealing decaying wooden beams above. The walls were dirty, cracks run in continuous lines. Some cracks were so severe, red bricks were left exposed. The paints were either chipped or washed out. The walls were dull, dirty, sorry-looking shades of grey. The fences were more rust than metal.

The building in the far left was divided into living quarters each with two bed rooms, two by two-and-a-half meter in size, a two-and-a-half by five meter living room, a one-and-a-half by five meter kitchen sat in the back. There were five quarters in that single building.

The building next to it was divided into two large rooms of equal size, each ten by fifteen meter. The third was one long hall. At the back were six lavatories and three bathrooms which everyone had to share. A kitchen sat at the back right corner.

The building in the far right was shorter just fifteen meters long to make way for two houses. The houses were government-owned and rented to low ranking public officials. The houses were small but lovely with fresh coat of paints, undamaged ceilings, complete set of tile roof and well manicured gardens.

The Ahmadis were placed at the building with one long hall. Once more they found themselves having to share a cramped out space with people they barely knew. Again they had to sleep in cold, plastic-mat-covered floor. But this time there were no gunshot waking them up in the middle of the night, no angry mob out to spill their blood. There was no guard telling them not to leave, no rumor and pressure for them to abandon their faith.

Ahmadiyya officials were free to walk in and out, telling their followers to stay strong, to be patient as their leaders worked to find a way out. From Jakarta came Abdul Basith, their Emir. The supreme leader of the Ahmadiyya congregation in Indonesia. Two things concerned him. The local government had said that the Ahmadis could only stay at Transito for two weeks maximum. Somehow, the displaced Ahmadis must be given a place to stay.

His other concern was children like Malik. He was worried that schools in Mataram would not accept them and they would not be able to continue their education. For smaller children like Safir, he felt it was best that they stayed with their parents.

And so it was agreed, school children fourth grade and up were to be sent to a boarding home in Java. Just a few days since their arrival to Transito, forty eight children would be separated from their family.

As an Ahmadi, Zubaidah had the obligation to follow her leader, but sending her eleven-year-old son Malik out on his own to live with complete strangers for who knows how long proved to be too much for her.

She must have combed Malik's hair many times over that morning, rubbed his diamond-shaped face with a gentle touch. Zubaidah was tearing up, unable to contain her emotion. Malik was also in tears but Zubaidah wouldn't let Malik's tears ran down his face, wiping his eyes continuously.

A bus came, parking inside the complex. The bus was adorned with artwork depicting a panoramic view of a forest. Amin Agus hopped on board. He was the Pancor congregation official tasked with looking after the children. Some of Malik's friends seemed excited. They never traveled outside Lombok. They didn't realize it would be months until they were reunited with their parents again. For some, it was to be their last time.

***

There had been more instant noodles coming their way but this time they had utensils. A place to cook whenever they felt hungry. With the exception of the second building from the right, the entire complex seemed lifeless. Not even a stray cat was roaming around. The only animals attracted to the complex were flies and mosquitoes, hovering around the refugees. But somehow the Ahmadis looked more alive. There was no joy at the police headquarters, only fear and uncertainty. By then, they only had to deal with uncertainty.

Mataram was a city, small but a city nonetheless. Everyone was too busy minding their own business. People were less fanatic about religion. In Mataram, mosques sat side by side with Hindu temples. There was no one calling them names, telling them that they were blasphemous. There was no one forcing them to leave Ahmadiyya, renounce their faith to the Messiah. The local government also didn't care much about the Ahmadis. Transito belonged by the central government, the Ahmadis were still technically under custody of the East Lombok administration. For the Mataram government, all that was left was a simple job of feeding them and they had ample stock of instant noodles.

People around Transito also didn't mind having Ahmadis in the neighborhood. They didn't care. But so was no one. The newspapers in Jakarta didn't put the Ahmadis and their plight as front cover news, burying the atrocities in the back pages. Stories about the Ahmadis went from 300 word fillers to 90 word briefs.

There was far more important news to cover. Newspapers and televisions were too busy comparing the recently impeached, controversial but reform-minded, moderate Muslim president Gus Dur and his replacement, a visionless, strong-headed lady whose rise to fame was much credited for having a very famous father, the country's first president Soekarno. Foreign media was more interested in Ambon where a bloody sectarian conflict had killed thousands and by then slowly becoming a terrorism recruiting ground.

For the Ahmadis in Lombok, the casualty of the violence numbered just one. It was never a hot subject for the media in Jakarta. The correspondents and contributors and stringers of national media reside in Mataram. Very few bothered to document the atrocities in far away East Lombok.

Mataram provided the Ahmadis much needed safety. But there was fear flooding Zubaidah's head. Fear that her son would not be OK. It is a long ride from Lombok to Jakarta. She wondered whether Malik would stand the long trip. She questioned whether Amin Agus is handy with the kids. What if Malik got sick? What if he misses his family? What if he doesn't like the new place? What if his new friends are mean to him? What if he doesn't like the cold weather of the mountainous Tasikmalaya? What if he doesn't like Sundanese food? What would he eat instead? But what if he feels at home there? Would he be too busy playing with his new friends and forget to call home? What if he decides to stay and never return?

Transito seemed very quiet without the children, half of them gone to West Java. The condition took its toll on smaller children like Safir, now with less friends to play with.

'When will Malik come back?' he asked his mother. 'Where is he?'

His mother smiled and gave his hair a gentle brush with her fingers. 'He's in Java.'

'What is he doing in Java?'

'Studying.'

'I want to study in Java too. Can we go there?'

'Of course. Which is why your father is working really hard. So we can have money to go and visit him.'

'I miss him.'

'I know son. I miss him too.'

As times passed by, Transito became more and more desolate. It was becoming more and more roomy. Their cleric Raehanudin was among the first to leave. The central leaders in Jakarta thought that since the Ahmadiyya congregation in Pancor was no more he should be reassigned to Sulawesi. Congregation leader Azhar moved to Surabaya in East Java to join his son.

For the rest of the congregation, they left because they had no where to go. They had no friend or family in Mataram. They were peasants and vendors. There were no fields they could plow in Mataram, no rice they could plant, no money to rebuild their lives.

Some returned quietly to East Lombok and stayed with their non-Ahmadi cousins and uncles, practicing their faith in secret. Some left for Java to become construction workers while the women worked as maids. Some got in touch with their friends in Sumatra and Borneo who told them there was work there as palm oil plantation laborers.

Some never said where they went and never to be seen or heard again. The Ahmadis are a very close-knit society with branches all over the world communicating with one another regularly. To disappear means they were Ahmadiyya in name only.

Some openly announced their departure from Ahmadiyya. They couldn't stand the fact that their leaders chose to 'resolve the problem quietly.' They were also told to keep paying their candah (contribution) to the congregation.

The Ahmadis have candah for everything. Candah for Ahmadis is more taxes than alms-giving. There is the compulsory income candah. They are made to give up one-eighteenth of what they earn to the congregation (far more than the one-fortieth other Muslims are obliged to set aside, and that is after they deduct their day-to-day expenses).

There are other candahs too. Every time they receive God's blessings, the Ahmadis are told to give candah. There is a candah for a newly born baby.

With all the candahs put together, the Ahmadis could be giving up to a third of their earnings for the congregation. The money goes straight to their international head office in London where it would be distributed back per country. Each national branch distributes the money to different areas and then to each local chapters.

London to the Ahmadis is like Rome to the Catholics. There sits the leader of all Ahmadiyya leaders, their Caliphs, one who presides over all things Ahmadiyya. It is a man whose words are absolute, whose photographs hang on the wall of every Ahmadi's homes.

Candah money from Ahmadis around the world would build Europe's grandest mosque with marbled floor and columns and climate control and automatic faucets. At the national chapter level, slightly less grand mosques and learning centers are built. By the time it reaches the local branch there was only enough to build modest mosques, finance the clerics and send a handful of children to Ahmadiyya schools so that they can become clerics and propagate their religion so that more candahs can be collected.

Alms are meant to distribute wealth from the rich to the poor but in some cases they work the other way around.

For some refugees, being instructed to resume paying candah was the last draw. The food they ate was not provided by the congregation, it came from their families and friends. The clothes on their backs were donations from the Red Cross and other NGOs. They were farmers with no land to farm. They had no money to start their own business. They had nowhere to go.

The leaders kept telling them to be patient. That was all their leaders did, aside from offering their prayers. Not seeking retribution and compensation, not voicing their concerns to the government, not telling law enforcers to do their job. The leaders kept saying that the Indonesian Ahmadiyya Congregation is a moral and spiritual organization and that helping them rebuild their lives was outside of their main function.

The leaders kept telling them that they have been generous and they should be grateful. They have been writing letters to the government about their plight and that they should patiently wait for a reply. The government never replied.

Patience is an easy thing to say when you don't live in a decrepit building with three-hundred others. Patience is an easy thing to say when you have somewhere to go. Patience is an easy thing to say when you still have a job, an income, a place to call your own. Patience is an easy thing to say when you are not the victim.

Unlike some others, Nasipudin and his family knew a thing or two about patience. He knew the virtues and powers of patience and the destructions brought by lack of it. The Koran is littered with stories about patience and the rewards that come after. The prophets and the saints were all driven from their homes. They were ridiculed, accused of blasphemy. Some called them insane. Others called them liars. Miracles would be performed in front of their eyes and they would dismiss them as witchcraft, trickery.

Patience was the prophets' most powerful weapon. They rest their fate to the All Merciful God. By His command comes calamity. Floods, plagues, balls of fire. Only the faithful, only the patient were spared.

And what good impatience brings? Isn't life but a stopping point? A proving ground of our faith and deed? Is the afterlife not eternal? What good is fortune when we denounce His blessings?

Nasipudin had a lot to rejoice, as pitiful as his family's condition may be. They were still together. They had not fallen sick. They still had their lands back home. They could sell it. They were offered protection and safety from his brother, given plenty to eat by the Marwans.

With their time at the Transito coming to an end the leaders had offered to rent houses for them and pay for the first three months. Some demanded more but he was thankful for the offer. Their leaders had told the refugees to find work and get back on their feet. Some took this as a sign they were abandoning their members.

But Nasipudin saw it differently. God has given him health and strength and mind to work and put food at the table. Would using them be a crime? Isn't providing for one's family the obligation of every man? Would sitting still and doing nothing count as being ungrateful for the health and the strength He has bestowed?

It was of course easier said than done.

CHAPTER 9

There were 80 families when they were first evacuated to Transito.
Only 30 families remained by the time they left. Their Ahmadiyya
leaders said that they can only rent 15 houses in low-income housing
complexes in and around Mataram. The leaders said they will pay
the first three months of rent. Beyond that point they would have to
come up with their own money.

'Don't go begging people for money! We must survive on our
own. Get a fresh start and get back on your feet!' the leaders said.
'Just because you are away from home does not mean we must
surrender. Does not mean we must wait for the government to do
something to change our lives. Rebuild your life!'

Bigger families would have a house of their own. Smaller ones
must share their homes with their parents or siblings or cousins or
aunties. The houses were small, no bigger than the individual
quarters in Transito's far right building. They had two rooms, each
three by three meter; a small living room, about four by three meters.
The kitchen and the bathroom were cramped into a two by five meter
space at the back.

Khaerudin and Suhaidi were the only family members with a
child. They stayed in Mataram while her sister Nurul and her
husband Asmi who had remained childless after years of marriage
went to Tangerang just west of Indonesia's biggest city Jakarta to
become domestic workers. Masitah, the teenage daughter number
five went to Ciledug (another Jakarta suburb) and landed a job at a
family. She became their maid, sometimes tending the family's
beauty parlor located at the family's home.

Zubaidah stayed in Mataram to care for her crippled daughter
Nisa and her two youngest sons Safir and Kasafuloh. Nasipudin said
he had got in touch with some Ahmadi families in the neighboring
island of Sumbawa who told him that there was work in some
plantations there.

Khaerudin and Suhaidi moved in together and had a plethora of work, never landing a fixed job. Suhaidi, with his confidence and lobbying skills were able to convince people to give him work at a market. He tried his hands at keeping other people's land, tending an empty property up for sale or rent. He became laborers for some construction work, carrying buckets of mixed cement, wheeling construction materials in carts to where they are needed by more skilled workers. Anything that only demanded power and not skills which he did not have.

Khaerudin knew carpentry and could have easily landed some construction work of his own. Mataram began to boom as Lombok opened its doors to tourism. Hotels and shops and restaurants and houses were being built all over town as tourists came attracted by Lombok's unspoiled beaches. There was plenty of construction work but Khaerudin was too shy to approach construction managers he didn't know and convince them to give him a job.

Every day Khaerudin simply pedaled his way across the strange new city in a bicycle the Marwans had given him. He cycled aimlessly for days, sometimes ending up in main streets and small dead end roads. In the afternoon, he would take his wife and son out for a ride. He built a basket from old wood so that his three year-old can sit at the front. He took them to the places he had seen earlier: metal workshops turning old steel gates into new ones, workshops building illegal mining equipments, workshops to recycle plastic, workshops to recycle papers.

But with no money saved and a wife who was eight months pregnant, desperation came seeping in and finally he mustered enough courage to go to a construction project and look for work.

'In the name of Allah the All-Caring and All-Merciful' he said before approaching a project manager.

At the first project he went to, he landed a job.

***

Faizah and Guntur decided they were not going to take the Ahmadiyya leaders' offer of renting a place in Mataram.

'Let's try to go to my hometown first. Maybe there is work there,' said Guntur to his wife Faizah.

Guntur's hometown was in Sumbawa in a sleepy port town of Seteluk, the first town anyone would see after they disembark from a short ferry ride from Lombok. There lies an area called Kelanir in the fringes of the town. It was only a fifteen minute drive from Seteluk by motorcycle taxi.

It would have taken them just two hours to get to Kayangan port in Lombok's easternmost point. The ferry ride would have taken less than an hour. But Faizah was anxious. She was never worried about the journey to Sumbawa. She was afraid of how people would treat them once they were there.

Faizah had never met her mother-in-law Saudah. She was told that Saudah was a very nice woman and that she shouldn't be afraid. But Saudah was not an Ahmadiyya. She observed the mainstream notion that Faizah's Messiah was an impostor.

Saudah lived alone after separating from Guntur's father. Saudah had six children of her own before marrying Guntur's father. From their marriage came an only child, Guntur. The marriage lasted less than ten years.

Faizah and Guntur woke up very early that morning. The bus to Sumbawa stops at a terminal some 10 minute drive. They didn't have any motorcycle. (It was either burned or stolen back in East Lombok). The cost of a motorcycle taxi ride was the same as a meal. With a goony sack full of clothes (they lost their suitcases in the attack too) and a dream they walked. It took nearly an hour to get to the terminal. The morning was cold but they were soaking in sweat, particularly Guntur who never worked the fields or did any manual labor.

The bus was packed with people sitting on a rundown seat covered in faux leather. It wasn't air conditioned. Speakers playing some Eurodance remix of a local song were the only signs of lavishness.

The bus had been parked in the same spot for hours. The driver refused to set off before the bus was full. When there was no seat left, he took out flimsy plastic chairs for people to sit in the hall. On the roof were canvas suitcases and cardboard boxes filled with who knows what. When the roof was overloaded with stuff, they placed bags, suitcases, boxes and packages in every nook and cranny inside the cabin.

It was an agonizing ride. The heat inside was enough to make a horse pass out. But people were accustomed to the heat. They were used to being cramped in a space filled with stuff and strangers. They had no choice. Faizah and Guntur certainly had been through worse. Just days ago they were living in a hall cramped with three-hundred others.

***

It was hard for Zubaidah to deal with separation. She had no way of knowing whether her daughters were alright in their new places. Nurul had a husband by her side who can take care of her. Zubaidah was anxious about Masitah. A teenage girl from a small town on her own in a cosmopolitan city of eight-million? Jakarta was full of temptation, full of lustful youths and the trappings of conveniences and ambitions which could make one stray from the path of God. What if she met a non-Ahmadi man and fell in love? Would she sacrifice her faith?

Zubaidah wondered if she had taught her daughter enough about religion. Masitah was nothing like Zubaidah. Zubaidah got married when she was 14 and had to grow up fast. She never knew what it was like to be young and attractive and single in a big city. She wondered if Masitah should have taken the Marwans offer to stay in Pancor and worked for them. At least Zubaidah knew the Marwans. They were very nice and would have treated Masitah like the daughter they never had.

She was worried about Faizah too. Would her mother-in-law be nice to her? Even if she knew that Faizah was an Ahmadi? Guntur converted to Ahmadiyya when he married her daughter. Would she pit the blame on Faizah for having her son leave mainstream Islam?

Zubaidah was worried about her husband. The two were inseparable ever since they got married. She was lost without him. She didn't even know exactly where he was, what kind of job he landed, would it be enough to feed their family or if he had found work at all.

Their money was depleting fast and she had Nisa, Safir and Kasafuloh to take care of. Zubaidah was becoming restless. She couldn't sleep at night as hard as she tried. Finally she decided to do something. Something she knew, selling vegetables. Maybe it was enough to feed her children. Maybe it was enough to pay the rent after three months of living for free. Maybe it was enough to send Safir back to school. Maybe it would keep her mind preoccupied from all the worries.

In 2002, two-hundred-thousand rupiah was equivalent to around twenty-two dollars. It was not much. Back in Pancor it was barely enough to provide her entire family with food for three weeks. In Mataram, it was enough for two weeks. And she only had to worry about feeding four mouths. It was all the money she had left. It was her only cash available. It was her starting capital to reboot her life.

She asked her sisters-in-law, Fahriah and Fatimah, her husband's younger sisters to join her to the market. It was a Monday. They left first thing in the morning to catch the first batch of vegetables coming from the farmers. They walked for thirty minutes in the early morning cold. The road was quiet. Except for the dogs barking at them, no one had woken up.

The market was already crowded with vendors and farmers and traders. It looked like they arrived too late. There were people pacing up and down the market with baskets and plastic bags filled with the best fruits, the best vegetables and the best meat. Some customers were beginning to arrive. It seemed like the women were lucky to get their hands at some second grade goods.

'OK. Who will buy the goods? Who transports them? Who is in charge of selling them?' Zubaidah told her in-laws who just had their first go at market life. 'OK. I will buy the goods.' Zubaidah said. It seemed fitting because she knew what to look for and what they were worth. She had mastered the art of haggling. She knew every trick farmers used to pass their fruits and vegetables as quality items.

'Fahriah... you stay with me and have the goods I bought transported over to Fatimah! Fatimah... you go and find us a nice spot over there so we can sell them!'

Zubaidah soon learned that the prices were different from Pancor. In Mataram, everything was more expensive. It was obvious. The fruits and vegetables came from far away in Lombok's interior. There were transportation costs the traders had to consider.

Zubaidah was able to buy vegetables for 1,500 rupiah a bunch. Fatimah sold them for 1,700 rupiah. They thought they were making a profit. They were wrong. They had to pay rent and sanitation fee which were double, sometimes triple than the fees in Pancor.

The women were thwarted. Their plan to earn some money failed disastrously. Upon arriving back home, Khaerudin asked his mother how it went. As if their faces were not telling enough.

'I started with 200,000 rupiah. Now, all I have left is 150,000 rupiah.'

Fahriah and Fatimah would never go with Zubaidah to the market ever again.

But Zubaidah was undeterred. That night, she asked Khaerudin to accompany her to the market the following morning. They agreed to walk to the market earlier this time hoping to find the freshest vegetables available. She could have gone alone but she was afraid of the dogs. That morning, the dogs did chase after them.

Zubaidah only needed company for the way to the market. Afterwards Khaerudin was free to do his construction work. By noon, Zubaidah walked home all on her own. When Khaerudin returned from work he asked her the same question as the day before.

'How did it go this time?'

'I only have 75,000 rupiah left.'

'Just hang in there mom!'

'Who said anything about quitting?'

***

The next morning she gambled. Buying what no one else would buy, selling what no one else would sell, jackfruits, a fruit people sometimes cook like vegetables to make soup. Jackfruits were more expensive than other vegetables. Zubaidah had a stroke of luck when she ran into a woman who was preparing for a feast. Jackfruit soup is a must have for any party here in Lombok. The woman eventually became a regular because she was selling good stuff for an affordable price.

On the fourth day, for the first time since she came to Mataram, she made a profit. On the sixth day, she gained back her initial 200,000 rupiah capital.

CHAPTER 10

Sumbawa is an island first gained notoriety in the 19th century as being the home of Mount Tambora, eruption of which was so violent Europe was without a summer for a year. It was also known as the island with four kingdoms, constantly at war with each other. In modern day a different war was fought, one between locals and a giant mining company. The giant company came and dug the earth for copper and gold, dumping toxic wastes into the beaches and drove all the surfers away.

The copper mine would make Sumbawa the richest district in West Nusa Tenggara. But the riches went to the elite few and migrating workers from other islands, while the locals had to deal with polluted land and water and drought and famine. It was one of the richest islands in Indonesia but with the highest rate of malnutrition and child mortality.

The buses from Sumbawa brought wave of people looking to escape the cycle of poverty and famine. The passengers were mostly heading to the airport in Mataram where planes take them to some foreign country in the Middle East or the rest of Asia. There they found work. Some returned with lavishly embroidered clothes and jewelries and expensive watches and electronics they could not find in Sumbawa.

Some returned poorer than before, having been ripped off by their placement agencies and forced into modern-day slavery. Some met abusive employers and returned with deformed faces or bruised and burned bodies. Some met extremely abusive employers and returned to Sumbawa in a coffin.

Guntur came from a long line of royalties whose status were then becoming more and more ceremonial. But even ceremonial royalties had better access to education. They had lands and influence which others didn't.

Guntur's family was well off, striking it rich by sending the poor and desperate to work for abusive employers in other countries. His other family struck rich by telling poorer people to risk cave-ins and mercury poisoning and arrest to dig for gold on the lands they never own. Guntur and Faizah took the same bus in search for a new beginning. But they were going the other way.

Faizah's worry disappeared when Saudah gave Guntur a big hug. She was worried sick when she found out Guntur had joined Ahmadiyya. She couldn't contain her emotion when she heard that people were targeting Ahmadis like Guntur in East Lombok. She grew more and more restless as the violence continued.

But her worry receded when she discovered that Guntur was safe and evacuated to Mataram. She was glad that his son's new Ahmadi family was looking after him. And so a son had returned home, bringing with him his new wife.

'Who's this?' she said with a wide smile giving Faizah a good rubbing on her upper arm.

'You must be Faizah? Welcome... welcome... It's so glad to meet you at last.'

Saudah led Guntur and Faizah to an empty room where the pair would sleep. She gave clean blankets and pillows. Saudah gave Faizah one of her nightgowns which she had only worn once or twice. Saudah gave Faizah a brand new set of mukena (women's prayer garb) and sajadda (prayer mat).

Saudah prepared the couple some dinner. On the table were roasted chicken, fishes, goat stew and curry. Faizah couldn't think when she last had such delicious meal. For weeks Faizah and her husband had been eating instant noodle and rice with water spinach.

'Do you like the food? Have some more!' Saudah kept telling Faizah the same thing over and over.

Saudah was nothing like her introverted son Guntur. She was a lovely woman who loved to chat. She was polite and smiling the entire time. She told stories of how Guntur was like as a kid. Saudah told how he never went outside to play with the other kids.

Guntur's half siblings came to see them once and a while. They were very cold towards Faizah. They shook her hand while looking the other way. Faizah tried to be polite, hiding her discomfort and asked questions. The half siblings only stared at Faizah without saying a word and talked to each other. Faizah thought how such a friendly woman like Saudah can have such spiteful children.

At his mother-in-law's home Faizah was summoned by one of Guntur's half-brothers. His name was Aleh. He was the oldest of the six and as the only one in his family who had performed the hajj pilgrimage, the one who knew most about religion.

He was a wealthy man, as was anyone who can afford to go to Mecca in Sumbawa. Aleh asked Faizah and Guntur to sit down with the rest of the family in the living room. He looked at Faizah straight in the eye.

'We know you are one of those Ahmadiyya people. I just want to let you know that we don't want your religion here. If you really want to stay then leave Ahmadiyya. If you don't want to follow our Islam then you can go back to wherever it is you're from. But you have to go on your own. Our brother will stay.'

Faizah hold her husband by the hand. Saudah was quiet. She knew this day would come but didn't expect it to be that soon. She was rejoicing the return of a son just a few days back. She was ecstatic to learn that he had found a very nice woman. But Saudah was too afraid to speak her mind.

Aleh outstretched his arm and pointed his index finger to a white cotton pouch. He wiggled his finger as if asking one of his brothers to fetch it. He grabbed the pouch, spilling its content on the living room's coffee table. It was full of money. One-hundred-and-twenty 100,000 rupiah note. Aleh said that Guntur's brothers and sisters had gathered all this money.

'We are prepared to give this you. All you have to do is leave Ahmadiyya.'

Before her eyes was the solution to all of their problems. It was lucratively simple. Leave Ahmadiyya and they wouldn't have to worry about money. It was the biggest sum of money that Faizah had ever seen in person. At that time, 12 million rupiah was enough to buy food for a year in Sumbawa. It was enough to buy the latest, most advanced scooter around.

They had no place to go and all they had to do was to say 'I will leave Ahmadiyya.' No more living in uncertainty. No more living in camps. No more sharing a hall with hundreds of refugees. No more running from attackers. They could take the money and stay in Sumbawa. They can be part of the family. They can say they had left Ahmadiyya and practice in secret. They can renounce the Messiah that day and ask for redemption later.

But the All Seeing God would know. They would rejoice here on Earth and suffer damnation for all eternity if they did. Faizah was sure of it. But she didn't know whether her husband agreed.

'I can't decide now. I must think this through with my husband because this is not an easy decision.'

They retreated to their room talking in whispers while the others waited outside.

'I will never leave my faith but I don't know about you. If you are willing to accept the offer, I understand.'

'I will follow whatever decision you will make.'

The pair got out of the room. They announced their decision. Aleh lifted his chin and took a deep, audible breath. The others shook their head in disbelief. Chuckling cynically in disappointment. Aleh gave Faizah a malicious stare.

'Then pack your bags! Leave this house… first thing in the morning!'

The brothers and sisters went back to their home, promising to return in the morning to see them head back to Mataram.

While packing their bags, Saudah came into their room with a canvas suitcase in her hand.

'Do you have a suitcase? I don't travel all that much. I don't see why I even bothered to keep one. You can have it. It'll keep your things nice and tidy.'

Faizah gave her mother-in-law a hug.

'It's not that we want to say goodbye. I really wished we could stay longer.'

'I know… I know… I wish too.'

She smiled at Faizah. Wiped the tears off Faizah's face.

'Here's a little something.' Saudah said while handing Faizah some money and some jewelries. The two hugged again.

'I want to see grandchildren, you hear. Please take a good care of my son!'

Faizah nodded

.

CHAPTER 11

The Bertais market in Mataram was the biggest in the whole province. It was a place where money changed hands. From traders bringing produce and tobacco leaves from other parts of the province to collectors who distributed them to all corners of the country. Money changed hands from customers to sellers. From people renting motorcycle taxis to the men operating them. From the car owners parking their vehicles to the attendants manning the parking lot. If Faizah was to earn some money, she thought, it was here.

The market was huge but hidden from view with rundown multistory shops sprawling in neat rows along narrow pathways. The buildings were old, occupied by rich middlemen and distributors and restaurants. The one closest to the main road were well maintained, with fresh coats of paint. They were the more expensive units. Occupied by printers and motorcycle dealers and automotive spare part distributors and banks. The varying types of the businesses they run were obvious to passerby, emblazoned high up in the air in oversize billboards.

Vendors like Zubaidah and Faizah were left to sell on the pavements and road and dirty ground, filling every available space they can find. For Zubaidah and Faizah, finding a spot was a constant battle. They were newcomers looking to make some money at the market but other vendors saw them as competition.

'No that's my spot. Get out! Get out! Find your own space,' said a woman who arrived an hour after Zubaidah and Faizah had set up her tarpaulin sheet on the ground to display her goods. The woman put her basket on top of their goods, crushing their vegetables and fruits.

Everyday, there would be more harassment from other vendors. Sometimes they were shooed away. Sometimes vendors threw garbage and discarded meat at them so that they would move. The message was clear: 'stay at the back of the market, away from our customers.'

Zubaidah and her daughter Faizah simply kept their distance from the mean vendors. They never argued or confronted them. They didn't want to make a scene. They were newcomers who had just been driven away from their hometown, out in the market trying their luck. The last thing they want was an enemy.

One day a vendor abruptly came up to their spot and shoved their basket to the side violently, spilling its content. A big tubby female vendor saw this and shouted from the opposite side.

'Hey leave her alone! Can't you see she was just trying to feed her family?' the woman screamed staring at the mean lady with a threatening look. The mean lady just kept her head down, slowly walking away to another corner of the market.

The nice woman helped them picked up their goods.

'Don't worry I got your back. I've been selling here ever since I was single. Everybody here knows who I am. If you're ever in trouble again just call me OK?'

The nice woman introduced herself as Rambik. She was one of the more successful vendors. She had her own stall. It was full of fancy fruits that nobody else sells. Grapes, oranges, apples. The fruits of Lombok's rich. Somehow Rambik trusted Zubaidah and Faizah and was always nice to them. The pair never knew why. Rambik often gave Zubaidah bananas to take home. Zubaidah's children couldn't remember the last time they ate bananas.

'My friend... She gave it to me,' Zubaidah told Khaerudin that day.

***

As soon as he got back from Sumbawa where he worked as a plantation laborer Nasipudin followed his wife to the market. Nasipudin also asked Guntur to come along. Guntur agreed. He had decided that he didn't have what it takes to be a construction worker. He was nothing like his brothers-in-law Khaerudin and Suhaidi. Before marrying Faizah, Guntur never worked as manual labor. For weeks he returned with sore backs, blisters on his arms and bruises on his shoulder.

Nasipudin knew Guntur needed a change of profession. His daughter Faizah had told him so. Guntur just nodded. Not saying a word while retaining his typical sorry looking face. Inside he was jumping over backwards in joy.

Nasipudin asked Guntur to stay close to him as they went from one shop to the next, one distributor's warehouse to the other, offering their services as porters.

'Excuse me sir… We are porters. Perhaps you might need some stuff to carry around. Perhaps you need our service.'

They were given the cold shoulder. Shop managers and owners told them to leave whisking their hands in the air while turning their backs at them. 'No… no… no… Don't need you here' one said. 'Leave us alone… We have our own porters,' said another.

Some were more polite. 'Oh you're porters? Well… we have no work for you here. But we'll look for you when we do.' They never did.

Occasionally some shop owners felt sorry for them. 'OK… I need these sacks of rice delivered to that black van over there. You sir… Get these vegetables over to that side! '

The sack of rice weighed 30 kilograms each. Nasipudin and Guntur had to carry them for at least 100 meter from the shop to the back of a waiting pick up truck while dodging customers crowding the frantic market.

They get 1,000 rupiah each every time they transported one sack of rice. Sometimes the man asked Nasipudin and Guntur to carry a sack filled with watermelon. The sack weighed 60 kilograms and they had to travel twice the distance to the man's storage unit. They would get 2,000 rupiah. (In 2002, it was equivalent to 22 cent).

***

Days turned to weeks turned to months. Nasipudin had made a few friends and had a few regular customers. But the market not only hosted vendors and porters.

'Hey sir… Do you have change for a twenty?' a man told Nasipudin one day. The man took out a 20,000 rupiah note from his wallet and held it in his hand for Nasipudin to see.

Nasipudin took out his money and gave him the change. The man thanked him and walked hurriedly before disappearing into the crowd of market goers. There was something odd about the man. There was something odd about the 20,000 rupiah paper note that he gave too. He gave the note a good look. He walked over to his wife's stall and showed her the note.

'I think this is fake. Does this look fake to you?'

'My God… it does look fake. Where did you get this?'

Nasipudin just smiled and never replied. He could have easily given the note to some unassuming person and he would get his money back. He tore the note apart, afraid it would lead others to fall into the same trick. He smiled some more, without anger or grudge or remorse. He thought that it was just one of those days.

***

Guntur wasn't very happy working as a porter at the market. It was still backbreaking labor. After hours of working he would walk away with barely enough money to feed himself. Muscles for hire are never certain how much they would make. But at least this way he could be close to his wife. He had a goal in mind which kept him going. To save enough money so he could buy a motorbike. That way he can become a motorcycle taxi driver. The pay was just as lousy and the hours just as long. But he didn't have to do hard labor ever again.

Seeing Nasipudin's working so hard made Guntur eased a bit. At 50, Nasipudin should be staying at home or do other stuff instead of punishing hard work. Some refugees half his age didn't share his view or went home complaining the whole time. Guntur adored Nasipudin. He admired how he gave all the money over to his wife as soon as he got it. Not once tempted to keep some money for himself.

One morning Nasipudin was hired by a man from Bali to load some baskets full of fruits on to an awaiting minivan. The man had bought a lot of stuff. But it was a simple job and Nasipudin thought maybe he could charge him somewhere around 5,000 rupiah. But Nasipudin and the Balinese man never negotiated a price. He was willing to take whatever the man felt like paying.

'Here you go!' the man said while taking a bank note from the right pocket of his trousers. He handed Nasipudin the money and swiftly turned his attention elsewhere. Nasipudin just grabbed the money gently and put it in his shorts without even a hint of curiosity as to how much the man had given him.

Casually, Nasipudin walked back into the market, over to his wife's stall to hand her the money he had just earned. He gently took out the money.

'You got 50,000?' Zubaidah said as soon as she saw the note's bluish color.

'Oh my God... I think that guy just handed me the wrong note.'

Instinctively, Nasipudin ran to the parking lot where he last saw the Balinese man. His van had already exited the parking lot and was beginning to accelerate down to the main street. Nasipudin chased after the van while shouting for the man's attention.

'Sir... Sir...'

The van stopped, jerking up and down as the driver hit hard on the brakes. The Balinese man leaned over, sticking his body out of an open window on the passenger's side of the car. He turned his head towards Nasipudin. Nasipudin hurtled closer with his arm outstretched. Hand holding the man's 50,000 rupiah note.

'You gave me too much.'

The Balinese man was shocked to learn that he had given Nasipudin virtually all of his pocket money for the day. He was even more surprised to see Nasipudin ran nearly the entire length of the market to chase him and give him back his money.

'Thank you... Thank you so much... Others would've just taken off with my money and pretended like nothing was wrong.'

'It wouldn't be right.'

'I see... What's your name?'

'Nasip'

'Well Mr. Nasip... I guess I will be seeing you again.'

The man did meet Nasipudin again. Many times over. He became a regular. He wanted no other porter touching his stuff. He would tell all of the friends he knew at the market about 'Honest Nasipudin.' They too became Nasipudin's regular. They wanted no other porter touching their stuff.

CHAPTER 12

It must have been a shocking scene for Nurul as her bus made its way through the traffic. The streets of Jakarta were wider than the biggest rivers in Lombok. Resting along its edges were tall buildings with tinted windows to keep the prying eyes of passerby away from the busy people inside.

The buildings were so tall, from the ground they looked to be piercing the sky. Some were lackluster boxes of concrete while others designed to inspire awe. Nurul was at awe nonetheless looking at both kinds. She might have even tilted her head upwards with her cheek resting on the glass, leaving a patch of sweat and moist.

She must have wondered how much money was poured into making just one. They must of moved mountains to build all the steels, turning hills into lakes to provide for its cement, turning forests into a barren land to build all its furniture.

They must have been homes and working places of the very rich and smart. Occasionally she saw these people entering and exiting these buildings. The men were in ties and suits and leather briefcases and matching shoes. The women in tight fitting skirts and colorful tops with ruffle fronts. She probably imagined the way they smell, clean and fresh with the fragrance of some exotic foreign flowers noticeable from far away.

Not a sweat on their foreheads as they moved from their air-conditioned office to their air-conditioned cars, heading straight towards the hippest shopping malls, buying the latest designer clothes, sipping a cup coffee worth her day's salary while gossiping with their friends about the trivialities of life.

She probably wondered whether poor people like her were mentioned in the chatters of the rich. The wools on their back came from remote farmlands, the spices on their plates brought by middlemen who became rich inflating their prices one-hundred-fold. The gadgets and gizmos on their hands contained gold mined by people risking life and limb.

It was clear to her why so many peasants come to Jakarta. This was the capital of everything, of glitz and glamour, of wealth, of knowledge, of extravagance. People like her and places like her home were mere objects to be exploited. To Jakarta's rich, smart and powerful, the poor were not people. They were workforce, they were stakeholders, they were liabilities, they were subjects of research, they were statistics.

From time to time, squatter homes appeared, hidden behind the glossy tinted walls of buildings. There lived those who came from rural lands, hardly making a living. They sweat to serve the rich while staying invisible. They washed clothes which cost twice as much as their monthly salaries or drove cars worth many times more than their houses, lands and fields back home put together.

Nurul knew her place was among the servants and not once dreamed of living in tall apartment blocks and marble-clad mansions. And why should it matter, she would probably thought. Why must possession, position and profession define who we are? Isn't everyone equal in the eyes of God? Isn't faith the only thing separating those who deserve salvation and those worthy of damnation.

The bus was moving slowly, its pace ground to a crawl. Traffic had always been a nightmare in Jakarta and the day she set foot in the metropolis was no exception. Occasionally she asked people to consult their watch. She had been navigating Jakarta's roads for nearly two hours. If she had been home she would've traveled from Mataram to Pringgabaya, Lombok's eastern edge.

'Jakartans must be mad,' she must have wondered. The roads were gridlocked and chaotic, filled with honking cars and unruly drivers trying to overtake each other.

Their times must have been more precious than their safeties, she must have thought.

Occasionally, fighting occurred. Motorists arguing with other motorists over the most trivial of things. A scratch which cost a few thousand rupiah to repair. A near brush. A misunderstanding. They cursed and shouted and sometimes jabs were exchanged. Cars and times were more precious than patience and forgiveness.

The road soon went from smooth to one infested with potholes, the building replaced by rows of factories, the shopping malls by decaying two story shops, the luxury cars by trucks. It was clear she was no longer in the home of the rich. It was a working class neighborhood filled with small houses for rents and boarding homes of the laborers.

It was a city named Tangerang, which overtime fused with Jakarta and other suburbs to form one giant megalopolis. Like its inhabitants, Tangerang was a servant with Jakarta its master. The two were minutes apart but with very different faces. It is funny how moving slightly from the center of power and prosperity starts to vanish. Faraway towns like Mataram were left to feed on the crumbles of the bread of wealth.

But there were big buildings and luxury homes in Tangerang as it desperately tried to match Jakarta's symbols of wealth. But not its taste. The malls were gigantic and flashy with splashes of contrasting bold colors painted on top of second grade materials clad by faux marbles. The designs were bland with classical columns awkwardly meeting modern forms. The houses were worse, big and intimidating and colorful and ostentatious with ornately decorated furniture placed haphazardly across the interior.

Nurul's employers' home was probably no exception. Big houses in Tangerang had five bedrooms, most unoccupied, two story with fake bronze railings running on each side of the stairs. The living room was huge but lack grandeur. Oversized couches and sofas clustering on one end and on another a big stretch of dead, unused space.

No matter how distasteful, Nurul was at awe. She had never seen a house this big in Pancor. But she was not impressed by the man's wealth. She worried if she could clean the house all on her own.

A man went up and greeted her. He was a lawyer, piling his wealth from those in running with the law, making money from disputes, divorces, accidents and tragedies. The lawyer was an Ahmadi but was careful not to reveal his identity. The man never thought about representing his persecuted brothers and sisters in Lombok. He never thought about using his lawyering skills gifted by the Divine to defend his religion. It would've been a career suicide. His clients would run away. So he did what he thought was the next best thing, hiring a desperate Ahmadiyya couple to be his maids.

***

Malik was ecstatic to see a familiar face. His brother Khaerudin had traveled all this way from Lombok to Tasikmalaya to pick him up. He dreamt of coming home but never so soon. Khaerudin told Malik that their mother had found him a school in Mataram. Since Malik had graduated from fifth grade, their mother thought it would be best to finish his elementary school there.

'So I get to go home?'

'Yes.'

It had been months since Malik felt so happy. He was homesick. As much as he liked living in mountainous Tasikmalaya. As much as he enjoyed meeting new people or waking up to an icy cold morning. As much as he loved the opportunity to get back to school and made new friends, it was never home.

The Ahmadiyya family hosting him was very nice and Malik also enjoyed the company of their children. But he was starting to become bored of eating the local Sundanese food. He didn't fit well with some local Ahmadiyya kids. They made fun of him by pretending to teach him some dirty Sundanese words which he didn't understand. The kids laughed and talked to each other in Sundanese. They were united in faith. But sometimes cultures clash.

Malik said goodbye to his foster parents in Tasikmalaya. In a true Indonesian tradition they asked for each other's forgiveness. Malik if he had been troubling the family while he was here.

'You haven't. Of course you haven't.' the parents said.

The family asked for Malik's forgiveness if they had been a bad host.

'You weren't. Of course you weren't.'

And so Malik and Khaerudin hopped on a bus traveling two-hundred-and-fifty kilometers northwest to Jakarta. The bus ride took six hours. They took a train to Surabaya, a 780 kilometer journey east. They took another bus which took them to Denpasar, Bali, a further ten hour journey by land plus one hour on a ferry.

From Bali they took another bus to Padang Bai seaport. It took them ninety minutes. They hop on a ferry to Lombok. It was a five hour journey across the Bali Sea. From Lombok's Lembar port another one hour bus ride took them to Mataram.

Malik returned to see that the Ahmadiyya congregation in Mataram had ballooned. Two months back, in May 2003, 14 families from Sambielen had been resettled to another housing complex in Mataram called Cakra.

For two years they had been driven from one town to the next. First they were forced to leave their village Sambielen, then from the safety of a police station in Medas. Finally, after a year of resettling in a village called Empan in Sumbawa they were driven away again under fear of violence and harassment. They were kept for four days at a police station in Sumbawa. Another four days in an unused government boarding home. And finally, they were transported to Mataram.

Malik also learned that his family had welcomed two more members. Khaerudin had welcomed a son named Rafik Wahyu Ahmadi. His sister Faizah also had a son, born just four months back. The son was named Muhammad Azmi Salim.

Rafik and Azmi had good Muslim names. Muslims in Indonesia believe that names were prayers. Wishes of what the newborn would grow up to be.

Rafik means 'friend' in Arabic since a friend helped pay for his labor. Wahyu means 'revelation.' Ahmadi, as the name suggests, was his religion.

'Muhammad' was taken from the name of their revered Prophet. Azmi means 'determined' in Arabic. Salim means 'safe,' 'righteous,' 'in God's protection.' When combined, the names seemed to symbolize perseverance, optimism, refusal to give in to misguided temptation and oppression. Nearly a year has passed since they were driven away from their home. They were the things that Malik's family knew so well.

From the day he was conceived, Azmi's life story had always been about perseverance. Ten months back his mother had to flee to safety when she saw hateful men descending upon their home. Ten months back his mother had to share a hall with hundreds of people who were also driven from their home. They were many pregnant women in the hall. From the haunting shock, the stress, the lack of rest, the poor hygiene, most had miscarriages. But Azmi somehow stayed in his mother's womb, refusing to die.

Faizah learned that she was pregnant during her second visit to Sumbawa to see her mother-in-law Saudah. After their painful goodbye Saudah came to Mataram in the hopes to see Guntur and Faizah once more. She brought rice. Five sacks each weighing close to twenty kilograms.

Saudah came with one of Guntur's half-brothers. Together they saw Guntur praying so devoutly, not missing any of the five compulsory praying times. Saudah saw how well Guntur recited the Koran. Her son had found religion and Saudah had Faizah and her faith to thank for that.

Saudah convinced Faizah to come and visit her in Sumbawa assuring her that this time her sons and daughters would be more welcoming. Back in Sumbawa, Saudah said, people never thought about religion. Religion was a communal affair meant to please others. They went to Koranic recitals because their friends went to Koranic recitals. They invited people to pray for their newborns, their newly-wedded child and bless their new houses. They cared more on serving people good meal, wow the crowd with lavish parties and decor instead of ensuring that their prayers were answered.

Praying was for Fridays where people see them praying. Praying was for old people nearing their grave. Praying was asking for divine intervention in the midst of adversity. Praying was for assistance in attaining earthly desires. Possessions, career advancements, love. Praying was never about adherence. Never about devotion. Never about gratitude for things men took for granted. Never about the afterlife.

'But Ahmadiyya people are different,' Saudah told Faizah. 'I think my son has found his place. With you. By your side. Among his Ahmadiyya friends. I'm sorry we treated you the way we did. We heard many things which turned out to be untrue. I really admire your religiousness. We never pray as often as you do. Whenever we get a little busy we forget about praying. But Ahmadiyya... you pray even when you're gravely ill. Not once did you come up with an excuse not to pray.'

Saudah smiled and told Faizah. 'Will you come and visit me to Sumbawa?'

Faizah nodded. Before long she was on her way to Sumbawa. Saudah showered Faizah with gift when she arrived. Gifts also came from her husband's half-siblings. But the best gift of all was when Saudah gave Faizah's belly a good rubbing.

'I think you're pregnant. I really think you are'

She was. Saudah's midwife friend in Sumbawa confirmed that she was.

Faizah and Guntur went back to Mataram with excitement. She was to become a mother and Guntur, a father. But they also felt tormented, worrying how they will feed the baby when they can barely feed themselves.

Azmi means 'determined.' Salim means 'safe,' 'righteous,' 'in God's protection.' In God's hands the would-be parents entrusted their future baby's fate. God in turn intervened. Leading Faizah to meet a midwife who happened to live not far from her home in Sweta.

When Ahmadiyya mothers were rejected by hospitals and other midwives because of their faith, Faizah found one who was really nice and welcoming. Everywhere else, Ahmadis were told to leave their faith before deeming them acceptable for the government's free health care for the poor program.

Faizah expected that she would be treated the same. But through the unseen power of fate, she wasn't. Faizah expected to be charged with a lot of money for her labor, forcing her husband Guntur to work harder than his body allowed him to. With all their power, their months of hard work, they could only yield 400,000 rupiah. She was worried it wouldn't be enough. All the other mothers had told her that they had to dish out at least twice that. But through what many would call destiny or perhaps coincidence or perhaps an act of God, she didn't have to.

'Mam, forgive me... How much will this cost?' Faizah asked the midwife weeks away from labor.

'Don't worry about that. You just worry about your health and the baby's. Those are what matter.'

And when the time came, with a newborn baby wrapped in blanket in her arm, she asked again.

'I only have four hundred [thousand rupiah]. Is that enough?'

The midwife smiled as Faizah handed her a pile of notes. The bank notes were full of wrinkles and stains and writings and ink spills and marks and cracks and holes and chips. Some notes had exchanged hands so many times they were turning into fragile, mushy, grayish pieces of paper.

The midwife took the money and began counting, holding the notes like a fan before Faizah's eyes. She folded the money and handed it back to Faizah.

'This is my gift for the baby.'

CHAPTER 13

Masitah and Nurul both lived in Jakarta suburbs and they met occasionally. At times the sisters called each other to check how they were, comparing stories about their lives as maids.

'How is your employers? Are they nice?' Masitah asked her sister.

'They're nice. They're treating me OK. How's yours?'

There was some truth in Nurul's reply. Her employers were treating her fairly. Nurul and her husband Asmi were paid generously for sweeping the floor, washing the clothes, cooking meals and cleaning the cars. They could save a lot and didn't have to worry about feeding themselves or paying rent. Nurul told her sister that she could even send some money to their mother back home.

But what Nurul didn't tell anyone was that working for the lawyer was a backbreaking labor. It was not like Nurul never did any hard work before. As a child Nurul and her sister Faizah followed her father to the fields and rode at the back of her father's water buffalo as he plowed the land. When her father was done plowing, they helped him plant vegetable seeds, watering them or reaping the vegetables when they are ready to be harvested. In the afternoon the sisters returned home. When they were little her father used to let them ride his baskets which he carried on his shoulder so that they didn't have to walk the long journey home.

In the afternoon, Nurul and Faizah helped her mother with the dishes, taking plates and spoons and forks and dirty pans and bowls to the back of the house. They fetched water from the well, with a bucket filled with water weighing 10 to 15 kilos. Occasionally they dropped a few plates from their tiny hands filled with soaps.

Their mother would just simply pick up the shattered glasses carefully and threw them away. Their mother could have scolded them or stopped them from doing the dishes again. But she wanted to teach her daughters the importance of hard work to succeed in a man's world.

As a teen, after finishing elementary school, Nurul worked. She washed people's clothes and swept their floors. People would pay her as they please. Sometimes generous. Sometimes heartless. But she never complained. She just pressed on and did what she had to do.

But in Tangerang things were different. She never felt so exhausted. The house was too big for a single maid. At 4 a.m. she woke up, getting herself ready for the day's chores. Her boss left for work as early as 6 in the morning. By that time she had to sweep the floor, mop it, cook the family breakfast and iron their shirts. Nurul's husband Asmi had to wash the family's many cars, one for each household members, each with its own driver.

After the man of the house left for work, after the children had gone to school, Nurul had to do the dishes, washing the plates and glasses and frying pans from grease and stain. She then mopped every piece of furniture in the house, making sure that every nook and cranny of the intricate woodwork was spotless clean.

Her husband gave the garden some trimming, cutting every inch of grass on the massive front and backyard. He then watered the plants. Asmi was old and could only do a half day worth of work.

By noon, Nurul had to cook lunch for the lady of the house and her children who were returning home from school. The kids sometimes threw away their bags, left their sweaty clothes on the door and stepped the floor using their dirtied shoes. Nurul had to tidy up some more.

She ate after everyone else had their meals, feasting on leftovers and the food they did not like. She wasted no time and washed their clothes. A day's worth of laundry was piling high consisting of nightgowns and pajamas for sleeping, school uniforms, and after school day clothes, post-afternoon-shower night clothes and on weekends, their best outfits for going out or special occasions.

The washing took hours and it was almost dark when she finished ironing them. After a 15 minute break she hit the kitchen, preparing the family supper. Cutting chilies and making pastes using pestle and mortar. Separating vegetables from their stem, dicing up meat, preparing the broth and making soup.

By nightfall, she was exhausted. Occasionally some family members made some late night requests. 'Make me a glass of milk!' 'Fix me coffee!' 'Find my earrings!' 'Make me some toast!' 'Watch the house, we are going out! Open the door when we get back!' It was usually 10 p.m. when she was done for the day and could finally get some sleep. After six hours of sleep she had to do her job all over again.

Nurul never told Masitah the amount of work she had to do. She never told her mother when she called home every month. She didn't want anyone to worry. Especially her mother who would overreact and tell her to come home. Mostly because she doesn't like to complain. Hours of sweeping caused her right wrist to sore. She sometimes cut herself while cooking. She grazed her knuckles while using the washing board. She burnt herself while ironing. She only stayed quiet, licked her wound and soldiered on.

The pay was good though. She thought if she could only hold on for another year or two she would have saved enough money to buy a nice little place in Mataram. But as it turned out she had to wait a bit longer.

During one of her weekly call to her mother in Mataram, Suhaidi asked to speak to her. He said his friend found a job for him in Malaysia. He said he needed money to pay for placement, training, housing and living expenses before he got his first paycheck there and asked if he could borrow eight million rupiah. Nurul replied that she only had six million. So she gave the money to his brother.

Nurul waited for a month to hear back from Suhaidi. Two months passed and even her mother didn't know what her brother was up to when she called her. On the third month Nurul finally got a hold of Suhaidi.

'Suhaidi… What happened? I thought you will give me my money back after a month.'

'Yeah… about that… I didn't get the job in Malaysia.'

'What happened? I thought you have already secured your spot for that work.'

'I don't know… Someone was willing to pay extra for that last spot I guess.'

'So will you give my money back?'

'Well… Here's the thing… I kind of spent it on a motorbike… But I will give you your money back. I promise.'

***

The dirt road in Ketapang was winding. It was covered in sands brought in from the trucks moving to and from a local sand mine. The sands were everywhere in Ketapang. They were on the road, covering people's rice fields and farms. On the porches of people's home.

But the area's charm was irrefutable. Far on the horizon, Mount Rinjani stands gallantly, towering above the landscape dominated by terraced rice fields, dotted by rustic homes and luxurious villas. Rinjani is a picturesque volcano, frequented by travelers from afar drawn by its unobstructed view of the ocean.

When weather permits, the mountainous island of Bali is revealed, far across the sea. From Ketapang, Rinjani appears in the form of a deep blue silhouette, wrapped by faint traces of clouds. Mists run gently down its curvatures and slopes like the tender touch of a lover. The cuddle of a mother to her young.

It was the first time Nasipudin set foot in Ketapang, located right across West Lombok's southeastern border with Mataram. He didn't come to view Mount Rinjani, but he couldn't help to be a tad bit at awe. His real reason for coming was to see six previously empty houses which by then had been occupied by his Ahmadiyya friends.

The houses were lovely, occupying each a hundred square meter property. Aside from the one house on the left side of the road, the other five houses sat in one neat row connected by a small beaten path. Empty pieces of lands infested with tall grasses and wild shrubs encircled the houses.

The houses were gated by nice redbrick walls. They each had a front yard roomy enough for a couple of motorcycles and a garden. They had front porches to relax and enjoy Ketapang's fresh air. They had two bedrooms and a spacious living room. They each had a kitchen, a bathroom and a well.

Nasipudin was told that a property developer built the houses eight years ago and was planning to build more on the vacant lands they have bought, thinking that people would be drawn by the location's unobstructed view of Mount Rinjani.

But there were no buyers. The spot was said to be haunted. Just meters from the complex was an old burial ground, a small hill filled with centuries old graves shaded by dozens of frangipani trees, believed to be infested by ghosts. Only the caretaker of the complex actually lived there, occupying one of the houses. He was said to be so tormented by the undying spirits wandering his homes he took his own life. No one had lived there since. Until their Ahmadiyya leaders heard about it.

'How did you like it here?' asked Jauzi the provincial leader of Ahmadiyya. 'When we heard about this place we knew it was the ideal place for our congregation to resettle.'

Jauzi told Nasipudin and the other congregation members that Shabri, a mid-ranking police officer and an Ahmadi who lived in Mataram was the first to discover the place. Shabri and Jauzi asked people from the neighborhood as to who owned the abandoned complex and got a name: Stephen Lianto, a businessman of Chinese descent.

Stephen was deeply in debt over the botched venture and had been living from one address to the next. Shabri and Jauzi spent the next three months tracking him down going from one part of Mataram to the next. He wouldn't answer the door when they first came but after explaining that they were trying to buy the property off his hands he was ecstatic. More than happy to let the housing complex go and cut his losses.

The Ahmadiyya congregation purchased the 2,300 square meter housing complex from the property developer for the price of 50 million rupiah, half the price of other properties in the area. The complex was then divided into 21 units by the congregation.

For the properties with already built houses the congregation charged 12.5 million rupiah each, those without 8 million. The Ahmadiyya Congregation claimed to be a moral and spiritual organization but at the time it became a property developer turning a handsome profit from people who wholeheartedly follow their every instruction.

But even then the price was a steal. It was so lucrative that Shabri bought one unit for himself. Two units were reserved for the Ahmadiyya missionaries and clerics serving Mataram. Former officials, elders and wealthier Ahmadiyya refugees from Pancor and Sambielen were given priorities to buy the properties.

Awaludin, who used to be a wealthy businessman back in Pancor built three two-story homes for himself and his children. Mahmuludin, who once operated a big rice distributing shop in Sawing occupied the house with the best view.

Impoverished people like Nasipudin were next to be offered. They didn't get the same priority because they were mere congregation members. But Nasipudin thought the offer was a sign that his Ahmadiyya leaders did care about refugees like him. Nasipudin expressed his interest in buying two empty lots totaling at 200 square meters to host his big family. The leaders put Nasipudin's name on the list.

After doing so little to help the refugees ensure that their properties back home were fairly compensated, doing little to advocate for their protection, doing little to help them rebuild their lives in Mataram, doing nothing to help the pregnant mothers and sickly elders in need of healthcare. After forcing the refugees to keep giving alms to the congregation despite knowing that they could barely feed themselves, people like Nasipudin were told to pay the congregation the full retail price for the properties. The ever obedient Nasipudin accepted.

The price might be a bargain but with his pay as a market porter there was no way he could afford it. The leaders then told him he could sell off his lands back in Pancor and raise the needed money. It was as good as saying 'You will never go back!' The ever obedient Nasipudin, a foot soldier in an extremely hierarchical organization called Ahmadiyya, complied.

And so Nasipudin got in touch with his brother back in Pancor. Told him to find a buyer for the only possession he had, the rubbles of his former home, his lands, his whole fortune, his safety net, his retirement plan.

He was desperate for cash. So desperate he was willing to let them go for a fraction of the retail price. A land speculator bought his property after haggling the prices even lower. The speculator argued that his property was once the scene of an attack and therefore undesirable. Nasipudin had no choice but to accept.

The money he had garnered was still not enough. He would starve himself just to pay back the congregation. He took up loans from families and friends. Unknowingly, he had put all of his eggs into one basket. All of his chips onto one table. That table was called Ketapang. It was a gamble. The sort of gamble that was all or nothing. Nasipudin didn't understand the risks. His leaders never told him the risks. Never ensured him that this time he would be protected, the safety of his family and his property would be guaranteed.

The ever obedient Nasipudin never asked.

CHAPTER 14

It had been five weeks since Nurul last had her period.

'Could it be?' she must have asked the heavens. 'Please God, let it be true!'

The heavens said nothing, not providing Nurul with any signs. Nurul had been praying for a child. She was beginning to worry that she might never produce one. Nurul was 27 and her friends and siblings already had children of their own. His older brother Khaerudin had two sons already. Faizah had a son after a marriage of less than a year. Suhaidi, five years her junior, had a daughter who was then four.

Nurul had been praying for a child. She already had a failed first marriage because she was childless for two years. It was a huge blow when her first husband remarried and immediately had a child. She pretended not to care when neighbors, cousins and her former in-laws began whispering. They were saying her first husband made the right choice by leaving her. They were saying that she was infertile.

For the first few months since her divorce she cried at night, hiding her sobbing face underneath a blanket. She was a strong woman but a woman nonetheless. And who would not cry when those around them passed judgment and made cruel remarks behind their back? And with her marriage to Asmi entering its fourth year, she was starting to worry the remarks were true. She prayed to God they were not. Asmi had repeatedly said it was OK not to have a child and that he loved her all the same. But she wanted a child so much.

'Please God, let it be true!'

It had been nine weeks since she last had her period and finally she had the time to have herself checked at a maternity clinic. Her heart skipped a beat when she learned that her prayers had been truly answered. A child was growing inside her womb and her joy was growing with it. She returned to her masters' home with a new found energy. She found a new habit, gazing at her own reflection while rubbing her belly. Occasionally whispering to the baby in her womb, how precious it is to its mother and father.

She had big plans for the child. A house to call their own. Nurul was to cradle the child whenever she could. She was going to bathe the baby, gently wiping its body with a warm, soft towel. Nurul was to play with the child, hoisting it up and down. The baby was to laugh. She was to buy toys for it to play. She was to teach it words. She was to watch it grow. She was to teach the child how to pray. It will recite simple verses from the Koran. The baby was going to school. She would take it there and pick it up after school. She was sending it to Koran recital classes on weekends for Ahmadiyya children. The child was to have many friends.

Nurul would attend the child's graduation after graduation. She would shed tears of joy. The baby would finish high school, earn a degree in University which either Nurul or her husband ever set foot on. The baby would grow up into adulthood. The child would have jobs and success. The child would marry, someone of the same faith. Together they would build a family. The child was to have children of its own.

But first Nurul must work and work hard she did. Nurul smiled as her wrist sore from sweeping the floor. Nurul cried happy tears when she burned her hands while ironing. 'It is for the baby,' she thought. Her sweat. Her pain. Her aching body. Her life. 'It was for the baby's future.'

The pregnancy was entering its fourth month. Her belly was getting bigger. She rubbed her palm across her stomach, trying to feel the child so that it would feel its mother's presence. But somehow she noticed a difference, like there was something wrong.

She just sat down quietly that night, fatigued. Her arms were aching so badly she could feel her own pulse running down her vein. For some reason she never felt so tired, so lifeless. She tried to change her sweaty clothes but couldn't find the energy to get up. She reached for her nightstand, grabbing hold of its edge to pull herself up. She was sweating and sweating badly. She struggled but somehow couldn't stand on her two feet.

Suddenly she felt an excruciating pain in her stomach. The sting was so harsh she felt it in her spine as it ran through her nerves and into her brain. The pain caused so much shock in her body that for a split second she lost all her senses. Her vision went from dark to dizzying bright white. She could hear her ears ringing. The room was spinning before her.

Seconds later, she collapsed, slamming all her weight onto the floor. There was blood. She slipped in and out of consciousness. She saw the floor was blood red. Her long nightgown was blood red.

'Please God!' she must have whispered with every breath, panting heavily. She was bleeding. She was in tears.

'Please God!' her whisper louder. She ran her hands into her groin.

'Please God!' She was panicking. Her hands emerged as blood red.

'Please God!' She mumbled. Her face drowning in tears.

'Pleaseeeeee!!!!! Gooodddd!!!! ' She screamed, crying her lungs out.

***

Faizah and Guntur built themselves a makeshift home at the market. They were given a two by three meter plot of land and a building which was originally used by her family for storage. The semi-permanent home was made of wood serving as poles and beams, covered in woven bamboo. It sat at the edge of the market, leaning against the wall of a two-story kiosk. Faizah and Guntur bought sheets of corrugated zinc to serve as roof.

The zinc roof made the house felt like a steaming oven during the day. Drips of rain turned into a constant, earsplitting roar. Water would seep through the holes used to tie the roof together with metal wires. The kiosk next door constantly sent its rain water to Faizah's home, occasionally flooding the ground around it in ankle deep water. Guntur had to dig a small makeshift gutter around the house to keep the water from overflowing inside. Sometimes the gutter failed to serve its intended purpose.

The house had no flooring. To keep their six-month baby away from the damp soil below, Azmi was put in a hammock made from a single piece of batik cloth suspended in the air tied to a chain of rubber bands to make the hammock swing and bounce up and down. The pair slept in a hard kapok matress on top of a wooden frame which Guntur hand built. It was a hard life, especially for their six-month old baby. Everyday they had to bear the foul stench of rotting vegetables and discarded meat. The noise of rain and chattering crowd, haggling prices up and down. At night it was cold. The freezing night wind penetrated through the fine gaps in the woven bamboo walls.

It was no place for Azmi. It was no place for Faizah and Guntur. But they had little choice. The landlords at Sweta had decided to raise the rent.

Nasipudin also felt the pressure from the planned raise, racing to finish his house. He was certain Ketapang would be his new home. He was certain Ketapang was different from Pancor. People seemed to be more receptive of the Ahmadis. It was safe. The village chief in Ketapang welcomed the Ahmadis to his home one day. He served them drinks. He served them snacks.

'You will be safe here. If anyone rejects your presence I will talk to them,' he told the Ahmadis.

For Nasipudin and many others it was the reassurance they had wanted.

Soon, Nasipudin began digging for the foundation of his new home. He had divided his land into five. One for Khaerudin. One for himself. One for Masitah when she decided to get married. One was for Suhaidi and one for Faizah when she ever decided to get out of the market and build her own home.

He worked at the market in the morning, carrying people's groceries and goods on his shoulder and back. In the afternoon he went with Khaerudin or Suhaidi to Ketapang. There were sands in the ground. The dug earth was enough to build him around 50 sand bricks. From the dug earth of his well he would get 50 more.

Abdullah, the man from Pancor's Kelayu neighborhood often came in to help. Abdullah had bought a property for himself but hadn't mustered enough money to start building his own house. He was living with Mataram's senior Ahmadiyya cleric Syamsir Ali in a missionary's home. He was an experienced construction worker. He was able to build bricks with speed. With no plans to build his own home he helped others building theirs.

Mahmuludin, who was among the first Ahmadis to settle in Ketapang helped by providing workers food and drink. The other settlers also came to help. Sometimes with snacks. Sometimes with construction materials. Sometimes with their own strength and hands. Sometimes with loans. The leaders came with no more than moral support. A pat on the back. A prayer. But Nasipudin was grateful for all the help he could find, even though they were more spiritual and moral than actual.

One day Nasipudin had a pleasant surprise when he visited Ketapang. The return of a daughter.

'What are you doing here? Why didn't you tell me you were here?' Nasipudin said hugging and holding Nurul repeatedly.

'Mom told me you were here,' Nurul replied, gazing at an army of workers busy building their new houses with a wide smile. 'As soon as I heard that you have bought us a place here. I had to check it out. I think I just dropped my bags and rushed my way over here.'

Nurul probably took a deep breath, filling every miniscule space in her lungs. It was a breath of joy. It was a sigh of relief. She was glad to be home. Glad to discover her future included a house to call her own.

As she exhaled, so too exited the troubles in heart. Miscarriage is known to scar all mothers to be. Back in Jakarta, she couldn't bare to look at her room, the place where she lost her unborn child. She couldn't shake off the thought of blood when she stared at the white tiled floor too long. She couldn't sleep. She had nightmares. Days were spent sobbing. Her husband saw this. As the first chance they got, he told their employer of their wish to return home.

Nurul didn't talk much on the long road home, even as their bus was finally entering Mataram. But when her mother said Nasipudin had bought a land in Ketapang it was like life was once more sparkling in her eyes. Right then and there in Ketapang, she felt she could finally move on.

Nasipudin picked up a shovel, which Nurul would have immediately snatched it right out of his hand.

'Here let me do this!'

'No... But you just came back home. You must be exhausted.'

'Dad, let me do this!'

Nasipudin relented, smiling and shaking his head. He knew there was no stopping Nurul once she set her mind.

'Alright... But if you're tired... don't force yourself! Get some rest!'

'Dad... you know me... Have I ever been tired?'

A few weeks after Nasipudin got another surprise. The return of Masitah. She was eighteen when she left for Jakarta. She was twenty when she returned.

Masitah told her father that she couldn't stand being alone away from her family in a foreign city. When news first reached her that her father was building a house of their own she immediately resigned from her work and bought tickets to Mataram.

Soon the houses were built. Nasipudin slowly began moving his stuff from his rented home in Sweta to Ketapang. He moved the big furniture first, cupboards, beds. He brought carpets. He brought a kerosene-powered cooking stove. He brought plates, glasses and cooking utensils. He brought clothes.

Malik was graduating from elementary school when they moved. Zubaidah had found a junior high school for Malik located just meters from where the dirt road met a highway connecting Mataram to the northwestern part of Lombok. Zubaidah also found an elementary school further down the dirt road in Ketapang for Safir and Kasafuloh who was entering school age.

Malik and his brothers were careful not to reveal their identity as Ahmadis. Ketapang was predominantly Muslim although there were Hindus around. The Ahmadi children soon made new friends. They were treated just like any other kid.

The adults were also treated equally, just like any other neighbor. The Ahmadis staged thanksgiving for their new homes. The non-Ahmadi neighbors came to celebrate. They shared stories, jokes and laughter.

Ahmadi and non-Ahmadi together worked to pave the dirt road with asphalt. They worked together to erect street lamps so that passerby wouldn't get scared traveling pass the scary old cemetery at night illuminating the dark shadows the frangipani trees casted seen from afar as eerie images. They worked together to build the community's first ever mosque where Ahmadis and non-Ahmadis prayed together.

CHAPTER 15

Among the main creeds in Ahmadiyya was obedience to the
government, not challenging the ruling power and adhere the rule of
law. It sits above prayers, determination of faith, submission to
God's command and His will, the act of humility and courtesy,
placing religion before all else. It comes before compassion for all
God's creature. Above brotherhood for followers of the Messiah. The
credo must be observed by all Ahmadis and must be practiced until
the day they die.

But what to do when the government refused to guarantee their
own safety? When the government refused to ensure freedom of
religion and tolerance? When the people claiming to be their
protectors turned out to be the oppressors, the persecutors, the
intimidators, the discriminators? When authorities condoned acts of
violence? When law enforcers provided impunity for the attackers?

A new president came to power in 2004. A smiling general
named Susilo Bambang Yudhoyono. Backed by his newly-formed
political vehicle called the Democratic Party. It was a nationalist
with only 7.4 percent of seats at the House of Representatives. With
a parliamentary power so small, Yudhoyono knew his reign would
not survive without a coalition. And soon he began handing out seats
in his cabinet to people from nationalist parties and the moderate
Muslims to the ultra-conservatives and the hardline-affiliateds.

It was important for any Indonesian government to form an
alliance with Muslim groups. In a country where 80 percent of the
250 million population are Muslims, not affiliating with Muslim
groups were political suicides. Everyone understood this. People kill
and die in the name of the holy and divine.

All there is to do is tell these religious fanatics what is unholy. Who is their God's enemy. In 1965, it was the communists. It took so much as a whisper, a baseless accusation before a man (regardless he was a true communist or not) was brutally murdered by machete-wielding religious radicals and gun-totting soldiers. And soon the numbers pile up. 1,000 dead. 5,000 dead. 25,000 dead. 100,000 dead. 500,000 dead. Before long no one bothered to keep track.

The New Order regime which rose to power after the anti-communist purge knew the power of religion. During the regime's 32 years in power they tried to muffle the power of religious groups. First the regime outlawed what the religious groups had strongly advocated against, blasphemy and atheism. The regime formed a coordinating body on religious beliefs to investigate cases of blasphemy.

All Muslim-based parties were then merged into one, allowing the regime to have full control on their political activities. To thank them for staying away from politics and challenging its absolute power, Muslim groups were put together under one organization: the Indonesian Council of Ulemas (MUI). They were rewarded for their loyalty to the regime by being given the power to issue edicts as well as the lucrative authority to issue halal certificates which every restaurant and fast food franchise holder and food and drug manufacturer needed to lure the Muslim-majority customers.

There were still however militant Muslims, radicals, those aspiring to turn Indonesia into an Islamic state, those who disagreed with the state's secular ideology. The regime used its spies and informants to keep them well in check. The regime organized a heavy military crackdown in 1984. The regime muffled the rest by facilitating their wish for martyrdom and sent them to Afghanistan, assisting the Mujahideen to repel the Soviet Army. Those the regime cannot control were locked behind bars or kidnapped.

The New Order regime cared little about Ahmadiyya. They numbered just a few hundred thousand and their creed was to obey the government. When the Rabita Alam al-Islami (the World Muslim League) issued an edict, decreeing Ahmadis as non-Muslims, accusing them as blasphemers and agents of Western imperialists and Zionists in 1974, the regime warned mainstream Muslim groups in Indonesia to stay away from openly attacking Ahmadis.

As compromise, the Ahmadis were barred from joining the newly formed MUI. They were barred from holding massive open sermons and gatherings. But the regime guaranteed their safety. They were not going to let Ahmadis be persecuted. That would risk destabilizing the country or worse, emboldening the dormant religious fanatics and militants. So when the MUI issued its own edict in June 1980, nothing happened.

In 1997 the regime began to crumble. The absolute power of Suharto and his cronies' massive influence were beginning to wane in the face of a crippling economic crisis. The international community who once saw Indonesia as an economic miracle was divesting their money away from the country. The rupiah lost its value to a fifth. Companies had to close and the banks which financed them collapsed. People lost their job. People were going desperate. People were beginning to criticize the government, demanding Suharto, who had ruled throughout the New Order to step down. They wanted his children and cronies tried for corruption. They demanded the military to head back to the barracks and stop meddling with Indonesian politics.

In a desperate attempt to hold its grip on power, the regime turned to the very groups they initially tried to control, the hardliners, the militants, the religious fanatics. A massacre occurred in East Java targeting animists and observers of indigenous religions. A riot targeting Chinese in Jakarta. An ethnic-clash between indigenous Dayak groups and Madurese migrants in Borneo. The aim was to warn people that change was dangerous. Criticisms create instability. But people persisted. The regime had been in power for three decades and people were getting tired.

In 1998, Suharto resigned. Replaced by his Vice President, a Muslim scholar named Habibie who ran an interim government tasked with preparing the country's first free and fair election. The election rejuvenated Muslim groups' long-suppressed desires to enter politics.

The fall of Suharto also attracted the renewal of the long infamous call to establish an Islamic state, denouncing democracy as a Western product, in favor of the more Islamic system of caliphs. Such calls were once considered treason under the New Order but with the return of fugitive firebrand clerics and former Afghanistan combatants who have now joined terrorism groups, the calls were alive and well.

In 1999 the country has a new president, a pluralist, a reform-minded, moderate Muslim scholar named Abdurrahman Wahid. He was better known as Gus Dur, the leader of the country's biggest Muslim organization, the Nahdlatul Ulama (NU).

The NU succeeded in blending Islam with Indonesian traditional values. But the militants sought a more fundamental form of Islam and for the country to enforce a strict and literal interpretation of the Koran. The fundamentalists saw Gus Dur's NU and tolerant view as sinful modifications. The hard-line views grew stronger as countries in the Middle East started pouring their petro-dollar into the country. Soon boarding schools became attracted to the petro-dollars and announced themselves to be as ultra-conservative as their Middle-Eastern benefactors.

Gus Dur tried to reform the military. Shattering the Army's dominance. Split the military from the police force. Gus Dur made many enemies in the military. Some generals began working together with the militants, the hard-liners and the fundamentalists. Out of nowhere, there was a riot in Ambon in Eastern Indonesia. That riot soon grew into an ethnic clash. The fundamentalists began recruiting militants to be shipped to Ambon. The military provided assistance and even allowed the militants to be transported using their warships.

Another conflict erupted in Poso, Central Sulawesi. A bomb detonated outside the Filipino Ambassador's home. A car bomb exploded at the Jakarta Stock Exchange. Churches were bombed on Christmas eve 2000 in Jakarta, Sumatra, West Java, Central Java and Lombok. The string of violence led Gus Dur to be impeached in 2001.

Yudhoyono learned from Gus Dur's experience how fragile his powers can be. He learned to be more compromising, more accommodative to the hard-liners' demand. He knew that religion was not a force to be taken lightly. He began to cooperate with the hardliners. Sending his ministers and top police officials to attend their gatherings.

To bring stability back the government and the conservatives worked together as partners. Turning people's attentions away from full blown religious conflicts. From picking up arms and turn to terrorism. Together they introduced new enemies. Vice, immorality, blasphemy. They needed a scapegoat. Some group of people which everyone saw as evil, deviant, blasphemous. And what better victim than a small minority group whose creed was to obey the government?

***

For days Suhaidi tried to avoid his sister, Nurul but eventually the siblings met. They were after all living in their new homes in Ketapang. Suhaidi came one day with a sporty looking motorcycle he had tricked out and modified. He sped across the narrow alleyway, attracting people's attention as he nearly skidded his wheel while making a hard left turn to his family's complex.

Nurul would look at Suhaidi from head to toe. It was clear that Suhaidi was no longer a small town boy from Pancor but a stylish, big city man from Mataram. A brand new T-shirt fresh from the store tightly snuggling his muscular arm. A digital watch was wrapped around his wrist. A metal chain glistering around his neck.

He wore a pair of brand new, tight fitting, blue jeans, acid washed to make them look they were worn. From the pocket of his jeans was a key to his motorcycle, bought from the money Nurul had lent.

Suhaidi was busy with his new phone. A luxury still in Mataram in 2004. Suhaidi stretched his legs straight as a board to allow easy access to the phone. The beeping noise was getting louder, playing a monophonic tune of some popular Western song. Suhaidi put his index finger and thumb into his left pocket, leaving the other three fingers exposed.

His sisters just couldn't take their eyes off Suhaidi's pockets as the phone got irritatingly louder. Any seconds longer Nurul might scream and snatched the phone right out of his pocket. Faizah just held her breath. Their mother was clearly annoyed.

Their irk grew more apparent as Suhaidi finally got hold of his phone but didn't immediately pick up the call. He took another second or two to reposition his body, right leg remained stretched, the left folded tight to his body providing a resting place for his elbow. With his right hand he hoisted the phone up in the air to get a closer look at the numbers on the screen. He then transferred the phone on to his left hand. The beeping was getting louder.

The sisters sighed as Suhaidi finally answered his phone. With no signs of remorse, Suhaidi gleefully shouted at his phone. 'Hellooo!!!' He laughed and giggled while slowly turning his back on the women.

He took his motorcycle key out of his pocket and grabbed it tightly. Seconds later he got up without excusing himself and slowly approached his motorcycle. His cheek still pressed against the phone. Suhaidi was again on his way.

Faizah could only shake her head. 'That kid came without saying hello and went without saying goodbye,' she would have said. 'I bet he's out to meet his girlfriend. '

Nurul was perhaps puzzled. 'He has a girlfriend? '

'That's what people at the market said. For some reason he keeps coming to the market. We see him almost everyday but he pretends he can't see us. Just keep on walking back and forth. Always on the phone. They say he has a girlfriend at the market. I don't know. I've never seen this girlfriend in person.'

'Does dad know?'

'I don't know. You know Suhaidi. Always sweet talking his way out of trouble. I think dad is suspicious. We all are. But I guess dad wants proof. He wants to see it in person.'

'God... What's got into him? Suhaidi I mean.'

'Suhaidi has always been Suhaidi.'

'What do you mean?'

'You didn't know he had a girlfriend while we were still in Pancor?'

'Nooo...'

'He did. You remember when Yuni was born and all of the sudden he bought all those expensive clothes and toys for her. They were from his girlfriend.'

Their mother must have felt she had enough from her daughters over what she considered to be gossips. She expressed her displeasure at the topic by leaving the house and heading over to the neighbors. She didn't believe it was true. At least she wished it wasn't. But the signs were all too telling.

'God, have I failed as a mother?'

***

From the main road came a group of cars carrying passengers in their best outfits. Batik shirts; colorfully embroidered headscarves; ornately decorated caps; long-sleeved, collarless, sparkling white, cotton shirts; spotless clean leather shoes. Traveling from Mataram.

From deep in Ketapang came the neighbors. Men in equally impressive attires. Some preferred to be more casual. Some men chose to look religious, wearing checkered sarongs ankles left exposed. Leather sandals with wide straps. Wrapping on their neck were checkered cotton scarves. Some used it to cover their heads, framing their weather beaten face and hiding their white skull caps.

Nasipudin wore a short-sleeve shirt with lime green batik motif sitting on top a black background. From afar it looked like neon-colored shrubs were growing on his torso. The contrast made him look even shorter. The checkered, maroon red, oversized sarong which he wore underneath it made it worse.

A small woven-rattan, top hat made his diamond-shaped face seemed even more angular. He was never a tall man and a group picture with Ahmadi officials highlighted that fact. Ahmadiyya provincial leader Jauzi and Ahmadi cleric Syamsir both wore light blue checkered shirts. Syamsir's shirt was a bit darker but at a glance you could swear they were wearing the same thing. In front of an unfinished home, wooden frames on top of what would be a concrete floor, they have their pictures taken.

At an empty lot they gathered. Ahmadis and mainstream Muslims. Ahmadi leaders from Mataram and Ahmadi followers from Ketapang. They formed a large circle with small wooden markers as its center. Four tall markers formed a perfect square with equal distance from each other. Between them were wooden stakes, buried halfway into ground with the top halves tied to each other to form long rectangles which overlapped one another.

Prayers were sent by men holding their hands up at chest height. Palms opened close to their body. From the mouth of the Ahmadi cleric, Arabic words were spoken, followed by a few sentences in Bahasa Indonesia.

Another series of Arabic words concluded the prayers followed by an audible 'amen' from the crowd. They gently brushed their palms onto their faces as if the prayers were invisible things they had to shove inside their head. God must have smiled that day, smirking cynically at the humans He had created and the futility of their plans.

With one rectangle guiding them, men with shovels began to dig making a ditch nearly knee deep. A bucket filled with cement mixture was readied at one end. Next to it were a dozen red clay bricks. The first few bricks were reserved for the most honorable of guests. Ahmadi leaders, community elders, neighborhood officials, clerics. God must have smirked once more. Men and their honors. How fragile is one's life? More fragile is one's honor. Even more is one's plan.

One by one the clay bricks were laid over a layer of cement. The most honorable and the most dignified laid them, carefully, neatly placing them on top of each other as people snapped pictures of them with then slowly fading point and shoot film cameras and more modern digital cameras and still fuzzy phone cameras.

The cameras didn't just record the groundbreaking ceremony. One picture was of an elderly man, back deformed, spines curving forward. He was shirtless, revealing spots-laden, soft, floppy skins. He was smiling, his mouth a hollow chamber missing its teeth.

There were pictures of a bashful child, standing in front of a pile of lime sand bricks stacked taller than his height as if ready to consume him whole. He was staring deeply at the lens with his hand holding a biscuit on his mouth. His arms were tightly pressed to body, curling, making him smaller. As if trying to hide. As if trying to run.

Other children were more enthused. Laughing hard, they jumped and ran and showed the camera their toys. Showing off their fighting skills learned from the cartoons they watched and comic books they read. The display made for dynamic photographs, the children's motions represented as blurry, colorful lines.

There was one picture of an empty alleyway connecting the single row of Ahmadi homes, sandwiched between bamboo fence and brick walls. Pictures of homes under construction in various stages of completion. Others were of those already standing, occupied. With lawns straightforwardly fenced with bamboo stakes sticking out tall enough to keep chickens in and cats away.

One home had its front yard converted into a garden of cassava and papaya trees. One yard was a garden of flowers. One yard was a concrete parking space. One yard was covered in concrete slabs covered in plastic roof held together by metal frames.

The last yard belonged to Shabri, the Ahmadi police officer, sent to live with the congregation to ensure their safety. Shabri was the community's eyes and ears, listening and monitoring for any signs of trouble. He was also their mouth, acting on the community's behalf to lobby government officials and the law enforcement agency he worked for. Shabri also acted as the community chief taking care of the Ahmadis' civic affairs. Ketapang's Ahmadiyya cleric Abidin, was Shabri's administrative deputy in the neighborhood.

Khaerudin was Shabri's number three. Many doubted he was the right man for the job. He maybe the most senior of the Ahmadiyya youths in Ketapang. But he was never any good at lobbying or even talking, particularly to strangers. He was such a nervous man when he opened his mouth, he rushed to get the words out. But he was always good with money. He was trustworthy. And so people voted him to become the neighborhood's treasurer.

Shabri, a small but muscular man with intimidating look and bushy mustache, had the bigger corner home. He had converted his yard into a mushalla, the prayer home for all 21 Ahmadiyya families in the community. Such is why he never locked his gates. Why his house was always full of life despite his work required him to travel far very often.

The house played host to a thanksgiving feast after the groundbreaking ceremony that day. Ahmadis and non-Ahmadis have their pictures taken picking up plates, spooning up rice from a huge bowl, goat stew from another, shrimp chips from the next. Everyone seemed happy, even Khaerudin whose forced smile radiated a hint of awkwardness. There were happiness, there were togetherness. The harmonious life of Ahmadis and their non-Ahmadi neighbors captured in a single frame.

None of them lasted long. The ground was broken to make way for a mosque. An Ahmadiyya mosque. From the national headquarter in Jakarta an instruction had come. No Ahmadi should pray in mainstream Muslim mosques. They cited cases and reasons why they shouldn't. No Ahmadi should pray with those accusing them of blasphemy.

The bricks laid that day were for a house of worship meant only for the 21 Ahmadiyya families living in Ketapang. It was planned to stand less than a kilometer from a non-Ahmadiyya mosque, frequented by the Tuan Gurus and the high clerics. Men who won't put their anti-Ahmadiyya rhetoric to rest. The Ahmadis in Ketapang had been welcomed. They were accepted based solely on their ability to blend in, to keep a low key.

God must have smiled that day, smirking cynically at the humans and the futility of their plans.

CHAPTER 16

There was a huge commotion one morning, coming from Suhaidi's home. Suhaidi's wife, Sri had threatened to leave him. Suhaidi grabbed Sri by the arm as she walked past their front lawn. Sri's face was all red. Her eyes were pools of tears. Sri said nothing. She didn't want to talk to Suhaidi, the husband she no longer trusted. Inside she was screaming for Suhaidi to let her go.

Suhaidi must have repeatedly asked Sri to chat in the privacy of their home. His voice a soft whisper. But Sri replied by telling Suhaidi to let go, telling him that she wanted to go to Jakarta and join her father and stepmother there. Her words incoherent though. The sadness which came after betrayal and infidelity made her unable to control her speech. Her body was shaking. Her head felt light. Adrenaline had made her heart pumped blood into her brain more than it should. Sri was so upset she must have at some point screamed the word, 'divorce.'

Suhaidi grabbed her arm even tighter. She tried to wrestle Suhaidi. He was strong but all the rage in her head gave her added strength. Sri screamed and screamed each time she had the chance to hurt her husband. She was venting her anger.

The fight attracted attention. Everyone couldn't believe what they were seeing. Suhaidi was well known as a womanizer but they never knew the quiet, obedient and submissive Sri could be so aggressive, so full of anger. She must have had it with Suhaidi. He must have done something so terrible Sri must have reached boiling point and just lost control of her emotion.

Khaerudin's wife, Suryani watched in silence. As a sister she knew she had to help Sri. But she was unsure how. She just wept and wept.

Suhaidi's father watched in disbelief, observing silently their every move. Nasipudin immediately intervened when Suhaidi raised his hands, ready to slap his petite wife.

Suhaidi probably kept staring at his wife, too afraid to look his father in the eyes. He eased his grip. Sri's arms were bruising red. It would be a matter of time before the bruises turned blue.

Suhaidi went and started his motorcycle. He hit the gas hard and raced across the pathway, nearly hitting his wife and father. In a matter of seconds, he was gone.

Nasipudin looked at his daughter-in-law, Sri and gently took her over inside. She was so shaken only crying was heard from her mouth. Nasipudin didn't dare to ask, as curious as he may be as to what had happened. None of their neighbors also dared to ask, just whispering to each other about what they assumed was going on.

'Uh oh… I think Suhaidi got caught cheating,' a neighbor might say to his wife. His wife would probably tell him such words were meant to be spoken in private. Deep down, she was agreeing.

At the privacy of Nasipudin's home, Sri was gradually able to stop crying. Suryani came to Nasipudin's home to check on her sister. Zubaidah poured a glass of water for Sri. But Sri wasn't ready to share her story. Everyone could see this, choosing to keep their mouth shut until Sri was ready. It was Nasipudin who broke the silence.

'I just want you to know that we support you all the way. I want you to know that we are your family too. Whatever you need… anything at all… we will be there for you… always.'

Sri just nodded. Nasipudin looked at his daughter-in-law with a smile and the piercing look of a wise man. He wasn't expecting Sri to talk much. He understood she needed space and time to think.

'I will talk to your husband. Don't you worry! We will be there for you! You are the mother of my granddaughter.'

***

That night Nasipudin called Suhaidi. It was late and he was nowhere in sight. Going out with his friends perhaps? Wandering Mataram's streets aimlessly? Whatever he was doing, Suhaidi was not answering his phone.

Nasipudin tried calling everyone he knew. He asked Faizah at the market if she had seen him or heard news of her brother's whereabouts. He called his nephews and sons of neighbors whom Suhaidi normally hanged out with. He sent text messages to Suhaidi's phone.

'Ignoring your father I see. If that's the case you can stop calling yourself a son.'

Suhaidi, as brave and reckless as he was, knew it was the ultimatum he could no longer ignore. Within minutes he gave his father a call. He was trying to explain himself but his father was not interested in his excuses.

'I will be at my house. And I expect you to be here this instant and meet me,' were Nasipudin's only words.

Suhaidi knew he was in trouble. For his father to summon any member of the family for a private talk meant only one thing: a scolding was imminent.

Upon arriving at his father's home Suhaidi was quizzed. Not of where he had been and why he didn't answer his phone but whether he had eaten. Suhaidi knew that his father was furious. For him to ask whether he had eaten can only mean that the scolding was to be so bad he would lose all appetite for food once his father was done.

Who knew what Nasipudin said to Suhaidi. It is a secret only the two shares. But Nasipudin must have asked Suhaidi to join him and the the two soon went for a stroll. Suhaidi was taken to somewhere quiet. A place away from their neighbors.

At the quiet place Nasipudin, angrily, quizzed Suhaidi about the rumors he had heard that Suhaidi was cheating on his wife. Suhaidi had no choice but to confess. It was true. He was seeing someone else.

Nasipudin must have been outraged. His voice perhaps grew louder and louder, scolding him, highlighting his past sins. How Suhaidi has failed him as a son. How Nasipudin and Zubaidah had to repeatedly clean up for the mess he had created. Nasipudin asked Suhaidi if he was insane, for seeing someone else when he doesn't even provide for his wife and daughter.

Nasipudin then told Suhaidi to break up with this other woman.

Suhaidi said he couldn't which left Nasipudin in shock, thinking that either Suhaidi is challenging his authority, he was choosing this other woman over his family or worse, the girl must have been pregnant with Suhaidi's child out of wedlock, a cardinal sin in Ahmadiyya.

Suhaidi assured Nasipudin that he was not sleeping with the other woman. He knew his boundaries as an Ahmadi. Nasipudin couldn't tell if Suhaidi was telling the truth. But he gave Suhaidi the benefit of a doubt.

'She's planning to sue if I don't marry her.' Suhaidi must have said.

'What do you mean she's going to sue you?'

'I kind of lied to her… I've been borrowing money from her… and I kind of said I wanted to marry her but I needed to sort some things out with my wife…'

Nasipudin couldn't believe his ears. He couldn't believe his son had played with the poor girl's heart and lying to her to get what he wanted. Perhaps he was planning to trick his wife and his whole family and secretly marry this girl. Perhaps the girl was smarter than Suhaidi thought and wouldn't settle on anything less than an official, lawful marriage. Perhaps worse, that he was really eyeing to divorce Sri.

Nasipudin then spoke: 'This is your mess. I am NOT cleaning this up. But whatever you do… I AM WARNING YOU… I will NOT let my granddaughter grow up without a father… You hear me? I will NOT let your wife Sri be a single mother. I will NOT let you throw her into the streets and starve or force her to be with her step mom in Jakarta. You hear? Am I being clear?'

Suhaidi was tearing up. 'Yes dad. '

***

It had been almost three years since the Ahmadiyya were driven away from their hometown in East Lombok. Since then the Ahmadiyya leaders had done nothing but writing letters after letters to government agencies and law enforcers.

Everyone was too afraid to speak out and put public pressure for resolution and justice. Standing up against intolerance was too risky. For the tolerant non-Ahmadis, it meant siding with people accused of blasphemy. For the Ahmadiyya leaders in Jakarta it meant having their identity as Ahmadis fully exposed. It meant the risk of losing their job. For the bureaucrats, it meant losing petro-dollars from rich Middle-Eastern countries.

Silence, as things unfold, came at a hefty price.

The militants were getting stronger. Launching attacks after attacks on innocent civilians. Sparking conflicts in places like Ambon and Poso. Further deepening the religious divide. The hard-liners were given spots at the country's top Muslim bodies, infiltrated every mosques to spread their divisive and intolerant messages, passing edicts after edicts on vice and blasphemy. The moderates were pushed further and further aside. Their influence waning as they meddled with politics.

No one spoke for the persecuted. For the Ahmadi leaders in Jakarta, doing their best was to offer prayers and moral support and a few lectures on patience. Silence has allowed intolerance to spread like wildfire. And then, it came to their doorstep.

The day was July 15, 2005. A hard-line Muslim group of more than two thousand strong had descended upon the Mubarak campus in Parung, the southern suburbs of Jakarta where the Ahmadiyya congregation is headquartered. It was also a place where they teach future clerics and old ones convene before they were stationed to other parts of the country. The hard-liners attacked the massive gated compound, pelting rocks and empty bottles. The attackers were determined that the Ahmadis should vacate the premise, promising that no harm would fall upon them if they converted to mainstream orthodoxy.

'Ban the Ahmadiyya! Death to those desecrating the prophet!'

Four police trucks came. Followed by four buses. Just like in Pancor police were there not to stop the attack but to drive the victims away from their own building. All four hundred men and women trapped inside Mubarak campus were told to get on the bus. They were to be escorted to safety. They agreed after police promised to safeguard the premise.

The convoy moved, slowly through the crowd of attackers, wielding wooden planks and bamboo poles carrying banners saying 'Disband the Ahmadiyya.' Some attackers banged and hit the trucks filled with petrified Ahmadis. It would be a full twenty minutes before they cleared the skull caps and white garbs wearing crowd. Minutes which seemed to last forever.

The intolerant had the first say about what happened. Shaping people's perception about the Ahmadiyya group.

'They have angered the Muslim community. Their faith had shaken the very core of Muslim beliefs,' said Amidhan, chairman of the Indonesian Council of Ulema (MUI) in front of the press.

'We have examined books and scriptures used by the Ahmadiyya and found that they have another prophet after the final prophet Muhammad which is the founder of the movement, a man called Mirza Ghulam Ahmad. They have different shahada. They have a different holy book. A book named Tazkirah. Therefore we are warning the entire Muslim community about this fraudulent teaching and ask those already falling victim to this fraud to return to the righteous form of Islam. We have petitioned the government to issue a ban on the Ahmadiyya group.'

The Ahmadiyya leaders felt the pressure. They realized the government was not going to do anything to ensure that they can practice their religion freely. They realized people would be provoked with what the MUI was saying.

From the shadows they revealed themselves to the masses, making allies with other moderate Muslim groups they once tried to stay away. Together they formed the Alliance for Tolerance and the Freedom of Religion and Faith (AKKBB). The Ahmadiyya leaders still thought their group was more supreme and more righteous than other groups, secretly calling the others defiant.

They allied themselves with Christians who were struggling to build churches amidst government intervention and harassments. Behind closed doors the Ahmadiyya leaders still told their followers that Christians were infidels and that their Messiah Mirza Ghulam Ahmad was sent from the heavens to destroy the Cross.

But they had a common goal. They had a common enemy: hardliners and intolerant groups. And so they banded, joining hands, reluctantly, half-heartedly. An enemy of the enemy.

They sought help from a human rights defender named Adnan Buyung Nasution, a senior lawyer who founded the Indonesian Legal Aid Foundation (YLBHI). Adnan agreed to advocate for their plight. But his juniors had mixed feelings about the Ahmadiyya including then YLBHI chairman, Munarman, who had been defending terrorism suspects and siding with hard-line groups. (Munarman was eventually fired from YLBHI in June 2006 and joined hard-line Muslim groups the Islamic Defenders Front [FPI] and orchestrated an attack against an AKKBB rally in 2008).

The Ahmadiyya leaders sought approval from Muslim scholars, using their mouths to speak against the onslaught of intolerant messages. They found help in scholars like Dawam Rahardjo, Azyumardi Azra, Ulil Abshar Abdalla and former president Gus Dur.

'There are no fundamental difference between the Ahmadiyya and other Muslim groups. They have the same Islamic creed. They pray just like other Muslims. They read the same Koran. But there are lies saying that they are not,' Dawam told the media.

'Despite our differences the government must ensure that their constitutional rights of religious freedom are guaranteed,' Azra said to the media.

Even Ahmadiyya's national emir, Abdul Basith was forced to speak 'Ahmadiyya simply believe that the promised Messiah has come. The Sunnis and Shiites believe that a Messiah shall come. We believe it had. We believe Mirza (Ghulam Ahmad) to be the promised Messiah. If the others don't believe Mirza to be a Messiah then it is their faith,' Basith told the press.

But aside from the few tolerant faces, the rest of the Muslim community was condemning the Ahmadiyya.

'We are both minority Muslim groups. But don't compare us with the Ahmadiyya. They have another prophet after Muhammad and this is blasphemy,' said the Shiites.

'We agree that the Ahmadiyya should be disbanded but it must be done peacefully without violence,' said the moderate Muslims.

'We are not deviant. Please differentiate between the Indonesian Ahmadiyya Congregation and the Indonesian Ahmadiyya Movement. The former observes the Qadian version of Ahmadiyya and thinks Mirza Ghulam Ahmad was a prophet. Whereas us observes the Lahore version of Ahmadiyya and thinks Mirza Ghulam Ahmad was a mujadid. A reformer of Islam,' said the Indonesian Ahmadiyya Movement.

The wave of intolerance grew and people were either openly expressing disapproval but secretly agreeing or the other way around. Within a few days after the attack on the Mubarak campus, it was no longer stoppable. The MUI had issued a fatwa, an edict for all to follow. A reaffirmation of their earlier fatwa made 25 years ago. That the Ahmadiyya was deviant. That they should be treated as non-Muslims. They should not be buried as Muslims. They should not have their weddings officiated in Islamic ways. They should not call their houses of worship mosques. They should not call their prayers shalat. They should be banned from wearing Muslim clothes and celebrate Muslim holidays. They should not call themselves Muslims at all.

They also banned those defending tolerance, the secularists, the pluralist and the liberals. They would call the three groups by a derogatory abbreviation 'sipilis.' Like the repulsive infectious disease.

But the calls were modest compared to what was happening on the ground. In sermons, clerics called for pillage, rape and murder. 'Desecration of religion. Desecration of the holy Prophet. Desecration of the Koran,' and all the other terms to incite hatred. To ignite fury. To fuel mistrust. To spark conflict.

And so violence began to spread, affecting one Ahmadiyya stronghold to the next. There were destructions. There were intimidations. There were threats. Soon they would make their way back to Lombok.

Perhaps Nasipudin's Ahmadiyya leaders should have spoken sooner. They should have stopped entrusting everything to the government. They should have stood up and defended what was rightfully theirs. They should have advocated for the Constitutional rights of all religion. They should have said something when other minority groups enjoyed persecution. They should have done something when those accused of blasphemy were going to jail for something they believed in. And now the intolerant groups had grown larger. The wave of hatred unstoppable.

But what was Nasipudin to do? A foot soldier in a hierarchical organization named Ahmadiyya. Who is he to defy the wishes of the congregation leaders? Who is he compared to the National Emir? He is nothing compared to the international Caliph. Their commands were absolute. His duty was to obey them. If the leaders were wrong? Then may God, the All-Compassionate God, have mercy on them all.

CHAPTER 17

The Friday sermon echoed across Ketapang, its words were barely comprehensible as it bounces off hills and people's houses. The speaker masterfully played with people's emotion. He started with a soft spoken voice, gradually making it louder as he built up his argument before exploding into a roar. It was a fiery sermon, with occasional growls as the voice grew louder. The tone peaked and dipped with carefully planned pauses to let people reflect on what was being said.

The Ahmadis were having a Friday prayer of their own, gathering at Shabri's yard in front of the foundation of their would-be mosque, construction of which were put on hold indefinitely as attacks occurred in other villages and towns.

The Ahmadis' sermon was soft and plain. There were times when the sermon faraway overpowered the one observed by the Ahmadis. The Ahmadis were curious to see the man behind the faraway sermon but at the same time respectfully followed their own.

Then came a few familiar words. 'Ahmadiyya…,' the rest were inaudible. 'Blasphemer… And would we stand… Insulting our Prophet Muhammad… Blood… It is our rightful duty… Blood… Ahmadiyya… Blood…'

The Ahmadi cleric quickly wrapped up his sermon as the congregation grew restless. The sermon faraway continued to be heard as they got up to pray. By this time they must have figured out it was coming from the non-Ahmadiyya mosque further down the road. The mosque the Ahmadis helped build.

The Ahmadi cleric recited short verses from the Koran. He was also curious about the sermon faraway, anxious to conclude the week's Friday prayer procession.

Once their prayers concluded, only a handful of elders stayed for after prayer recital. The youths immediately got out of Shabri's home to investigate. They wanted to hear what was being said and who had made the sermon faraway.

'If you don't banish the Ahmadiyya people from here then by God I will send my pupils here and drive them away ourselves,' the sermon heard as the Ahmadis inched closer to get a better listen.

The day was October 19, 2005. It was in the middle of the holy month of Ramadan, a time to reflect on one's sins instead of others. A time to constrain one's emotion instead of inciting hatred.

Shabri, the hot blooded Ahmadi police officer, readied his pistol, anticipating the animosity to come. He took his motorcycle out on the main road and waited. Suddenly he spotted Khaerudin, his most trusted wingman at the complex.

'Let's wait to see who it is [that gave the sermon],' Shabri told Khaerudin, who was probably struggling not to let his fear show.

'And do what?'

'We're going to follow him. See where he is heading. I want to see if he was bluffing or not.'

'And what do you need me for?'

'You're coming with me!' Khaerudin looked confused. Inside his heart was racing.

'Just a quick look. We'll keep our distance. I just want to see where he is heading after this. Maybe he's got a few thugs ready to strike. Maybe he's having a meeting somewhere after this. If this guy is really up to something we'll know.'

Khaerudin's fear was starting to show. Shabri placed his hand over Khaerudin's shoulder.

'Relaaaaxxx!!! I'm a cop. Nobody's going to touch me.'

'What about me then?'

'Yeah well.... I got my gun.'

Suddenly a sedan drove past them coming from the mosque's direction.

'That's him. Let's go!'

Shabri started his motorcycle and told Khaerudin to hop on the passenger's seat. Once the car was a tiny spec at the end of the road they began their pursuit.

They followed the car as it made a right turn. They passed rows of villas and holiday homes, past stretches of rice fields, past upscale restaurants and car wash. They rode passed a metal bridge, past a crowded four lane street. Past garbage trucks, fancy cars and tricked out motorcycles. Past political banners, and colorful murals. Past a mosque with a bright blue dome shaped like an onion. Past an orange Hindu temple.

In front of a restaurant the car made a right turn, decelerating as it ground to a complete stop at the restaurant's parking lot. Shabri decelerated and slowly drove up to get a better look. He stopped his motorcycle at the side of the road directly across the restaurant. He could see the cleric in his car.

His driver went inside and emerged a few minutes later with three tall and muscular men. The men went inside the car. Two were sitting next to the cleric at the back.

'I think that's his bodyguards,' Shabri said. Khaerudin pretended to express interest. All he could think about was going to the safety of his home.

Soon, they were on the move again. The car had turned towards the opposite direction. Shabri raced to make a U-turn. He didn't know that he had been spotted. It became obvious to Shabri that his cover was blown when the car decelerated in front of him and pulled over to the side. He made no intention to turn back and instead decided to confront the cleric. He positioned his motorbike parallel to where the cleric was sitting.

The window started to roll down revealing the cleric who was stretching his arm to the bodyguard on his right who immediately called off his intention to get out of the car.

'Hey! Why are you following me?'

Shabri casually replied. His cynicism obvious. 'Oh... c'mon. I'm just a fan. I just want to tell you what a great sermon you delivered just now.'

'Are you one of those Ahmadiyya people?'

'As a matter of fact I am.'

'I got nothing to say to you. ' The cleric whisked his hand, telling his driver to move.

'Assalamu alaykum!' Shabri yelled a courtesy call to the cleric as a fellow Muslim, a well wishing for God's protection.

'Whatever you say, dog!' the cleric said as his bodyguard rolled up the window.

Shabri just smiled, a wide grin running ear to ear as he balanced his stationary motorbike. He looked at Khaerudin with the corner of his eye.

'Now there… is a religious leader of impeccable manner. We should all follow his example!'

Khaerudin laughed. There was a sigh of relief in his laughter. Any minute more he would have been pissing his pants.

Shabri and Khaerudin returned to Ketapang. Enthusiastically, Shabri told their friends of their earlier adventure as the sun set. His friends had come to his home to enjoy their fasting break meal. Shabri told the joke he made to Khaerudin after the cleric set off. Everyone laughed. It was the last time anyone had so much joy on their faces. For chaos was upon them.

As the men shared jokes. As the children gathered to recite verses from the Koran. As the women were in their houses watching soap operas. Came the sound of flying rocks crashing into the tiled roof. The sound of windows smashing. The sound of a mob, in the dozens, descending upon them. The sound of people shouting the word 'Attack! Attack! '

The sound of crying children and screaming women. The sound of people hurriedly fleeing to safety. The sound of panicking mothers calling out to their sons and daughters. The sound of bushes being stomped by escaping people. The sound sandals snapping and feet stomping across a muddy rice field. The sound of elderly women falling into the ground as they lost their balance. The sound of a crying homeowner pleading the attackers to stop. The sound of brave Ahmadi youths trying to retaliate.

Then came the loudest sound of all. Three gunshots firing into the air. They were followed by the sound of the attackers scrambling away, retreating. It was the last time Shabri fired his pistol.

***

The men didn't get much sleep that night. Some chose to sleep on their porches while others forced themselves to stay awake to watch for any sign of trouble. The women had trouble sleeping too, worrying about their family's safety and future. Zubaidah noticed that her last son Kasafuloh didn't talk much after the attack, avoiding people and never answered any question. He was there at Shabri's house attending a Koran recital when the attackers stroke. He witnessed the mayhem with his own eyes. He must have been shocked.

Kasafuloh was refusing to go to school despite his brothers and sisters saying it was OK. Zubaidah tried to go along with what he wanted despite her husband feeling otherwise. A lot of the small children in Ketapang skipped school that day. But somehow Kasafuloh didn't want to play with them either.

Kasafuloh was in third grade. He went to the same school as Safir who was in fifth grade. He also shared the same school with Khaerudin's son Hafidz who was in first grade. The school was further down the road and nobody thought it was best to go pass the mosque which a day before was home to a message of hate. 'The cleric must have supporters there, ' the parents thought.

Their leader Shabri hadn't given the all clear either. He was obviously too busy minding other things. Like so many other men in Ketapang, he too had not slept but by morning he was already assessing the damages done, the people injured and making dozens of phone calls.

Nurul also didn't get much sleep. The rest of the women were busy minding their children. So the childless Nurul thought she must do her bid to help by making coffees and fried snacks for those on watch duty. This morning she thought she would just help her dad plowing the nearby plot of land her dad had rented for the year and maybe after helped the neighbors whose homes were damaged in the attack.

But just as she was about to fetch water from the well to clean up, a sobbing was heard from further down the alleyway. A woman had suffered a miscarriage. Her pregnancy was less than 10 weeks old and the pain was not as severe as Nurul who lost her child less than 5 months before she was due to give birth. But still she empathized.

Dramatization:

Nurul was probably just about to go over the poor woman's home when Suhaidi fired up his motorcycle, cranking up the throttle to check how his engine ran. The roaring sound was earsplitting. The smoke from his exhaust nauseating.

'Where are you off to?' Nurul must have asked his brother.

'The doctor. I got to take my wives to check on their pregnancies.'

Minutes later out came Ramlah, Suhaidi's second wife who was five months pregnant. Ramlah smiled at Nurul's way while rubbing her belly. Nurul smiled back as she stood by the door, watching Suhaidi as he lifted his motorcycle's back end and positioned it to point the other way. Out came Suhaidi's five-year-old daughter Yuni followed by her mother, Suhaidi's first wife, Sri who was two months pregnant.

God really works in a mysterious way, Nurul must have thought. For she couldn't understand why her irresponsible, trouble-making, polygamist little brother was soon to have three children while she had not been blessed with just one.

'OK, now you just wait there until I get this bike out,' Suhaidi told his wives. 'Yuni... Yuni... You sit here in front of daddy, Sweetheart. Good girl.. Now Ramlah, you sit behind me! You need help getting up?'

'I'll just wait for you to get back,' Sri told Suhaidi. She understood that Ramlah was further in her pregnancy but she was also upset seeing a woman sitting on what used to be her seat in their motorbike.

'No, there's enough room,' Suhaidi said. Ramlah gave Sri a stare as she wrapped her arms around Suhaidi.

'I think I'll just wait.' Sri was thinking why she didn't just leave him when she had the chance.

At one time she did. But she found out later that she was pregnant and her in-laws convinced her it was best that she stayed. Suhaidi was not letting her go either, simply making promises about him eventually buying off land from his sister Faizah so that she didn't have to share a house with Ramlah. She couldn't stand Ramlah. She couldn't stand her fake smile which she put on whenever the two wives were not alone. And to think that Suhaidi was giving Ramlah her seat? What's next?

'C'mon! There's no time to go to the clinic and back to pick you up, ' Suhaidi argued.

Reluctantly Sri agreed.

Suhaidi and Ramlah waved goodbye to Nurul. Sri, still upset, stared at the air in front of her.

CHAPTER 18

Four days had past since the attack and it seemed nothing was ever going back to normal. The neighbors tried to avoid the Ahmadis the best they can, pretending they were strangers when they happened to wait for the same bus down at the main road. They hastened their pace when they passed the row of Ahmadi homes. They couldn't help their curiosity to look but immediately kept their heads down when some Ahmadis looked back at them. The Ahmadis tried to say hello, but the neighbors just looked the other way, pretending that they can't hear them.

The Ahmadis could only reminisce the days when the neighbors visited them regularly, chatting over the trivial things that had happened in their lives, asking for help or favors, borrowing stuffs or money or discuss plans on how to upgrade the village. Back then, no one seemed to question what Ahmadiyya was all about. The neighbors never talked about religion and the Ahmadiyya's subtle differences with the mainstream. The neighbors never let that differences affect their social interaction. They never seemed to care. Everyone was just neighbors. Everyone was simply residents of Ketapang.

Perhaps the neighbors were afraid to talk to them after all the chaos that occurred. Perhaps they were threatened. Perhaps they were provoked by what the clerics had said about the Ahmadis.

Whatever it was it was keeping Malik's friends away from him at school. Even those he used to hang out with and whose lunches he used to pay. Malik never said he was an Ahmadi but his friends knew where he lived, among the people whose houses were hurled with rocks. The blasphemers.

'I never thought he is one of those Ahmadiyya people. He seemed so nice,' heard one of the whispers behind his back.

'I know right.'

They made it sound like all the kindness of an Ahmadi never mattered. As if someone's faith dictates how they should behave. Worse still, they made it sound like a raping mugger of the same faith is holier than a loving Ahmadi.

Malik thought of confronting his friends at school and tell them they were wrong, that what the things their clerics said about Ahmadiyya were not true. But as soon as he approached them, they walked away.

And so everywhere he went he just stayed with Zakir, his fellow eight-grader from school, his cousin, his Ahmadi friend and by then his only companion.

'Is your brother OK?' Zakir must have said to Malik in between classes.

'Who? Safir? He's OK, why?'

'He was standing up to a sixth-grader who was picking on smaller Ahmadi kids at school. You don't know this.'

'No... no... no... I do... I do...' Malik was lying. His mother never told him that the previous day his nephew Hafidz, Khaerudin's son was picked on by a sixth grader for being an Ahmadi. The first-grader was pushed to the ground by a kid almost twice his age. Safir tried to stop this kid but as a fifth-grader standing up to someone older he could only use words. The sixth-grader responded with a threat, verbal but a threat nonetheless.

'You think the attack the other day was over? Think again, dog!'

Safir got shoved to the side. The sixth-grader went on and picked on another Ahmadi kid. This time limited to a few name calling.

Hafidz was crying. So loud that the teachers agreed Safir should take him home. Hafidz's mother was shocked to see her son crying. He had only been to school for a few months. She was afraid that the ordeal would make him stop loving school. Suryani never said anything to Safir but Safir's mom made him promise that he would always look after the smaller Ahmadi children in his school.

'You're the biggest one in your school. We parents can only take you kids to school, pick you up and protect you while you kids are home. We can't do anything once the kids are in school,' Zubaidah said to Safir.

Zubaidah never told his other son Malik about what happened. She never said to him that she and Suryani went to meet the school's principal that day demanding that something be done about the bullying kid. The school said they could do nothing. They never wanted to. When Zubaidah asked the school to never let that happen again, the school also made no promises.

Zubaidah never told Malik that his youngest brother Kasafuloh had missed school again. It had been days since Kasafuloh spoken any word.

Malik must have regretted why his mother never told him these things were happening. He also regretted why he never bothered to ask how his brothers were doing. Why were these facts oblivious to him? Was he too busy with life as a teen? Malik used to play with his brothers everyday. They used to go everywhere together. Had he outgrown them? What kind of ignorant brother had he become?

'God, forgive me!' Malik would probably say in his heart.

***

Hours later the school bell rang. Zakir was already waiting for Malik in front of his classroom. The two had decided it was best not to stay long after school. And so they walked home under the scorching sun, in sweat-drenched uniforms.

Right at the corner where Ketapang's dirt road meets the busy main road was a bench made from solid concrete. There the boys sat, waiting for the trucks heading to nearby sand mine to come and give them a lift home. In Ketapang, the trucks were the only mode of transport. It was either hitching a ride on the trucks or walk home and get covered in dusts as they pass.

Zakir and Malik's eyes were transfixed to the direction where the trucks would come. They didn't realize that one kid from school was targeting them. From behind, the kid, whom Malik recognized as his senior Nuriyadi, struck a punch to Malik's face. He was thrown to the ground.

'What's wrong with you?' Malik said to Nuriyadi.

'You're an Ahmadiyya. Get up and fight.'

Malik blocked blow after blow. It was not that hard. Nuriyadi was not at all as good as a fighter as he was a loud mouth bully. He wanted desperately to fight back and lay a punch or two to shut Nuriyadi's big mouth. But Malik knew harming him would only bring unwanted attention against him and other Ahmadis. So he pushed Nuriyadi, making him fall hard flat on his back. As Malik tried to pin Nuriyadi, Nuriyadi signaled his awaiting friends to help.

Malik and Zakir were mobbed. Zakir was thrown into the mud. They tried beating Zakir but the mud softened the blow. After wrestling and struggling for his life he was able to run to safety. Malik was less lucky. He was surrounded and outnumbered. Amidst the chaos his only reaction was to cover his head using his arms. They beat and kicked him repeatedly.

Then two trucks came. They stopped. Malik thought the drivers would try to get off their trucks and help stop the assault. But instead the drivers offered them a lift. Malik could breathe a sigh of relief as he lied helplessly on the ground. The beating had stopped. The kids were boarding the two trucks' beds. The world was spinning before him. He was bleeding heavily. He didn't get a good look at the assailants but he could tell they were at least three dozens. The trucks took off and left him.

Malik tried to pick himself up. He could feel warm blood was gushing out of his nose. He could feel the sore on his neck, the aching on his back, the pain in his stomach, the sting in his eyes and the dirt on his bleeding mouth.

He limped his way home, taking the long way round along a small creek which ran to the back of the Ahmadi housing complex. It was a safer and more discreet route. It also provided him the opportunity to clean his wound, get the dirt out of his uniform. He didn't want his mother to worry. His sisters Faizah and Masitah would cry hysterically if they found out. Once he was all clean, he thought he could tell them that he fell into the stream and hurt himself.

But Zakir had already told them what happened. Suhaidi had gone out to search for Malik, waiting for him on the dirt road he usually took to get home. Everyone else was already waiting anxiously for his return. At the first sight of Malik they went hysterical.

'Look at what they did to my boy. Why did they do this to such a sweet child?' his mother wailed.

'If I find them I swear I will beat them,' said Suhaidi.

'Hush… Don't be ridiculous. You want more trouble than this?' Masitah must have told her older brother.

Suhaidi instead went to Malik's school with Khaerudin to talk to the principal.

'This incident is out of my jurisdiction. It happened after school and not within the premise of the school,' the principal responded.

It made all the school kids in Ketapang thought twice about going to school. Nasipudin made Suhaidi and Khaerudin keep a close watch of all of the Ahmadi children in Ketapang.

Nasipudin tried to calm his son down, reigniting his dimming spirit to go to school. At night he called Malik for a three way conversation with Zubaidah.

'Son. I know what happen to you is bad. Be patient. This is a test for us. A test of our strength, a test of our courage, a test of faith, a test of our conviction. This is a consequence of being an Ahmadi. But remind yourself this: God has a special place for the strong. A special place for the courageous. A special place for the patient. A special place for the faithful, ' the wise Nasipudin said to his son. 'You have a duty as a student. You have a duty to your fellow classmates. Don't hate them. They are resentful for they are ignorant. Care for them. Be nice to them. Our sins no matter how small we must redeem. People's mistake no matter how big we must forgive.'

And so that's what Malik did. The first day back at school he immediately went up to Nuriyadi.

'If I have done you wrong forgive me,' Malik said extending his hand.

Be it pride, be it pure resentment towards Malik, Nuriyadi would not shake Malik's hand, looking the other way and kept on talking to his friends.

***

Very early in the morning, Shabri got up and began packing his suitcases. It was to be a final farewell. His superiors at the Mataram police headquarters felt they had enough of Shabri knocking doors at various government agencies urging them to protect his people. The plan was set, Ahmadis must move away from Ketapang and Shabri, it seemed, was standing in the way.

And so his superiors reassigned him to a Sumbawan district of Bima. It is a hostile place miles away from anywhere. It is a place set in perpetual state of conflict. Neighbors fighting neighbors over the most trivial of things. It is a place forsaken by those in power, even the provincial government. It is no place where anyone wants to be. A place where all unwanted government officials and police officers end up.

Most likely, Khaerudin was at a loss for words when he found out that Shabri was leaving.

'Who will lead us?' he must have asked Shabri in a soft spoken voice.

'You will,' Shabri would have replied, tapping Khaerudin in the shoulder.

'I'm not a leader.'

'Now, who says that? When that poor elderly man was too sick to work and build himself a new home, you took the initiative to raise money and you went door to door asking people to donate money and volunteer. When that poor woman lost her pregnancy, you immediately called the hospital, making arrangements and such. Nobody asked you to do it… but instead, out of the goodness of your heart, you take the lead. You put everyone else above your own need. Being a leader is not about skills or influence or supporters or any of those things. It is what you do with them that matters.'

Khaerudin nodded. He wanted to believe that what Shabri said were true but the thought of failing people's expectation petrified him. He would be a leader of a very small community. But with an attack so fresh, with the assault on his own brother? He was unsure what to do if such attacks were to happen again. In a time of danger one wrong move would spell disaster. Would he cope bearing the consequences of his actions?

Shabri could see Khaerudin's mind began to wander and reminded him that he could always rely on his Ahmadiyya brothers. God will not forsake those who sincerely pray. In time of doubt, in time of uncertainty, in time of need, God will show the way.

For the first time Khaerudin's mind was at ease. For the first time he was able to smile.

The whole community gathered to bid farewell. Shabri greeted them, shaking their hands goodbye one by one. He made sure his last farewell was to Khaerudin, the interim leader of the community.

'You take care of yourself. God be with you,' he said to Khaerudin who was tearing up.

'You too.'

***

The test of Khaerudin's leadership came in many forms. Sick elders, kids being bullied at school, mothers denied of healthcare, rumors of another attack.

'God, help us. Give us strength. Show us the way,' he said.

And soon he composed himself together, drafted a letter demanding for police protection. He asked his brother Suhaidi, the better speaker, to accompany him. He went over to Jauzi's place, the only person he knew who had a printer, five kilometers away in Sweta to print the letters. He made copies at a local photocopy shop. He bought folders and envelopes using his own money.

He told Suhaidi to take him to the Ketapang Subdistrict Police Office. The brothers drove to the Lingsar District Police Office, warning them about a possible attack. He gathered enough strength to open his mouth to total strangers, police officers, explaining them what had happened and what he thought might happen.

The threat of harm made for many sleepless nights in Ketapang. The men stayed up late all night watching for any signs of danger. The subdistrict head had called for a meeting with the Ahmadis telling them to leave for their own safety. The once friendly village chief turned his back on them. The firebrand cleric returned speaking in a mosque not too far away.

'We shall give these Ahmadiyya people three months. Wait until I get back from my hajj pilgrimage. We shall drive these blasphemers then,' went the cleric's sermon.

Khaerudin reported every threats, every intimidations, every call to violence. Police responded by sending a couple of unarmed officers. They came, they chatted with the Ahmadis, they lingered, sometimes asked for 'cigarette money' for staying overnight. They left after they failed to get what they wanted.

The threats were mostly just that. One afternoon, dozens of people came, traversing their way across an empty field sitting at the back of the Ahmadi housing complex. They were heading to the creek down the slope. But one Ahmadi woman swore that they were out to attack the Ahmadis and screamed her lungs out.

The cry sent people scrambling out of their home and into the fields. Suhaidi led a group of youths to investigate, slowly approaching the dozens of people who came to the creek. They were fetching water and washing some bowls of rice. False alarm.

One moonless night, from afar were a row of lights and a distant call. The lights grew bigger and bigger as they inched closer, the call became clearer and clearer. 'Attack... Attack...' There were engine roar and chanting and loud cracking noise. The men on watch duty immediately rushed from home to home waking everyone up.

People panicked. A woman frantically ran outside, holding a pillow tight thinking it was her baby. Some people tried to run in the dead of night in pitch black condition and hit a wall, hit a tree, fell flat on their face, plunging into the muddy rice field. Some managed to make their way to the bushes and hid in horror.

And then terror turned to confusion as it became clear to them that the row of lights were no more than a few youths lining up four motorcycles in one row. Behind the motorcycles was a pick up truck carrying a sound system, a young man speaking on the microphone and a few people hitting some snare drums. The roared their engines to create the illusion of an attack.

As the group of posers disappeared, the Ahmadis got out of their hiding places. An elderly Ahmadi man was standing with a bow, his hands trembling uncontrollably, his breath heavy and show. He had released an arrow.

'My God. What did you do?' People asked.

'I was panicking. I think I hit the wheel of a motorbike.'

'God.... Thank God you didn't hit anyone. Can you imagine if you did?'

'I'm sorry... I'm sorry... I was panicking.'

CHAPTER 19

The day was February 4th, 2006 and the threat somehow felt different. From the night before police had been deployed. A truck full of officers with fiber glass shields and helmets and firearms were told to stand guard in Ketapang. The Ahmadis sensed there was something big about to happen. Police who used to dismiss and sideline their demand for protection was suddenly so quick to respond, so alert, so vigilant.

When morning struck, after the children had gone to school, more officers came. They parked their police trucks in an empty field more than two hundred meters away from the Ahmadi housing complex. The officers left their gears inside the trucks and marched along the unpaved road carrying nothing more than their police batons strapped to their belt.

They encircled the housing complex, forming a human barricade separating the Ahmadi complex from the rest of the neighborhood. There were meetings and sermons and calls on the speaker happening deep down in Ketapang. The venue was the mosque the Ahmadis helped build.

'To all able-bodied Muslims, to those who will not tolerate blasphemy. Please join us!' a call was heard.

The Ahmadis tried to investigate but police woouldn't let them pass the barricade. They made sure the Ahmadis stayed where they were. The only place they could go was to the main road, out of Ketapang.

Khaerudin immediately contacted Jauzi, his provincial leader. Sulaeman, who went to Borneo to work after his home in East Lombok was ransacked, was there at Jauzi's place as was another man named Iqbal. Sulaeman came back to Lombok after the first attack in Ketapang in September. His father-in-law Mahmuludin had his house badly damaged in it and Sulaeman's wife begged him to return from Borneo so they could be with his aging father. After getting a call from Khaerudin, Jauzi informed Sulaeman what happened.

'Ketapang is about to get attacked again,' he said. Hearing this, Iqbal suddenly fell ill and collapsed to the floor. Sulaeman and Jauzi took Iqbal to the hospital. During that time Jauzi's phone kept ringing and ringing.

'Yes, we will immediately go there. Yes, I know... I know... Hellooo?... Can you hear me now? Iqbal... He's sick... We have to go to the hospital... Just hang in there OK?... We'll be there as soon as possible... ' Jauzi must have said as Sulaeman drove as fast as he could, navigating Jauzi's car around the traffic. 'Khaerudin... Khaerudin... You keep me posted OK! I'll send someone over there. '

Jauzi kept fiddling his phone with one hand and with another trying to stabilize Iqbal who was going in and out of consciousness. Jauzi flipped through the phone book inside his phone, trying to find someone, anyone who could help. He dialed a number on his phone. No one was answering. He dialed another number, another person he thought might help. That call too went unanswered.

Jauzi chuckled. 'Why is nobody picking up the phone? '

***

As soon as the crowd began flocking to their complex, Khaerudin and Suhaidi wasted no time, transporting their children over to Faizah's makeshift hut at the market. Khaerudin's son Hafidz was still in the bathroom completely naked when Khaerudin dragged him over to his motorbike. Khaerudin didn't even bother to dry his son's wet naked body. Khaerudin's wife Suryani, carrying their two-year-old toddler Rafik, sat on the back.

Suhaidi's second wife Ramlah, by then eight months pregnant, insisted she should come. Ramlah had a brother working at the market. Their late parents' home was close and she thought she could easily hide there in case people were starting to target Ahmadiyya and violence spread out from Ketapang.

Sri, still upset about sharing a husband with Ramlah, said she would stay. Suhaidi was upset Sri was being so stubborn not to come but there was little time for argument. Ramlah took Sri's daughter Yuni to safety.

Zubaidah was not sure what to do. His son Malik was still at school as was Safir and Kasafuloh and she was anxious to know if they were alright.

'This is your fault,' Zubaidah said to her husband Nasipudin.

'What? What are you talking about?'

'If you hadn't insisted that the children must go to school this morning I wouldn't be this worried. At least I would know where they are, if they're safe.'

Nasipudin just shook his head in disbelief and calmly smiled. He felt the same way, had he known he would've asked his children to stay. But who could foresee what God had planned for His creation? Nasipudin knew that deep down his wife understood the reason behind his decision.

'Come, let's go inside. They will come home soon. Stop worrying,' he said.

Zubaidah followed her husband into their home. Masitah must have been there at the living room looking after Nisa, whose muscular dystrophy had only allowed her to make the simplest of movement.

Zubaidah would have watched Masitah as she gently combed her sister's hair with the gaps between her fingers. Nisa's hair was silky smooth with golden glow reflection of the sun shining from the doorway. Nisa raised her right arm. Her crooked hand seemed as if she was also reaching for her sister's hair. Masitah probably stared deeply into Nisa's eyes, smiling as she continued to comb down her hair. People said Nisa didn't have a mind of her own because of her illness. But for a second Zubaidah could well have sworn Nisa was smiling back at Masitah.

Nasipudin must have seen what happened too. He took it as a sign from God. It must have been a miracle, he thought. God's way of showing how lucky they were to be together. God's way of showing that nothing else mattered. The houses which his family had built brick by painstaking brick. His entire fortune which he had mustered from every dirty crumpled bank notes he had saved. They all seemed less important.

No one in the room said anything. Trying to grasp every precious second they had. Danger was imminent. The enemy just meters away ready to strike. But there was no fear. For they sensed that God was with them. Nasipudin prayed He always would be.

Minutes later Malik came riding a bicycle with Safir on the back and Kasafuloh sandwiched between them. Someone at school told him that people were preparing to attack his home. He took the initiative to pick up his brothers up from their school.

Nasipudin smiled some more for it was another of God's blessings. When Malik entered junior high school he distanced himself from his brothers. He was feeling like he became too old to play with his two younger brothers. But right then and there, with danger lurking, they were finally reunited once more.

Suhaidi came, a short time after. On the passenger seat was Guntur, his brother-in-law. Khaerudin's motorbike was also spotted, with him his wife Suryani who insisted she shouldn't stay with Faizah at the market because she wanted to be with her sister Sri.

Nasipudin turned his head over to Nurul. She was standing by the door, shedding tears at the sight of her two brothers, like all her grudges against Suhaidi had disappeared. Perhaps she was thinking of the chance of losing her home. The one she built with her bare hands until her arms sore and filled with blisters.

Whatever it was, Nasipudin felt elated. With the exception of Faizah his family was complete. They were together. Faizah was making a huge sacrifice. Putting her family above all else to look after all four of his grandchildren. Making sure they were safe.

'I give myself to You, God. Whatever plans You have for my family. I give myself to You,' he whispered a prayer.

***

For hours, Malik paced up and down the alleyway, following his older brothers and cousins. Suhaidi kept telling him to stay home and not on the frontline.

'I can fight,' Malik said.

'No... you go home.'

'But I want to stay. I can fight.'

'If you really want to make yourself useful, go home. Protect our mother.'

Malik reluctantly complied. Suhaidi tried his best not to look at Malik. The smart and hardworking Malik. He's the only hope the family had, Suhaidi thought. Khaerudin had formal education but lacked ambition. Himself the other way around. Suhaidi would do anything to make sure Malik was alright. His father would not forgive him if he didn't.

Malik walked slowly home but couldn't keep his eyes away from what was going on down the dirt road. There were screaming and yelling. The crowd was chanting words of hate. Reciting verses from the Koran which he also read. Funny how the victims and the attackers were both quoting from the same book to justify their actions. As he got closer to home, that very book was placed in his hands.

'Malik... ' It was his mother, placing a Koran in his hands. 'Will you guard this?'

Malik took a deep breath as if somehow he had found his place in the world, his role in this chaos.

'OK mom. I will.'

***

Hours passed with hardly any incident. The attackers didn't make a move. Staying behind the human barricade of men in uniform. Suhaidi was desperate for a drink. He was starving for food. The sun was scorching hot. Some of the attackers were starting to wander around out of boredom, some chose to sit, fatigued, keeping their heads covered by their scarves. Even the man on the bullhorn couldn't find more words to keep his men's spirits alive. Suhaidi thought he would return briefly home and drink some water, have a bite to eat.

As he walked home an officer approached him. 'Excuse me, where can you find cigarettes around here? '

'If you walk down the road for about ten minutes there's a shop.'

'Well... see... we can't leave our posts without permission. I was hoping you'd go.'

The officer gave Suhaidi some money. 50,000 rupiah, enough to buy five packs.

'Just get me one pack if it's not too much trouble.'

Suhaidi picked up his motorcycle and made his way to the shop. He bought the officer his favorite brand. The shopkeeper gave him change. He kept the pack of cigarettes and the change in his pocket.

Upon returning to Ketapang all hell had broken lose. Rocks were flying haphazardly from all direction. Some wood plank-wielding attackers were chasing down an Ahmadi man across the rice fields. Suhaidi raced his motorcycle right to the edge a ditch separating the road from the fields. He leapt out of his motorcycle, letting his favorite bike slamming to the ground, its back wheel still spinning.

With all his might he chased down the attackers like a tiger pursuing its prey. The attackers fled at the sight of Suhaidi, now filled with rage. They were scrambling, running for their lives. One dropped his wooden plank. Suhaidi picked it up, arming himself. Dodging rocks after rocks being pelted at him. The Ahmadi man was able to pick himself up and ran to safety.

From the distance, Suhaidi could see men, women, children running out of their homes and out of the rocks range. Amidst the chaos he couldn't be sure if his family was safe. One police officer had his face covered in blood. The officer's friends did nothing but waving their arms up and down telling the mob to calm down. The rest of the officers were too busy telling people to leave their homes. After a few intense minutes, the assault receded.

There were quarrels between a few of his Ahmadi friends and some police officers. Suhaidi couldn't make out what they were saying but from the tone, from the expression, from the loud voice, he could tell that they were expressing disappointment that police cared more about getting the victims out of their homes instead of stopping the attack from happening.

The officer just nodded and nodded while raising their arms in front of their chest telling his friends not to return to the front line. From the Ahmadi side of the barricade arguments continued. From the attackers' side more chanting and more yelling. Suhaidi approached his friends to see what they were arguing about.

Suhaidi was panting and sweating from all the running. He made a quick glance to the empty fields where the women and children were told to gather. His wife was there, his sisters were there, Malik was there keeping his brothers safe. His father was carrying Nisa standing next to his mother.

'Where's Khaerudin?' he must have thought.

He was surprised to see Khaerudin there on the frontline, meters away from the plank-wielding mob, arguing to a police officer. Khaerudin was not the timid older brother he once knew. Ketapang had a new leader.

CHAPTER 20

Suhaidi's stomach was contracting. He felt weakened. It was getting harder for him to concentrate or control his emotion. Khaerudin was also feeling the same way like his gut had taken a powerful blow. The two brothers were hungry.

Suhaidi whispered, 'are you hungry?'

'You bet. You too? '

'Yeah... Haven't eaten anything the whole day.'

The two waited for the officers, who were keeping the Ahmadis from coming back inside, to move away from the houses. At the first chance they got, casually they walked past behind them so not to attract attention. They planned to just play dumb if they got caught. Arguing that they didn't know they were not supposed to get back into their homes.

They made their way to their mother's home. Zubaidah had prepared a feast earlier that morning, thinking it might well be their last meal. Swiftly they opened the door and let themselves in. The food had not been touched, neatly tucked under a clean handkerchief. Underneath was fried chicken. Their mother had slaughtered all the chicken they had when the threat of an attack was heard. The rice was still in its cooking jar, still on and plugged to the power socket on the wall.

The brothers made sure no one was looking when they grabbed the plates from the kitchen at the back of the house, separated from the mob by a flimsy wall built from hand-made sand bricks. They scooped the rice, filling the whole plate. They took huge pieces of chicken. They were starving and it could be their last meal.

But nothing was entering their throat as hard as they tried to chew. The adrenaline. The rush of the moment. The thought of impending peril took a toll on their digestion.

Abruptly, with rice still lodged in their mouth, a rock, came crashing through the roof and landed on Suhaidi's plate. They had been spotted and more rocks were falling down on them followed by distant yelling. The brothers instinctively got out of their mothers house. It was only then the pelting stopped.

The brothers laughed as confused police officers looked at them. In a time of peril, they had time to think about food.

***

By the time Jauzi and Sulaeman and the rest of the Ahmadi leaders came, both the Ahmadis and the mob were well kept on opposing sides. They had been on guard for nearly an hour, observing each other's moves. Jauzi and Sulaeman quickly looked for the most senior officer they could find. It wasn't hard to see who was in charge. All they had to do was look for a police officer in dress uniform with badges on their shoulders, wearing tinted sunglasses and a dark brown cap.

The women and children were still in the rice fields. Too afraid to return home but unsure where to go. So they just waited. A thin headscarf was all that protected their head from burning under the scorching sun. The children were crying, begging their parents to return home or fetch their toys inside. The elderly were fatigued, minutes away from passing out.

Jauzi and Sulaeman were seen talking to the officer in command. Several Ahmadis approached to get a better listen. The crowd on the other side were chanting and singing. The officer made a few calls on his radio transceiver as well as a few phone calls on his mobile phone. He made some gestures to the Ahmadi leaders surrounding him telling them to wait. The leaders' faces made pleading expressions, mouth gagging to a frown, eyebrows drooping outwards.

A few government officials came, immediately joining the discussion. On their hands were folders containing pre-written sheets of papers and their copies. All that missing were signatures. The officials made three draft agreements, each with its own scenario: renounce Ahmadiyya and they could stay and live in harmony with the rest of the community, police would ensure the safety of their well beings and their properties. The second option was to leave Ketapang, never to return, their properties will be guarded, their religious activities made to bare minimum. The third is to stay and do as the Ahmadis please and the government and police would be absolved from any future responsibility to protect their lives or their properties.

The leaders chatted among themselves choosing the lesser evil. The youths tried to convince them that they should stay and fight for their Constitutional rights to practice their religion, to protect their homes, their basic human rights to live without fear and oppression. The youths argued that the mob was no match for the hundreds of armed police officers guarding them. The youths argued that they were prepared to die as martyrs. Ketapang was no Pancor. This time they weren't living in separate communities. They were united and strong.

But the leaders had a different idea. They weren't ready to have blood on their hands. They weren't prepared to make their own sacrifices, become the target, become the victim, part with their homes and possessions. They weren't letting their followers convert either, become part of the mainstream, renouncing their faith to the Messiah, leaving the congregation and their regular alms contribution. And so a decision was made.

'You will protect these people's houses if they leave?' one of the leaders asked the commanding police officer.

'Trust us.' It was a half-hearted pledge.

And soon men, women and children boarded the police truck, leaving behind the things they couldn't carry with them amidst the chaos earlier that day. The mob jubilantly chanted prayers. Praising God that the Ahmadis were leaving. The blasphemers were moving away from their neighborhood. It was what they wanted but with their wishes granted came another wish.

'God commands the Ahmadiyya's blood to spill,' the intolerant reiterated from time and time again. It seemed God commands Ahmadiyya's possession to be stolen too. As the trucks began to move, as they get into a corner, as they went out of sight, came more yelling, came the sound of pelted rocks, the sound of smashed windows and shattering bricks. At that moment they knew, they were refugees once more.

***

Words of the attack soon reached the market. Faizah wouldn't allow herself to walk out the door leaving the safety of her small makeshift hut which felt even smaller with the presence of four children. Her son Azmi and their three cousins. Her nephew Hafidz kept asking about their parents. Faizah was unsure how to respond, simply telling the six-year-old that his father and mother had some business to attend to and that later they would come and pick him and his brother up.

She was making promises she wasn't sure they could keep. The kind of lies told by parents to keep their children quiet. Truth be told she wasn't sure if they were safe. The rumors in the market were that more than 1,000 police officers had been deployed to Ketapang. It was an exaggeration for that would mean an entire police force in Mataram was descending onto Ketapang.

No one bothered to make an actual head count. But most agreed that in Ketapang there were more men in uniform than they had seen in one place. From mouth to mouth along the grapevine the number got more and more exaggerated. But no one was disputing that something terrible was happening. Faizah included.

'This is it,' she thought to herself. 'We are under attack.'

Azmi was growing restless, mumbling the very few words the two-year-old had just mastered. He was fighting over his toys with Rafik, Khaerudin's second son just a few months older than him but slightly smaller in size. Faizah struggled to keep the children quiet. She feared that their noise would attract unwanted attention. She knew how quickly people's attitudes towards Ahmadis can change in an instant once violence breaks.

Faizah prayed for her family's safety, her husband in particular.

She wondered where Ramlah was. Faizah hadn't seen Suhaidi's second wife since she dropped the children to her place. Ramlah swore that she was only picking some things up from her stall, transporting them to safety and return immediately after.

Faizah was looking to do some tidying up herself or perhaps salvaging a few of her parents' goods and hid them for safekeeping. But with hours passed and still no sign of Ramlah she couldn't leave the children unattended.

Faizah grew more and more anxious by the hour. She turned on her tiny, old, cathode ray tube television in search for news. The fuzzy screen displayed footage of Ketapang being attacked on the 6 p.m. news program. It appeared as a one minute filler story which no one in Jakarta thought to be worthy of more airtime.

Her heart stopped. When the children began gathering in front of the television to see what had happened she immediately turned it off. She didn't want them to see that violence was befalling into their family and friends.

But Faizah wasn't the only one watching the news. A female vendor the family knew ran towards her hut.

'Faizah...' she yelled in front of her hut. Faizah went out to meet the woman. She seemed anxious and concerned. 'I saw your mother's home being attacked. I saw your mom on television, standing near a burning house... What happened?'

'I don't know,' she replied.

From across the market was a commotion. It was Ramlah, being surrounded by men from the market.

'You must leave this place. You are an Ahmadiyya. If you won't leave I will drag you out of here and rape you,' the men said.

Faizah quickly came to her rescue. Screaming at the men.

'What are you doing? Can't you see she's pregnant with child?'

'I don't care. You too Ahmadiyya. If you don't leave I will burn your hut with you in it.'

The two were trembling but at the same time angry at their mistreatment.

'Pack your bags and go dogs!' one of the men said, hurling leftover vegetables and coconut husks at the two.

'Alright we're leaving. But we're human too. We're women. Can you show us some respect?' Faizah said in a high pitch voice of a woman consumed in hysteria.

'Don't you dare talk back at me! If we want to we can rape you right here and now. You think it's a sin for us to rape a few blasphemers like you?'

Faizah was stunned and slightly disgusted. Ramlah sobbing. Abruptly a sack filled with ten kilograms of shallots was hurled towards them, hitting Ramlah's pregnant stomach. The two were screaming hysterically.

It was then that the men came. Guntur, Suhaidi and Khaerudin. Just in time to take the women and children to safety. The harrasers didn't dare to come any closer once the men came. Perhaps because of Suhaidi, the man who had been actively lobbying for all market workers and laborers to get better pay and incentives. The man they considered to be one of their closest and most trusted friends. Suhaidi just looked at them, as if asking why after all the things that he did for them, they were mistreating his wife and sister. The others gazed emptily to the ground, afraid to look back, perhaps asking themselves the same question.

Soon they departed. Making their way out of the market. Faizah took nothing but her son Azmi, the clothes on their back, whatever cash they had and a big bowl of rice she had prepared for what was to be her family's only meal for the day.

From the market they drove past low rising shops and stores adorned with colorful signs emblazoning the wall and street lamp posts. They passed buses awaiting for passengers with big suitcases and carefully wrapped boxes. They passed a busy four lane street where cars fight for space with trucks and motorcycles. They moved past more shops lining up the streets.

Past vendors pushing their carts and setting up their tents, ready to lure hungry customers out for dinner. Past banks and offices ready to close for the day. Past weary faced workers driving home to their awaiting wives and children.

Past big statues manning a busy traffic circle. Past crowded intersections and traffic lights. Past a lonely street filled with rundown stores and squatter homes. Past a mosque with a bright blue dome shaped like an onion, past villas and hotels, past an orange Hindu temple, past a snaking small road, past schools and offices. Past a big metal gate welcoming them to a Mataram area called Majeluk. Following a manmade riverbank.

At one corner sat four buildings heavily guarded by police. They were buildings which Faizah once knew and never expected to see again. It was the first place she was taken to after they were driven away from East Lombok. A place where for two weeks in 2002 served as their temporary stopping place. A place which would later become their permanent settlement. A place called Transito.

CHAPTER 21

Blaring from the speakers of nearby mosques were the calls to prayer, a signal that dawn had arrived, bringing with it a new day. It was the first day after the attack, the first night spent in the refugee shelter known as Transito.

The sound was deafening, bouncing off the walls surrounding the Ahmadis, creating a unison chorus. The calls were sung into a beautiful tune, the tone dipping and rising, up and down a Middle Eastern diatonic scale.

Some felt annoyed for their dreams of being home were interrupted. For some, as simple as the words of the adhan may be, presented a sense of inner peace, a reassurance that although they have no possession left, their dreams shattered, their lives ruined, they still have their religion on their side, they were on a path of righteousness. Heaven awaited them on the other side. Their true homes were being built by angels with patience and virtue their bricks and mortars.

Not all agreed. The thought of losing everything was too much for a few others. Hours after the attack there were sobbing still. Disbelief that their houses were gone. Destroyed right in front of them. One day they were sleeping on their warm mattresses and suddenly they were forced to sleep on a hard wooden bed frame in a cold hall shared with a hundred plus refugees.

Nurul kept gazing at her arms. Somehow she could feel the blisters, bruises and aching she sustained long ago when her house was being built.

Suhaidi was still angry. He had secretly returned to Ketapang in the cover of night, watching from the distance as people looted his family's possession. They took out their television, clothes, furniture and the things they bought from money they painstakingly collected over years of hard work. It was only after they had taken everything of value and left behind the things they didn't want did they began to wreck their homes. Suhaidi even saw men stealing the hinges of their doors and windows.

Suhaidi was angered by the fact that all this time the Ahmadis had been nice to the neighbors. They had even helped them raise money for their mosque. The mosque which later became a meeting spot for the attackers, a home where malicious plans were conceived. He couldn't believe his friends at the market were trying to rape his wife. That they had hurled a sack of shallots at his unborn child.

Malik must have wondered what would happen if he stayed and fight. If his mother hadn't placed a Koran in his hands and asked him to guard it.

Khaerudin perhaps wondered what his friend Shabri, the community's leader before he was reassigned to Bima, would do had he been there. He wondered would the outcome be different if others were at the helm instead of him.

Kasafuloh was stuttering. His thinking was slow. He struggled to get the words out, speaking his mind. He chose to say very few words even to his family and the people he knew. It was plain to see that the series of attacks had traumatized him so bad it changed the boy.

Masitah became very ill. Ketapang was not the same as Pancor. This time they had to watch their homes being ransacked before their eyes. The attack shocked her so bad she wouldn't eat for days. At nights she lost sleep and wept. Sometimes the memory haunted her so much she vomited.

But as bad as the family was, there were others who were less fortunate. There were people who couldn't live with the fact that they lost their homes for the second time and slowly they lost their sanity. Men who were talking to themselves and shut themselves from the people around them. There were those who developed schizophrenia, seeing things that weren't there. They would sometimes have breakdowns and screamed frantically, frightening those around them.

There was no one in charge of their psychological states, no one to heal their wounds inside. There were only instant noodles from the Ministry of Social Affairs. There were only assistance, handouts and volunteers from the Indonesian Red Cross. The Ahmadis had been regularly donating their blood to the Red Cross, taught that it was better to give what the body could easily replenish to those who need it more. In return the Red Cross gave them blankets. Gave them tooth brush. Gave them fresh clothes. Gave them free medications.

The adhan continued to sound, echoing in the dusty white, tiled floor, the foggy glass windows, the crumbling doors and ceilings, the mold infested walls.

Nasipudin would have got up from his sleep, sitting at the edge of the bed frame. Eyes still close, halfway between dreaming and awake. Or perhaps giving the adhan a better listen. Unknowingly his body swayed, the full balancing function of his inner ears had yet been regained. Or perhaps he was moving to the tune of the adhan.

Arise he stood, slowly making his way to the washroom at the back of the complex. There were chatters, coming from the dozens of police officers keeping them from leaving the compound instead of pursuing the attackers and ensuring that they face justice for what they did. It was the victims who were locked, barred from going anywhere they please, doing what they want. It was the victims who had their freedom taken.

The officers busied themselves talking about sports matches, domestic affairs, problems at work. Gossiping about colleagues, making fun of their superiors. Expressing their hopes, their fears, their secret longing for some girl. They shared jokes which commanded laughter. There was coffee in a plastic cup. There was water in a plastic bottle. There were empty food wrappers littering the ground along with hoards of cigarette butts.

Nasipudin smiled as he walked past the officers. He knew they were just doing their jobs, taking orders from the bosses and their bosses. Like him they were pawns in a chess game while the true plotters stayed comfortably in the shadows, giving instructions from their marble-clad mansions.

Pawns never questioned why they were the first to die and why the kings hardly move an inch unless threatened. Let alone understand the schemes of things. How their deaths play a part to a greater purpose whatever purpose that may be.

The officers' leaders were not there of course, sleeping in their warm beds in air conditioned rooms, bodies wrapped in fluffy blankets on top of clean bed sheets. The Ahmadi leaders also returned home leaving behind their faithful followers in Transito.

'A leader must live separately from his followers,' the Ahmadi leaders would reiterate.

'Patience!' they simply said.

How can anyone tell a man who had lost everything to be patient? How can anyone tell a victim who knew that the ones harming them will never face justice to be patient? How can someone with a roof over their heads, warm beds to sleep in, well manicured lawn tell a displaced man to be patient?

Nasipudin needed no one telling him to be patient. He has pledged his loyalty to his religion, aware of the consequences which lay ahead. He had devoted a lifetime of servitude to God's command, submission to His plan. He had denounced all earthly desires and ambitions as illusions. Each day was a gift. God the owner of all things. His life, his family, his wealth, his possession borrowed from the Almighty.

He knew everything there is to know about patience. He lived and breathed patience. The earthly embodiment of an abstract concept so elusive to attain. He needed no teaching about patience nor a reminder.

Not the hypocrites. Not the people who don't practice what they preach. Those waging war were too afraid to go to the frontlines and risk their lives, staying in the shadows, fearing arrest and prosecution. Those asking people to make sacrifices were too afraid to make sacrifices of their own.

The adhan continued to sound. Nasipudin cleansed his body of earthly filth. He washed his hands, purifying them from the things he shouldn't touch. His mouth from the things best left unsaid. His nose to breath. His faces and eyes from the things he shouldn't see. His arms from doing sin. His head from ill thoughts. His ears from evil words. His feet from taking the path of the damned. The freezing cold water washed away grievances, grudges, doubts, envies, lusts leaving only good, conviction, faith, peace.

God's grace his true companion. God's kindness his true treasure. God's compassion his true protector. God's will his true home.

***

The Ahmadi youths in Transito were told to ready themselves, packing what few clothes they had left. An instruction had come from Ahmadi leaders who had finally decided they could no longer trust the government they once so blindly obey. The Minister for Religious Affairs had issued a statement to the press, urging the Ahmadiyya to stop calling themselves Muslims when he was asked what had become of religious freedom guaranteed by the Indonesian Constitution with the attack happening in Ketapang.

'The threat to religious freedom and tolerance comes from a group of people posing as members of a legitimate and officially recognized religion. This is what upsets people,' the minister said. 'If these people would only call themselves as non-Muslims there will be tolerance. They will be treated just like Muslims treating and honoring their non-Muslim neighbors.'

What the minister didn't say was that Indonesia only recognized six religions and there was no sign that the country was going to recognize the seventh. What the minister didn't say was that people other than the six religions had to practice their faith in secret and that they were having problems going to school, landing jobs and marry unless they lie and claim to be part of the six religions.

The minister also failed to mention that Pakistan had also decreed Ahmadis to be non-Muslims and that everyday people were being attacked, beaten or murdered for wearing Muslim attires. Ahmadi mosques were not allowed to be called mosques. Ahmadis had to tear down domes and minarets because they make their houses of worship resemble mosques. Ahmadis were going to jail for saying Islamic things like 'peace be upon you' or 'Allah is great' or 'praise Allah most gracious most merciful.' They weren't allowed to call their God 'Allah' they weren't allowed to call their prayers 'shalat' they weren't allowed to call their holy book 'Koran.'

They were ban from celebrating Muslim holidays. They had to fast in secret during Ramadan. They can't sacrifice rams in public during Idul Adha. If they do there would be reprisals, mob attacks, car bombs, carnages, chaos, murders.

The minister also didn't mention that the government was only interested in satisfying the Muslim majority. Permits to build Churches were being denied because of 'rejection from the surrounding community.' Buddhist statues were dismantled because 'they offend the major religious group in the area.'

The minister didn't refer to the attacks against the Ahmadis as 'attacks.' Downplaying them as 'ordinary acts of crimes,' a justifiable mishap. The attackers were certain individuals expressing their anger which unfortunately get out of hand. The hard-line groups were not intolerant people. They were partners of the government. The victims were not victims. They were blasphemers who provoked the mainstream, bringing calamity onto themselves.

As far as the government was concerned there was no persecution only vandalism. There was no hate speech, only freedom of expression. There was no threat to religious freedom, so long as the Muslim majority is appeased. Churches were not having problems obtaining permits. There were only land and communal disputes.

The government said the religious attacks were acts of crime and should be resolved according to law, handled by law enforcers whose independence can't be intervened. The law enforcers said the root cause of the problem should be addressed and that it was the job of the government.

The Ahmadi leaders knew they couldn't keep quiet like they did in 2002. They knew that something must be done or else violence would spread once more, coming to their own backyard as it did in 2005. The well being of the entire Ahmadiyya community in Indonesia was at stake. The Ahmadi creed of obeying the government must take the back seat or at least reinterpreted.

And so they sought help from the Legal Aid Foundation in Jakarta, contacting various human rights and religious freedom advocates. They got in touch with local and foreign media. They called up their friends in the government and the parliament. They phoned embassies and consulates.

'If this government can't protect us, ensure our rights to practice our religion then perhaps another government will,' said the National Emir to his followers. The message got relayed to every other leader below each quoting the Emir like they were their own words.

An instruction had come, passing down from one mouth to the next in the labyrinthine system of leaders and officials and units and functions and advisers within the Ahmadiyya structure. The men of Transito must apply for asylum in the hopes of thrusting the attack in Ketapang into international limelight. Just two days after the Ketapang attack, the youths would depart for Bali, meeting officials at the Australian and Japanese consulates there.

Suhaidi was perhaps having trouble sleeping. It was the opportunity he was looking for. A chance to become citizen of a foreign country. Imagine the adventure. Imagine the things he would see. Imagine the people he would meet. He was young and ambitious and didn't have the slightest dream to follow the steps of his father by becoming a poor peasant. He was destined for glory, he must have thought. Not the hollow and dull existence which he found in Lombok.

It was a golden opportunity he must have imagined. To see another country, experience a foreign culture. Not that people like him could never set foot in another country. There were many friends and relatives going to Malaysia or Saudi Arabia. But they traveled as maids, as laborers. They were no different than his peasant father. No different than his domestic worker sisters. Imagine having his asylum application accepted. Imagine going as citizens. Imagine what the food would be like. Imagine Australian or Japanese girls. Perhaps one was destined to be his next wife.

But before any of that could happen, he must seek permission from his two wives.

Sri was more forgiving. As an Ahmadi from birth she knew that a leader's command was not something to be refuted let alone refused.

Ramlah, the recent convert, was less understanding. A husband not being there by his pregnant wife's side with just weeks before she was due to give birth?

'What about our baby?' she must have said. 'Are you going to leave us just like that so you can have fun in some foreign country with your friends?'

'I must do this. Do you think I'm doing this for myself? I'm doing this for all of us. So we'd have a better future. So all of us won't have to keep running away, worrying if some people are going to destroy our house. Is that what you want?'

Ramlah didn't say a word. Tearing up and letting her disapproval and disappointment show. Suhaidi cheated on Sri to be with her. What's stopping him from doing the same again? Ramlah and Sri were living in the same city and yet he dared flirted, dated and married her. With Suhaidi given the chance to be far away from home who knew what would happen?

CHAPTER 22

It had been weeks since the Ahmadi youths left Lombok, drifting in limbo from one place to the next. One day they were greeted by diplomats at a foreign consulate in Bali. The next, those very same diplomats told them they cannot process their asylum applications and that they have to talk to their bosses in Jakarta.

One day they were in the spotlight, giving out a press conference at the National Commission for Human Rights, swarmed by microphones and tape recorders and television cameras, surrounded by people asking questions about who they were, what had happened to them and their families and their homes. The next day they were sleeping on the cold floors of the Legal Aid Foundation office.

One day they were chatting with dignitaries and politicians and former ministers. The next day they were no more than humble followers receiving instructional words at their leaders' houses. One night they were sleeping in private bedrooms of a government agency's guest house. The next they were cramped in an empty storage room of an Ahmadiyya mosque.

For every place they went there were questions, discussions, arguments, promises. Some doors were opened wide, some shut closed. Some officials were gracious to spare an entire day some didn't care to spend a few minutes. Some listened their words carefully. Some only cared to hear themselves talking.

None of the Ahmadi youths knew how long they had been in Jakarta. They had lost track of time. Perhaps a week had passed, perhaps two, maybe more.

There was another place they must visit called the House of Representatives, a vast complex sitting in the middle of the metropolis like an oasis of gardens, trees and man made lakes surrounded by a concrete jungle of towers and skyscrapers.

It was meant to be a palace of the people. Built from the money collected from the people, by the people, for the people. But the only people there were impoverished street hawkers resting under the trees to avoid the scorching sun. Men in uniform stationed to guard the complex and scrutinized every visitor. Low level staffers in safari shirts.

The rest were the so called 'people's representatives' in suits and ties and colorful dresses arriving in their luxury cars. In front of them were men in black outfits opening every door, carrying their briefcases. Behind them were secretaries and personal assistants in skimpy clothes.

The youths from Lombok were probably staggered to see such an impressive building complex. They had never seen so much marble in one place. Khaerudin the builder, pondered how they could make the main assembly hall into the shape of two massive green turtle shells merged in the middle, suspended in the air by two concrete arches at least 100 meters wide and 40 meters high.

A building sat to the right, towering at least 20 stories tall. It had rooms for all 560 lawmakers and their staff. Rooms for every commission and sub committee. Rooms for every faction and political party.

It had state of the art equipment and flat television screens. Furniture made out of exotic woods and rocks, intricately carved and professionally assembled. The carpets were velvety and thick, covering from wall to wall. Every inch which wasn't carpeted was granites and marbles.

Here the youths played a different role, watching silently as their leaders were being bombarded with questions and statements from members of parliament, some came to listen, some came to make their political statements and hear themselves speak, some for the so called 'attendance money. '

With the pounding sound of a gavel the hearing started.

The leaders began telling stories of how they were first discriminated, taunted, harassed, attacked and ultimately persecuted. Then they explained why the displaced was seeking for asylum.

'This is a disgrace, outright obscene,' said a nationalist party politician about the Ahmadis' attempt to get asylum.

'We want to be able to trust this government, believe that the law enforcers are there to protect the victims and enforce the law,' one of the leaders said. 'We want to believe that the government will ensure religious freedom but that is not the case is it? We want to believe that the government will guarantee our Constitutional rights, our rights as citizens of this country. But we have been proven otherwise.'

The Islamic-based parties responded. Comparing the Ahmadis to thieves.

'Let me ask you this… does a thief deserve to be free? Deserve to have his rights protected? Because the way I see it, this is what happened here. A group of people who have violated the Blasphemy Law. A group of people who have mocked other people's religion. Suddenly talking about their rights when they clearly have no respect to the rights of others?'

'I want to stress that we have not been proven guilty of breaking any law by any court,' the leaders replied.

The members of parliament laughed. A politician from a moderate Muslim based party responded with a question.

'But there are decrees from the Indonesian Council of Ulemas. There are studies by the Coordinating Board for People's Beliefs. There are decrees demanding that you stop spreading your religion.'

'Again we want to stress out that in the formulation of all the previously-mentioned decrees, there was never any attempt to verify and confirm such accusations with us. We were never involved in those decrees. They were one-sided decisions based on one-sided assumptions.'

The lawmakers then turned the hearing into a religious debate.

'Ahmadiyya believed that the promised Imam Mahdi (Messiah) has come as described in the Koran and the Hadith (saying of Prophet Muhammad). We believe that our founder Mirza Ghulam Ahmad was this Imam Mahdi,' said the leaders.

'And who is this Mirza? Is he your Prophet?' the lawmakers asked.

'We believe Mirza Ghulam Ahmad was an Imam Mahdi and that Imam Mahdi was the earthly embodiment of the second coming of Christ. In the Koran, Christ will come at the end of days to restore faith, to return Muslims back into the system of caliphs.'

'End of days? You said this Mirza guy was sent a hundred years ago. He's been dead a hundred years and where is this end of days?'

'There are signs. In the Koran it was mentioned that Dajal will come, he will be as tall as the sky and breathe fire. We believe that this is the figurative description of a jet plane.'

The lawmakers laughed hard. The youths standing at the balcony six meter above were clearly annoyed by the laughter.

'Wait. I want to get back to what you said about Mirza being Christ. Does that mean Mirza is also a prophet?' another lawmaker asked.

'First we must be clear as to what qualifies one to be a prophet. If you're talking about someone who is entrusted by God to carry new sets of rules for mankind then 'no.' If you're talking about someone who is sent by God, given revelations and should be revered as the divine messenger then 'yes.'

'So is he or is he not a prophet?' a politician from a conservative Muslim party said while his 'people's representatives' peers watched in disbelief, chatting and making jokes about their religion.

'Again, I said it depends on your understanding of a prophet.'

'I think I have heard enough. I think it is clear that there can only be one solution to this whole sham. Disband the Ahmadiyya!'

The politicians made a thunderous applause, some even shouted and whistled. The gavel was sounded again to keep the session back in order.

The Ahmadi leaders could only watched quietly in disbelief perhaps by the lawmakers' unwillingness to listen, their reluctance to have a mutual discussion, their refusal to look for a long term solution or just at how they shouted and screamed like juveniles.

***

The boat journey was long and tedious as it navigated across the Bali Sea. From the stern, a view of where they had been, Bali's Padang Bai seaport, dwarfed by the mighty Mount Agung. A blue sky hung above, stretching far beyond the mountains before dipping into the horizon.

There, in the far west, thousands of kilometers away where the sun would set was Jakarta, a place filled with promises and broken dreams. They have failed their missions, looking for a new beginning in a foreign land. Unsuccessful in bringing people's attention to their plight. It all seemed like an alien world for Jakarta offered a live far different from the tediousness of Lombok. There they were drifters, living the life of adventures and excitements. Meeting people they never dreamt of meeting. Going places they never thought of going.

Jakarta seemed like a dream and the vessel was their transport back to reality. Fore was where their wives and children, sisters and brothers, fathers and mothers awaited. Greeting them would be a life of peasantry as poor carpenters and construction workers, as refugees without a home.

It was hard for Suhaidi to return back home. He had set his eyes on Australia or Canada or Japan or some other foreign nations willing to grant him an asylum. He was sure he would never return. Reuniting with his family was the last on his mind. Perhaps he wasn't keen on leaving Jakarta and going back to Lombok, his birthplace, the site of his charred and ransacked home. Awaiting him was Transito which he had to share with a hundred others. Awaiting him were duties, as a father, as a husband, as a breadwinner. Duties which Suhaidi's father thought he had failed.

While he was away, his father had to feed his daughter Yuni. Look after his first wife Sri. His father had to care for his pregnant second wife Ramlah. His father had to lobby Ramlah's brother who insisted that she should leave Suhaidi and the life as a refugee.

In Suhaidi's absence, a child was born, a son she named Sultan. Ramlah was disappointed that Suhaidi couldn't be beside her when she gave birth to their son. She was devastated when Suhaidi didn't even send money for her labor. She was heartbroken that he didn't at least call.

She mourned and mourned, felt cheated and abandoned. When the time finally came to give birth, Ramlah's brother didn't have to argue much to convince her to leave Transito, to leave Suhaidi, to leave Ahmadiyya. There was nothing Suhaidi's father could do. Suhaidi's father understood.

Awaiting Suhaidi was a divorce paper and undoubtedly the scolding of his strict old man. Perhaps also the many 'I told you so's from his mother, sisters, uncles and aunties. The embarrassment of confronting his first wife. The solicitation of forgiveness. The promise of fidelity. The pledge for change.

Beyond that was still a mystery, a daunting uncertainty. What life awaited him in Lombok? The fulfillment of duties? Responsibilities of a father? Acceptance of fate? Surrender to the fact he was no more than what he was then? Suppression of a dream? Abandonment of a goal? Give up the chance for a better life?

On the port side was nothing but a calm sea, like a giant blue carpet dotted by colorful sails of traditional, wooden fishing boats. On the starboard, the jagged rock island of Nusapenida had been replaced by a series of tiny islets and passing tanker ships bound for the Indian Ocean. The Western tip of Lombok was spotted, presented as silhouettes of hilltops in different shades of grey accompanying the latter half of their journey home.

The silhouettes began to reveal more detail as the boat was about to do its job, ferrying the Ahmadi youths from Bali to Lombok across the Bali sea. Lombok was a land of strange contradiction for the Ahmadis. They were home but had no place to call home. Had no friend who would protect them. They were citizens to an absent government.

***

By the time they got to Transito, it was not quite the way they left it. There was something strange about the familiar. Each family had decided to partition the halls into small quarters, each at least three by three meters in size, for privacy, to stop disease from spreading quickly, to keep their children from running around, to feel less like a refugee camp.

They used old wood serving as poles reinforced by split bamboos forming multiple 'X's bound together by salvaged wires and nails. They used old cardboard boxes and plywood and sheets of fabrics as makeshift partition walls.

Necessity is the mother of invention and inside the quarters were little pieces of ingenuity. Couches from fruit boxes serving as wooden frames with old bicycle tires, cut to long strips, woven to one another and nailed to the frame serving as cushions. Shoeboxes tethered to the wall and repurposed as bookshelves. Lampshades made of coconut husks and broken bamboo baskets. Dead tree logs, cut, cleaned and sanded as stools. The root of a fallen tree cut into a coffee table.

Running through people's trash became a treasure hunt. Restoring broken furniture and salvaging unwanted goods became an obsession. Mismatching sandals were their footwear. Their credenzas were patched up cupboards with shelves and sliding doors from old plywood. They mended broken clothing hangers using wires and glues. They piled up bricks to serve as wood stove. They salvaged broken mirrors to look at themselves.

Life as homeless refugees forced them to become creative craftsmen, restorers, master repairmen. They fixed their own cooking pots and pans by melting tin. They mended their shoes by replacing their worn out soles with tire rubber.

But they were careful not to get too comfortable. The upgrades were simply ways to make Transito slightly more livable. Transito was no more than a stopping place, a temporary shelter until they could find a new, safer place to call home. Or so they thought.

With each passing day more and more people came to Transito. Human rights groups and University students with their researches: 'Religious Conflict and Their Effects on Women,' 'The Rising Intolerance and Their Effects on Children.' They conducted projects too: 'Letters to the President,' 'Drawings of Internally Displaced Children.'

They were reporters and journalists from Jakarta, Australia, the United States, Japan, European countries. They conducted interviews and took footages and photographs and returned with their heartbreaking, award-winning feature stories.

With each arriving guest came renewed hope that their plight would soon come to an end. But that is not how the world works. Not among the guests were those in power, the decision makers, the influence peddlers, the parliament members and lobbyists. Deaf ears for the many words spoken about Transito. About Ahmadiyya.

CHAPTER 23

The potholed road was becoming narrower. Masitah noticed that the lines of trees next to her were becoming taller and taller. The scenery went from crowded urban center to lush farmlands to barren wastelands filled with low vegetations to dark, dense rainforest. The trees along the road were joining at the top forming an arch which made the road seemed like a desolate, dark tunnel.

Occasionally she heard wild animals calling from deep within the forest. Their voices seemed alien for Masitah who never set foot in the jungles of Kalimantan, the Indonesian side of Borneo. Fear grew inside her. The trees seemed to be enchanted, waving in the winds as if closing in on her. Trying to consume her whole.

She grabbed the jacket of the man in front of her. The driver of the motorcycle which for the last few hours was taking her to her destination, a Central Kalimantan village named Pangko. The driver was a man she married just three months before. An Ahmadi named Muhtarom.

Masitah thought marrying was her way out of the miseries of Transito. So she asked her cleric to find an Ahmadi man for her. Muhtarom was asking the same to his cleric. A marriage was arranged.

In June 2006, Masitah met her groom the clerics had chosen for her. A man she only knew from photographs his family sent and words from the clerics. Masitah knew that Muhtarom's family was living in Kalimantan as a transmigrant. They owned several hectares of farmland and was growing a magic crop named oil palm.

She didn't know much else. She didn't even know what oil palm was. She had never seen one. She only knew that demand was strong for palm oil and people were earning money because of it. She didn't know that forests were being cleared because of palm oil. Endangered wildlife loosing their habitats and being poached because of palm oil. Forest fires and massive flood was caused by palm oil.

Muhtarom could never stand living in Transito and was constantly begging his new wife to come with him to Pangko.

The journey took forever and Masitah was beginning to regret her decision to come to Kalimantan. Hairs were raising at the back of her neck. Palms sweating. She was afraid of the darkness. Afraid of the sounds she heard from the forest.

There were remnants of a violent past still echoing in Kalimantan. Charred homes of the slaughtered dotting the landscape. The ground was once the scene of a massacre. The trees were silent witnesses to a time when everyone went mad.

The year was 2006. Mere years had passed since a bloody sectarian conflict swept across this entire vast island between the indigenous Dayaks and the migrant Madurese.

Five years back, 500 Madurese were slaughtered in a town not too far away. A town named Sampit. Madurese men, women and children were butchered like animals. Their meat savagely eaten in some cannibalistic ritual which everyone assumed was well in the past for this once head hunting nation.

The government spoke little of the tragedy, nor do anything to stop it. The media were too scared to run the disturbing pictures, to print the harrowing witnesses' remarks, to tell the unbelievably brutal stories from the people who were there.

Instead they retold the lies of some spokesmen who kept telling them that everything was fine, everything was under control. The media did nothing to verify these lies, too scared to risk the lives of their reporters, too scared of the truth and what the truth would do to the rest of the country, too scared of the prospect that words would fuel further animosity, spreading violence to other areas, other islands, other towns, other villages.

People were too ignorant or too afraid to believe they were real. People were too ignorant or too afraid to believe they could happen to this once peaceful land. People were too ignorant or too afraid to believe that human beings were capable of such palpable monstrosity to their fellow men. People were too ignorant or too afraid to believe that an entire island of Borneo, world's third biggest, has gone mad. People were too ignorant or too afraid to believe that humanity had lost its meaning.

Masitah included. Kalimantan was far from Lombok. With no media and officials dared to tell the truth about the atrocities it became no more than rumors to Masitah. But right then and there she could feel it. Feel the anguish of the fallen. The sadness of the spirits was in the air.

After five hours they arrived in Pangko. Masitah thought she should never have come. The first thing she did was ask her husband when they could go back to Mataram.

***

Dreams of freedom were put under suspension. Transito slowly began to feel like a permanent residence. A wave of discrimination followed. The Ahmadis found themselves unemployable because of their faith. The government refused to provide them with identification and residency cards. Making it hard to apply for jobs. They couldn't renew their driver's license needed to become motorcycle taxi drivers.

The Mataram government argued that they were still listed as residents of Ketapang and the West Lombok district government was the one with authorities to issue their residency cards. The West Lombok government argued that they no longer lived in Ketapang.

A cycle of poverty had begun, which disallowed them to rebuild their lives. Worse still, the Ahmadi parents found it hard to get their children transferred to another, much safer school near Transito. Many had to put their study on hold because there were not enough seats to accommodate the refugee children.

Transito was beginning to feel like a deserted island which hosted a group of marooned sailors. Detached from the rest of the world. One they could never get out of.

One by one the sick and elderly died in Transito replaced by babies born in Transito. The first was a boy named Ridho, whose name means 'acceptance of God's will.' The next were twins, whose names were inspired by the very place sheltering them: Transita and Transiti. Soon it would be Suhaidi's turn once more. His first wife was due for labor and the pair was penniless.

Nasipudin was determined his next grandchild would not be born without Suhaidi. Suhaidi had already abandoned his second wife when she gave birth to Sultan. Suhaidi's first daughter Yuni was old enough for school. There was no way Nasipudin was going to let his son Suhaidi abandon his family again.

Perhaps Suhaidi did work hard. Perhaps he had tried his best. But the money he had mustered wasn't enough to feed his family, let alone afford to pay the medical bill for his wife's labor. He borrowed money from his brother Khaerudin who made use of his time in Jakarta to look for construction work and collect as much money as he could. Still the money was short, only enough to live day by day.

But Suhaidi was not alone. There were many fathers who found themselves unable to make a living in Mataram. A family friend, Sayidin, even thought about selling his third son because he couldn't pay the medical bill. The hospital refused to discharge his wife unless he paid up. He begged and begged for the hospital to provide him with leniency. But the hospital insisted he should pay the full medical bill. He was ready to give up his newborn child, putting him up for adoption. Anything to get his wife out. Until a human rights activist came and put pressure on the hospital.

And then came time for Suhaidi. His wife's Sri was burning hot and frail from high fever. Transito's water was dirty. Their meal was only instant noodle. Suhaidi took his wife Sri to a local health clinic, the only place which accepted Ahmadiyya refugees for free. The doctors at the clinic said that Sri had signs of typhoid and malaria and had to go to a better equipped hospital or Sri could lose either her pregnancy, her life or both.

'I had no money doctor,' Suhaidi pleaded.

'This is a life and death situation,' the doctor argued.

Suhaidi tried to explain their condition, telling stories of persecution, discrimination and marginalization.

'Don't worry about the bill! Just take your wife to hospital! You can take care of the bill later.'

At the hospital Suhaidi was told that his wife's pregnancy was very weak and that she might have to undergo an operation. That she might have to stay as an inpatient for days.

Suhaidi again explained his condition, saying he could never afford the procedures the hospital suggested. The hospital told Suhaidi that they need letters stating his status as a refugee, as a victim of a religiously-charged attack.

He made calls, trying to pull strings from anyone who could help. He went to the Social Affairs Agency to meet up with an old friend.

'Is there a way? My wife is very sick at the hospital. I have no money not even to eat let alone to pay for her medical bill,' Suhaidi said.

Another agency official overheard. 'Hey, don't come here with your medical bill. We had enough problems just feeding you. Take your wife to the doctor not here,' the man shouted.

Suhaidi's friend took him to the back of the agency's office for a private talk. 'Just try. I don't know if you'll succeed or not. Try contacting the police because you are under their supervision.'

Suhaidi went to the police headquarter securing a letter stating that he was an Ahmadi being relocated under police supervision to Transito.

He took that letter to the Social Affairs Agency. He left with another letter and took it to the Transmigration Agency which is in charge of Transito. A week passed before he got all the necessary letters. By that time his wife had lost her pregnancy from bad hygiene. Sri was fine but the hospital bill reached 800,000 rupiah, a month pay if he still had a job.

Suhaidi went to the hospital management and presented all the letters he had garnered.

'Go ahead, just go on home! ' A hospital clerk said, discharging Suhaidi's wife without paying a single rupiah.

And so Suhaidi became the pioneer, the pathfinder. The man people turned to when they need someone to guide them through the red tapes of bureaucracy. Suhaidi took children, mothers and elderly to the hospital, explaining them the procedures they need to go through, going from agency to agency to acquire letters after letters.

His wife Sri was pregnant again. In 2007 a child was born. A baby girl. Suhaidi named her Hijwana.

***

Nasipudin braved himself to return to Ketapang. He was penniless, jobless and desperate. He was tired of eating instant noodles. He had rented a farmland for the entire year in Ketapang. He was curious what had become of his rice and vegetables. What had become of his family's homes.

Nurul spotted him getting up one morning, preparing himself for a long walk an hour away. She was curious where her father was off to.

'Ketapang?' Questions must have run inside her head when she heard her father's plan. There was a hint of fear for the unknown. The uncertainty begotten from a recent tragedy. Three months had passed since the attack but the trauma was still fresh in everyone's memory. But she felt compelled to join. Perhaps curiosity and the prospect of seeing what happened to her former neighborhood was too great a temptation to resist.

Perhaps she was just bored of the dull life in Transito. Her brothers Khaerudin and Suhaidi were again in Jakarta, having another go at seeking asylum as the leaders had ordered. Jakarta offered better opportunity for the men. There they found work. In Lombok there was only discrimination. Nurul wanted to join them but didn't have the money to go. And where would she go? Back to her old employer? The house where she lost her pregnancy?

'Can I join you?'

Nasipudin looked anxious. No one knew how people in Ketapang would react to their presence. He was unsure of his own safety let alone Nurul's. There were too many questions running inside Nasipudin's mind that he went silent.

'Well... can I?' Nurul asked her father once more.

'Sure.'

And so the two set off. Walking along the side of a winding road. Past a government housing complex at the bottom of a gentle slope sitting below the outer walls of a posh gated neighborhood. An electricity line ran above their heads, connecting poles after poles with sometimes broken street lights. A river ran along their right before flowing beneath them and switching sides.

They came across small alleyways of a congested neighborhood, one of which provided a shortcut to Ketapang, cutting their journey by about one fourth. But the alleyways were a maze of turns and corners and dead ends. A day would come when they master the labyrinth, but not that day. And so the father and daughter stuck to the main road.

A bridge was visible, forming an intersection crowded with motorists going from one direction to the next. Here they turned left, crossing the street to stay in the shades of small shops and houses as the sun shone from the East.

Here the road was more familiar. Up ahead was the tailor where they used to come to have their clothes made and mended. Up ahead was a barbershop where the men used to have their hair cut. Up ahead was Malik's school. Up ahead was the dirt road which led to their former neighborhood.

Once they arrived in Ketapang, what they saw was carnage. A house had been leveled to the ground with tiled roof and sand bricks and wood beams piling on top of each other. Another house was charred with trails of smoke rising to the roof, blackening the wall. All of the houses had been looted.

All that remains were children's books, broken plates and cooking utensils, pieces of clothes scattered on the floor. There were empty chicken cages. Charred motorbikes. Fallen furnitures. Bottles of kerosene next to a burned out bed. Pictures of the Messiah. Pictures of their caliphs. Smashed up windows. Broken doors. Holes on the walls. Missing hinges.

On the walls, molds started to appear. Wild shrubs began to encroach the interior. Tree branches started to protrude the roof. Tree seeds started to grow inside people's homes. On the walls was graffiti. Badly written writings made hurriedly, in charcoal of a burned out furniture or marker. A statement of a secret school crush. There were crude drawings too. The image of a man and a woman fornicating. A nude woman figure sitting beside the shape of a penis.

'Some kids were responsible for those,' heard a voice as Nurul and Nasipudin gazed in horror at the inappropriate drawings. It was a neighbor, presence of whom caught Nurul and Nasipudin by surprise.

He must have assured the two that he meant no harm. He convinced Nurul and Nasipudin that they were amongst friends.

'No one here has anything against your religion,' he said. 'Those attacking you were not even from around here. We don't know where they're from. Some drunk kids confessed that someone just came and asked them to do these things to Ahmadiyya. The one asking them claimed that he was asked to join by someone else. People here were just provoked. Most just stood and watched. Yes, a few joined the pelting and looting. But they didn't know anything. I'm not even sure they know what was going on.'

Nasipudin smiled to the neighbor and shook his hand.

'We understand. I'm sorry that we have caused you trouble.'

The man must have looked at Nasipudin in disbelief. A victim asking forgiveness from someone too afraid to stop acts of evil?

'People here were provoked. They didn't know what they were doing. They didn't understand why,' Nasipudin said.

The three started walking out of their former home and move towards Nasipudin's rented farmland. Along the way they met more neighbors. They exchanged smiles and greetings. Shaking each others' hands and giving hugs.

The neighbors asked how they were and where they were living. They were shocked when Nasipudin told them that they were homeless. The ward of Ketapang also came, embarrassed by the fact he couldn't do much to stop the attack. Or so he claimed. Perhaps to his boss and the firebrand clerics he made a different pledge.

Nasipudin inspected his crop. The tomatoes were dead but the sprout survived nicely and ready to be harvested. The rice was being eaten by pests and insects but the jackfruit tree was beginning to ripen and soon the fruit will fall, ready to be cooked. The rest of the crop was on the verge of dying with the weed and wild shrubs slowly exhausting the nutrients of the once fertile soil.

He went back to his former house to see if his shovel and sickle were still where he had left them. He returned with a spark of jubilance to learn that they still were. And soon they began cutting down the shrubs, plucking them all the way to their root. Picking up everything they could harvest.

They returned the next day, this time to fertilize the soil, restoring the clogged irrigation. They plucked the jackfruit right out of its tree, their meal for the next few days. The next day they brought seeds, lent from some farmers they met along the way.

They brought lunch to stop themselves from starving. They put their packed lunch at their former home, storing it for lunch time hours away as they worked the fields. They found a piece of plywood, still intact and clean. They laid the plywood on the dirty floor to serve as mat.

They lunched on the rubbles of their broken home, roof holed but still standing. There were enough tiled roofs to shade them from the scorching sun. They sat and feasted on the plywood, keeping their clothes from getting any dirtier.

The next day they found plates and utensils and goony sacks to transport their harvest. They found more usable plywood. This time enough to fix a door. This meant they could turn one room into a storage, to keep their plates and utensils and farming equipment.

The next day, they found brooms. They swept the floor and tidied the scattered trashes left from the attack. They ended up with a nice and clean place to lunch. The next day, they found more plywood. This time they could fix another door for more storage. They boarded up the windows for extra security. The next day they fixed the roof so water wouldn't ruin their storage and wet the interior with the rainy season just around the corner. They first used corrugated sheets of metal they found and eventually, replaced those with roof tiles salvaged from other homes.

Soon Nurul took her husband back to Ketapang, to help with the fields. Other people also came to help. By this time Nurul needed more plates, more utensils. Sometimes people spent an entire afternoon at their place. So they brought plastic mats. Sometimes they worked the fields and lost track of time and had to spend the night. So they got the electricity back running again. Before long, Nurul and her husband spent an entire week at Ketapang.

Eventually what began as a way to make their former home a more comfortable resting place and more secure storage rooms became a full restoration. The rubbles no longer resembled a broken house. Nurul gave her house a fresh coat of paint. To make their nights at Ketapang more bearable they bought a mattress. They bought new windows and cupboards.

It became more than a resting place. Became more than a storage house. It became a home.

CHAPTER 24

It had been months since Nasipudin last set foot at Bertais market. His son Malik had outgrown his junior high school uniform, so had Safir who was entering sixth grade and Kasafuloh who was about to be in his third year in school. It was not that he couldn't get the uniforms somewhere nearer to Transito but coming back to the place where he once worked was too irresistible. He wanted to see if he still had friends at the market. Testing whether the attack in Ketapang had made him no longer welcomed.

To his relief, that was not the case. Everywhere he went, people greeted him with smiles and questions of how he was doing and what he had been up to. There were few curious faces but not those with malicious intent.

It was as if nothing had happened. Like the attack on his people was all a bad dream people keen on forgetting. Where were the people who felt Ahmadiyya had offended their own faith? A rhetoric so often used by those calling for war. Where were the people who believed Ahmadiyya was a menace? Would they not kill an Ahmadiyya man at first sight? Where were the name calling and hostility?

Perhaps in their minds they also wondered why. Why make a fuss about how others are different? The texts from the Holy Book are divine and flawless. But not the minds which read and interpret them. How was this allowed to happen? What did these attacks even mean? An attack so carefully plotted and systematically executed? What was to gain from it all? Who benefited from all this?

Was it all a show of force? Were all the things said a baseless argument to incite fear and hatred? A tool so often used and abused for power and control. Was it all talk far detached from the grass root? Far removed from reality?

Nasipudin's uneventful return to Ketapang and Bertais the prime example. Nasipudin was an old friend, a vendor and market laborer like their own self and no more, no fewer. He was a good friend too. An honest one. All agreed. Religious differences set aside. For underneath everyone was human with human needs and human wants.

Nasipudin went from store to store. Meeting and greeting one friend to the next. Who could tell what were being said? But he returned to Transito with a job offer. Honest Nasipudin was back transporting people's goods.

Soon his wife Zubaidah joined him, braved herself to find a spot at the market where she could lay her plastic mat, put down her woven basket filled with vegetables and meat, laying the contents up for display and yelled to entice meandering potential customers.

Among the people passing before the pair was Ramlah, their former daughter-in-law, recently divorced from their son Suhaidi. Ramlah was carrying a baby, their grandson Sultan. Ramlah didn't smile back when Nasipudin and Zubaidah greeted her. She just pretended they were strangers, ignoring them completely. Nasipudin and Zubaidah were curious what Ramlah had been up to. They knew Ramlah was staying with her brother at their late parents' house, just a short walk from the market. Her brother was busy at work and now with an extra mouth to feed, Ramlah too was forced to find a job.

***

It was no place for such a small baby. Let alone unattended while his mother was cutting and grating people's coconuts. Sultan spent most of the time confined to a hammock, unable to move like a baby should when it is learning to move its legs and arms. No one to play with him so he could learn words or the meaning of joy.

There were bite marks all over his body from the many mosquitoes. Flies circulated and landed on his fragile body. He would cry constantly, craving for his mother's attention. The young mother responded with fury, a face betraying annoyance.

From time to time Nasipudin observed from the distance. Shaking his head and raising his thick bushy eyebrows. He felt like intervening. Sultan was after all his flesh and blood. But there was nothing Nasipudin could do. Perhaps Ramlah noticed her former father-in-law's prying eyes. Her indifference continued and apparent. Like telling Nasipudin to stay away, not to get involved in her life or her son's.

Months had passed and the dry season was at its later stage. Drops of rains began to pour like they always did at that time of year. They came as droplets, sized no bigger than a pin prick, width a little wider than hair. The droplets made a silent sound when they touched the ground and their muffled presence was nothing but felt. The falling water from the heavens has a way of washing down all scents, fragrant or foul, except for the fresh smell of clay.

With the dry season drawing to a close the baby's biological clock signaled that it was time for him to learn to crawl. He was getting restless. The small and feeble body moved from side to side inside the hammock like it was ready to roll over. Sultan kicked and elbowed the hammock's cloth like it was suffocating him.

As a last resort he cried. His mother came offering to bribe him with a pacifier and breast milk and his favorite toy. Anything to gag him up. But he wouldn't stop crying. The young mother didn't understand what was happening.

She yelled at Sultan in a language not understood by babies his age. His mother made another attempt to subdue Sultan, carrying the baby in her arms. Sultan quieted perhaps thinking his mother was about to heed his wish. He cried when he learned this was not the case.

Other mothers came with theories of what was going on. 'Maybe he's hot,' one would say. 'Maybe he doesn't like it in the hammock.' Ramlah's employer offered her to take the baby to a small room at the back of her store. Inside was a thin mattress stuffed with kapok, laying flat on top of a plastic mat. Here Ramlah put down her baby, here the baby stopped crying.

Soon he was rolling over, sometimes repeatedly until he fell to the ground. In the room he learned to crawl, strengthening the muscles in his legs and arms. Soon he was able to wander on his own, feasting his curiosity and the excitement of a newfound skill. He began touching stuffs, grabbing them and holding them in his tiny hands.

He wondered if these things were edible and put them in his mouth. He sometimes shook them violently up and down and tossed them on the floor. Sometimes he touched stuffs he wasn't supposed to touch. Sometimes dirt, sometimes dangerously sharp objects lying on the floor. No one was stopping him, not his ignorant mother, not his God-knows-where father.

Sometimes Ramlah did find her son playing with things he shouldn't be playing. Sometimes a passing vendor alerted her what was happening to her son. 'Ramlah, your son!' a friend shouted as Sultan wandered far from his mother's watch, playing on a dirty market walkway putting sands into his mouth. Perhaps in embarrassment, she laid the blame on the innocent child, slapping his hands hard or pinching him. Sultan cried to the horror of others, to the bemoaning of his grandparents.

As Sultan began learning to walk, her mother's ignorance grew. Sometimes she went places, leaving her son unattended. Where and why was anyone's guess. Sultan practiced his strides on the assistance of concerned friends while his mother was away. Sultan knew laughter from the teasing of playful strangers. Sultan learned words from passersby. Sometimes other vendors carried him and played with him. He became everyone's child. With customers mistakenly passed adoration 'what a cute baby you have' to someone who just happened to care for him. Sometimes he was nobody's son, playing on his own.

'Excuse me... Nasip... Your grandson...' a friend came one day asking Nasipudin and Zubaidah to follow her.

Nasipudin and Zubaidah were in shock to discover that Sultan was playing underneath a parked motorcycle, hands ready to touch a smoldering hot exhaust pipe, body ready to knock over the motorbike's kickstand. He was on the verge of burning himself or had his body crushed by the motorcycle's weight.

And so they picked Sultan up, keeping him out of harm's way. They waited for his mother to return. It seemed that she was unfit to be a mother, treating Sultan like a burden and not a son. Perhaps she saw Sultan as the bitter fruit of a failed marriage. Perhaps she projected her resentment for Suhaidi onto the innocent child.

Whatever the excuse, it was doing more harm than good for Sultan to stay with his mother, particularly if she intended to continue letting Sultan grew up in the market. A place ridden with disease, people and chaos. A place filled with cusses and curses. Tricksters and stealers.

When Ramlah returned, among the first things they asked was: 'are you seriously going to let your child grow up in the market?' preceded with a few small talks and an explanation of what had happened. The question was followed by an argument of what market life could do to such a small baby. Following the argument was an awkward silence, a deep thought from Ramlah. She was mulling on what to do, choosing the best of two evils.

Hesitantly, Ramlah agreed. Sultan was to be with their loving grandparents, a pair more fit to raise the child. And so that day, Ramlah went home alone and Transito welcomed another member.

***

Days turned to weeks turned to months. Soon, a year would pass since the attack on Ketapang. Life in Transito became more than the temporary solution the government pledged it to be. Slowly Transito was becoming less about a facility to host the transmigrants as it was originally intended, but home to the Ahmadis.

Before long people had forgotten what the place was officially called. Locals just scratched their heads when strangers asked for direction to get to a place called Transito. When people were asked where the Ahmadis lived they knew exactly where it was. A small complex right next to where the road curved. Where sat four decaying buildings with rusted out fences.

A dry afternoon was the only time when the children came out to play, merrily in their dirty old clothes. The clothes were passed down from one sibling to the next once they no longer fit to save money. Dawn was the time they all head out to the fields and market. First sign of daylight was when the children went to school. Late morning was the time mothers came outside to dry their rice. Fridays were the time officials and other Ahmadis around Mataram came for communal Friday prayers.

Beyond those times the place seemed lifeless, particularly from the outside. Inside was different. But not by much. A few elders could be spotted pacing back and forth across the hall, walking shirtless to and from their respective rooms, flimsily partitioned with cardboards and cloths. They were few signs of life, apart from the slow whispering sound of a radio, the crying of the newborn, the coughing of the sick.

The back, where the lavatories and wells and communal kitchens were located, seemed more exciting. Filled with chatters of housewives as they prepared meals for their children returning from school.

Someone had the idea of making individual kitchens made out of bamboos, corrugated sheets of metal and plywood boards in an alley separating the two buildings in the middle. They were tired of having their kitchenware stolen at night. Their firewood and coconut husks wet. They build fences and gates to keep their kitchens safe. Here they parked their motorcycles.

But the slippers and shoes weren't safe. The footwear sometimes got lost or stolen or taken by mistake or borrowed without permission. In either case they were gone. No footwear was allowed inside the hall. It was agreed that they should keep the tiled floor clean enough for the children to play on. But constant cleaning was required. The roof emitted choking asbestos and termite dusts. Heavy rains sent water leaking.

They were other minor inconveniences too. Sometimes there was no water in the lavatory, because someone at the two government houses which shared the same complex with Transito forgot to turn off their tap after watering their plants and gardens.

Twice a year, the refugees had to make way for the transmigrants who wore their shoes indoors. They took long showers and used up all the water in the bathrooms but never bothered to fill the water tank back or flush once they were done using the toilets. After the transmigrants left a week later the Ahmadis volunteered to clean up their mess.

Budin, the transmigration official in charge of Transito was certainly not going to help. He was busy making excuses to collect money from the Ahmadis. There were electricity bill which was never actually sent to the utility company. There were water bills for the water which came from a piped underground well.

There were sanitary fees despite the fact that the Ahmadis did all the cleaning on their own even for rooms they did not actually occupy. They were forced to pay rent for the bed frames donated by the government. They were made to pay maintenance fee for the kitchen that they built arguing that they were causing damages to the building's exterior.

Budin liked to steal things too. He rented unused bed frames to people outside of Transito. He sold off electrical wirings inside the unoccupied rooms. When his boss came and saw things were missing he pitted the blame on the Ahmadis.

But the Ahmadis never complained. Fearing to cause unwanted attention. Everyone had developed a habit of blaming the Ahmadis. Even if they wanted to expose Budin of his acts of corruption who would believe them? They risked making a foe out of the keeper for their only place of refuge.

***

Life was so hard fewer men volunteered to go to Jakarta at the instruction of their Emir. Many had given up hope of seeking political asylum from foreign countries, choosing instead to fulfill their immediate needs rather than chasing an uncertain future.

Many also saw the fundamental contradiction of applying for asylum while at the same time pushing for human rights groups and lawyers to advocate for their civil rights as Indonesian citizens. The contradictions have caused a split inside the very few people trying to defend them. It even caused a stir from within the Ahmadiyya. Some argued that they should give up their hopes of being a citizen of a foreign country but some argued that it was the best way to put the persecution against Ahmadis in Indonesia to international spotlight.

Khaerudin thought it was best simply because his leaders said it was best. But his brother Suhaidi was a firm believer that it was. Suhaidi wasn't interested in going back to Transito. He wasn't interested in life as an internally displaced person. He wasn't interested in staying with his wife Sri. His son Sultan he hardly knew. His newborn daughter Hijwana.

The first thing he did when he returned to Lombok was hanging out with his friends, chatting and laughing about old times, staying up late all night and at times never returned. In Transito there were only duties. There were only responsibilities There were only scolding from his father, the whining of his mother and sisters. There was constant comparison with his older brother Khaerudin.

There were praises how Khaerudin still managed to find work and earn for his family while the two were in Jakarta and met with reporters and dignitaries and activists. There were admirations on how unlike Suhaidi, Khaerudin took care of his family. A good provider.

Suhaidi chose to stay away from the talks behind his back. He busied himself by taking the sick to the hospital, delivering letters, meeting Ahmadis in and around Mataram, escorting guests. Every excuse he could find to get out of Transito.

People around him told Suhaidi to let go of his dream even some who at first believed in the cause. His friends at Transito had given up. But not Suhaidi. Not a few people in high places inside the Ahmadiyya congregation. Not the Ahmadiyya Lombok's adviser Syamsir Ali. Not the national Emir, Abdul Basith.

***

For days, Suhaidi didn't step out of his room in Transito. Lounging on his bed while watching the television. He turned the channel each time the television showed a travel documentary of countries he so desperately wanted to visit. He made excuses when journalists came to Transito asking to speak to the few remaining Ahmadiyya men still seeking to denounce their Indonesian citizenship.

One day, a call was heard from behind the curtain serving as the room's door. It was his sister Nurul, on a visit to Transito from her home in Ketapang. Nurul came to inform him that his son Sultan was crying. Nurul came to say that he needed to look after his son Sultan. That despite separating with his second wife Ramlah, Sultan was still his own flesh and blood.

'I thought mother adopted him,' Suhaidi must have said grumbling.

'Mother is busy with Kasafuloh, with Nisa, preparing stuff for the market, preparing for your meal.' his sister Nurul would have replied.

'Where's my wife Sri?'

'Seriously... You want your first wife to care for the child from your second marriage?'

'Where's Faizah?'

'Your sister is busy with her own kid. And she's pregnant now. She needs to rest.'

'Then why don't you look after him?'

'I did... That's what I've been doing while you're sitting here doing nothing.'

'And? Now you're too busy?'

'I have to go back home to Ketapang. I can't stay and watch for him all day.'

'Why don't you take him home to Ketapang then. It's not like you have a kid on your own.'

'Why... you...'

Suhaidi probably got up and began to raise his voice. He would perhaps yell at his older sister Nurul. Calling her names. Saying she had no right to lecture him about parenting. Saying to her that she knew nothing for she was childless. Saying that if she were fit to care a child, God would have blessed her with one long ago.

Nurul would have wept, unable to contain her calm. The words were cruel when said by strangers. When spoken by a brother they were barbaric. They were hurtful. The kind which evokes immediate tears. Utter disappointment. Her heart was more than broken. It was shattered.

There were perhaps the slightest feeling of remorse in Suhaidi. But words had been spoken and could not be unsaid. The broken heart of a sister could not be unfelt. 'I'm sorry' was perhaps the proper thing for Suhaidi to say. But instead he ran. Where to was anyone's guess. Perhaps hiding his embarrassment. Burying his guilt in the comfort of friends in places faraway.

Nurul, a strong 30-year-old woman, wept. Crying. The only time she felt that vulnerable was when her first husband divorced him and the time she had a miscarriage. She stayed in Suhaidi's empty room. Her legs seemed frozen to the floor. There must have been flashes of the past she thought she had forgotten. Bad memories and traumas rushed into her head. Like ghosts terrorizing her mind.

She felt like screaming. But the walls in Transito were not really walls. They were cloths and bamboos and cardboards and plywood stacked and nailed together. The quiet scream and the silent cry allowed her reason to slowly come back replacing her rage and sadness.

There was truth in what Suhaidi said, she thought. Perhaps she really should adopt Sultan.

CHAPTER 25

It was the third time Suhaidi and Khaerudin found themselves in Jakarta. This time the only other Ahmadi refugee who volunteered to go was their uncle Kamarudin. Kamarudin was their father's little brother but he was not much older than Khaerudin. Having uncles and aunties younger than yourself is a situation so commonly found in families with many children. It was hard for someone outside their family to imagine they were uncle and nephew. Particularly as kids. Khaerudin and Kamarudin could well be classmates in school.

Suhaidi never thought he would set foot again in Jakarta. He had almost given up hope of being granted asylum by another country. An instruction had come from their leaders in Jakarta and Mataram for them to try once more. Spurred by a series of attacks on Ahmadiyya communities in West Java.

Suhaidi, Khaerudin and Kamarudin were convinced that they were advocating for the whole Ahmadiyya community. For their families in Transito. For their harassed brothers and sisters in the rest of the country. For the Ahmadis in Pakistan and all corners of the globe. For the good of their country, Indonesia. For the restoration of peace and order. For the freedom of all religion.

But some saw the move as a selfish act. Doubting its assumed effectiveness. Would seeking asylum start a chain reaction which lead to a better life for all or would it backfire? Would it trigger more resentment, more acts of violence? Would it sanction more blood to spill?

Would the government finally act to protect the victim amidst international pressure? Would the government tone down the level of persecution to the outside world while domestically it secretly facilitates the systematic persecution of Ahmadiyya? It had been done before. Why must it end with three Ahmadis from Lombok being granted asylum? Asylum had failed to stop the blood elsewhere. Why should it work in Indonesia?

It was one of the reasons why the Ahmadiyya congregation's supporters dwindled.

Dawam Rahardjo, a Muslim scholar so vehemently defended Ahmadiyya's rights to coexist with other Muslim communities had been ex-communicated from the rest of Muhammadiyah, Indonesia's second largest Muslim organization. The organization he helped transformed into the 21st Century. Ulil Abshar Abdalla, a progressive Muslim scholar had a price on his head. Even the once revered president, Abdurrahman Wahid, was shunned for his stance on Ahmadiyya by Nahdlatul Ulama, Indonesia's largest Muslim group, established by his grandfather. Himself was a long time figure and chaired the organization for more than a decade. When it came to defending Ahmadiyya, the religious figures and scholars were on their own, no matter how much they were revered by their respective organizations.

The same went for politicians. Individually, they supported Ahmadiyya. They supported religious freedom. They supported all religious minorities. They decried all forms of injustice against them. But when asked if their political parties felt the same way. If their stance had the full backings of their party leaders, they all went quiet.

The Ahmadiyya leaders were anything but blameless as well. When victimized they were the first to cry for justice. First to press for the fulfillment of their constitutional rights. First to question about their right to freely practice their religion. Their right to live without fear.

They sought alliance from other religious minorities. Convincing them that they were fighting for the same cause. But when it came time for the other minorities to seek help from the Ahmadis, they did little. Even to show sympathy, camaraderie, solidarity. Only one or two Ahmadis came to meetings held by the Jakarta Legal Aid Foundation which spearheaded an Alliance for Freedom of Religion.

The only Ahmadi who consistently attended these meeting was its spokesman. A tall, bulky man named Mubarik Ahmad. He attended joint rallies with other religious groups while the Ahmadi leaders argued that rallying to criticize the government was against the Ahmadiyya creed. He fought against the one-sided foreclosure of churches because he believed it's the right of every religion to freely build their houses of worship. But the leaders kept telling their followers that their Messiah was sent to restore Islam's dominance over the world and destroy the Cross.

He criticized the sentencing of a self proclaimed prophet. An Indonesian woman named Lia Aminnudin who led a religion called Eden. Mubarik argued that the state had no right to interfere with people's beliefs. The Ahmadi leaders disagreed. Ahmadi clerics across the country told their followers that Lia Aminnudin was a fraud, a self proclaimed prophet, a blasphemer. The clerics told their followers that she deserved to be jailed. She deserved God's wrath. She deserved eternal damnation. All precisely the same words used by those seeking to persecute the Ahmadis.

The Ahmadi clerics told their followers that they hold the truest form of Islam, the one which guarantees their adherers total absolution of all sins. The only Islamic group to be spared from the horrors of hell.

What the clerics wouldn't say is that all Islamic groups claimed to be on the sole path to righteousness. All other paths, all other teachings, all other sects, all other interpretations of the Koran would lead to damnation.

In fact all religions do the same. Making their claim as the true owners of heaven. And who dare say otherwise? Who dare say it is never about which path they take but the determination to get to the ultimate destination, the overcoming of obstacles? Who dare say paths are not of importance when they are the paths?

They spread fear to retain power. Promising heaven to those who follow their instructions to the letter and hell to those who won't. They made it sound like paths are more important than the destination. They forgot that the interpreters of the divine words are mortals. Worst of all, the paths are one way. None has returned to warn the living that their paths would lead to peril. None has returned to advise that their paths would lead to bliss.

The Ahmadi clerics told their followers that the persecution of Ahmadiyya was the works of the Zionists who plotted to destroy Islam through the hands of other Muslims. The Shiites claimed that the Sunnis and Ahmadis are part of the Zionist conspiracy. The Sunnis believed the same about the Shiites and Ahmadis. Perhaps they are all complicit. Perhaps there never was any conspiracy. Perhaps they are all right. Perhaps they are all wrong.

The leaders tried to hide these facts from Khaerudin, Suhaidi and Kamarudin. There was a decision to shield these humble peasants from what was really going on. From the duality of their teachings. From the inconsistency of their struggle. From the fact that their supporters were dwindling. The fact that their prominent lawyer Adnan Buyung Nasution had been appointed as presidential adviser and couldn't advocate them as actively as he should. The fact that even the top leaders were starting to second guess that the asylum attempt would serve its intended purposes.

Came a wealthy Ahmadi man. Neither Suhaidi nor Khaerudin and Kamarudin knew much about the generous man, except for the fact that he came to them one night asking many questions about their home, their life in Transito, their effort to seek asylum.

Suhaidi, the brave and confident youth, acted as their speaker. His words were calm and polite but well structured, logical and detailed. He was a skilled story teller. He had the gift of a seasoned salesman, a skilled negotiator. It was easy to see why friends liked to be around him. Why girls fell in love with him. He was a good judge of character and adjusted his tone and speed to suit the person he was talking to. Like a showman, he could read his audience, deliver what they wanted to hear while occasionally passing jokes, sometimes compliments so people would be transfixed to his words.

He was not like Khaerudin. Khaerudin maybe older, maybe more educated but hints of his old timid self still radiated. His delivery dull, his words uninspiring, his chain of thought not well connected. He went back and forth presenting his arguments and missed important details. He provided too much information and sometimes too few. He avoided eye contact. His gestures betrayed nervousness. When presented with tough questions too hard to comprehend or answer he rambled about unrelated things.

The wealthy man seemed more interested about the asylum attempt asking fewer questions about anything else.

'So you guys are really adamant about applying for an asylum are you?'

The three nodded. Explaining that they had nothing left.

'You're ready to leave behind your family?'

The three nodded once more, this time with apparent hesitation from Khaerudin and Kamarudin. At this point the wealthy man could see that Suhaidi was the man more eager to leave the country. More willing to leave everything behind and never looked back.

He sensed that the other two only did this because they were told to do so by their leaders. He wondered whether they were willing to go all the way and make sacrifices necessary. At this moment he grew fonder of Suhaidi. Not just because of his words. He asked more questions but was more interested in what Suhaidi had to say. Ignoring the other two.

'So what are your plans? What are you going to do once you get there?'

Suhaidi replied, 'We don't know yet. Maybe get in touch with the congregation members there. Maybe look for work and send some money back home.'

The wealthy man smiled. 'Does any of you speak English?'

The three looked at each other. 'Not much. Only what we were taught at school. But that was a long time ago,' they responded.

The smile on the wealthy man's face grew larger. 'How could you possibly expect to talk with the Ahmadis there? Are you going to speak to them using Sasak?'

The three seemed embarrassed at how ill equipped they were. They were too focus on applying for asylum they overlooked one important detail. Everyone was so transfixed with the process they forgot to ask themselves what to do once they're there.

The wealthy man offered to find a private tutor to teach them English. They were delighted, Suhaidi especially. For it rekindled their spirit thought long lost. It made them believed their effort would not be in vain. They felt they were closer to their goal.

***

The day was August 17, 2007. People were commemorating 62 years of Indonesian independence. In an act of respect for the government mandated by their creed, the Ahmadis in Transito also observed Independence Day by raising Indonesia's red and white flag. There was no jubilance. There was no pride. It was their second Independence Day celebration in Transito, the home of the persecuted.

They pondered the meaning of Independence. A nation is built to free people from the shackles of oppressors. To liberate them from injustice. 62 years… Was this the nation their fathers and grandfathers fought for? Was this the nation their forefathers had envisioned? A motherland which wanted them gone? A land where people couldn't practice their beliefs?

It was a moment of sorrow for the Ahmadis. It had been one year, six months and thirteen days since they were exiled to Transito. One by one the sick and the elderly called Transito their death place.

Meanwhile, new babies were born. Nasipudin had welcomed three grandchildren while he was in Transito. First Sultan, then Hijwana. Then came the time for Faizah to birth another child. A son named Barahin Ahmad. Born four months back. It appeared that Transito was overrun with babies. The joy of having their own home in Ketapang was celebrated with the conception of a child. But the joy was short lived. Their homes were reduced to ruins and with it their dreams. A child conceived in joy was to be born in wretchedness.

There were separations too. Many months before, Malik asked permission to go to Taskimalaya, West Java. A town he once spent a year as a child to continue his education after they were driven away from their hometown Pancor.

'I don't want to be a burden. I know our family couldn't even afford to buy food,' he said one evening. 'I know high school here can be expensive. So maybe I should try and apply for a scholarship from the congregation.'

'I understand son. The most important thing is for you to continue your education.' Malik's parents stared at their smart boy with teary eyes. 'We're going to miss you. We will always love you.'

Nasipudin stuttered and got emotional. 'I will…' His voice crackled and for a moment he was lost for words. Then he rephrased. 'If God is willing… If God gives me the strength… Gives me long life… I will try to find money so you can go to college someday.'

'Father… You don't have to… I will get another scholarship so you don't have to worry about me… Ever.'

Malik expressed his desire to apply to Mubarak campus, a facility just south of Jakarta where Ahmadi clerics are trained. Many people from Lombok had studied at the Ahmadiyya campus. They became missionaries, flown to far corners of the archipelago, some to countries like Cambodia, Vietnam and Papua New Guinea to propagate their religion, spread the wisdom of their Messiah: 'Love for All and Hatred for None.'

His father quizzed him as to why he wanted to be an Ahmadiyya cleric. Malik was smart enough to choose any profession he liked and be successful. Malik responded by telling a story of what happened to him during the attack the year before. Back when his mother handed Malik a Koran and told him he should guard it. His mother gave him that Koran so that Malik didn't join his older brothers on the frontline. She was well aware that Malik felt he was old enough to fight. Malik however saw it as a sign. His task in the world was to protect the Koran. To spread its message to the world. To reaffirm people's beliefs.

Nasipudin was happy his son decided to devote his life to their religion. The ultimate sacrifice. Being an Ahmadi cleric means to be free from the obligation to pay candah, a contribution to their congregation. A huge percentage of their income. Obliged to be paid no matter how little they earn. 'Our Messiah taught us that we must pay candah as long as we can feed ourselves,' clerics would say about candah. It was another way of saying 'no matter how poor, no matter if you're homeless and sleep on the streets, pay up until you starve.'

Being an Ahmadi clerics also comes with perks. An entitlement of a missionary's home. A salary from the congregation. A right to demand the best of education for their children. A privilege to live differently from their poor followers. A chance to become a leader, an emir, a caliph. A chance to see the world.

But it also comes with great expense. There is no way of knowing where a cleric would be stationed. In an inhospitable area a cleric is among the first to be targeted. A cleric must be able to lead his community. To get through tough times. To give them strength. To give them hope.

Many didn't see these tasks. Many didn't bother to make sacrifices. They whined that their missionary houses are too small and ordered for a total refurbishment. Complained that the local congregation could only afford to provide a motorbike and not a car. When comes the time their followers ask for help and protection, they told them to pray and be patient. When criticized they accused the critics with being jealous and warned that envy is a sin. Yet so is gluttony.

But first Malik had to finish high school. And before that he must go to Tasikmalaya.

His father regretted that he had no money to pay for his travel. But the smart and resourceful Malik told his father not to bother. He had saved enough to buy a bus ticket to Java.

He bought a basket of mandarin oranges while in Mataram where it was cheap. He sold the oranges once he got to Java where they cost more. With the money he got selling oranges he bought a train ticket.

He stayed over at people's homes using his Ahmadiyya connection. Sometimes he stayed at Ahmadiyya mosques. He swept people's floors, washed people's cars. Any work he could find to save and make money. As long as he didn't beg, didn't steal or didn't defraud others.

'Even if you see even a dirty, old rubber band lying on the street, if it is not yours don't even think about keeping it,' his mother often said to her children. Malik followed that message by heart. The message: 'Don't take what is not yours! Don't do what you are not supposed to!'

And so Malik went. There was a feeling of sadness, gladness and pride rolled into one in Nasipudin and Zubaidah's heart. Their son dreamed of being a cleric, a profession they so devoutly respected.

But the start of a new school year meant there were other family members they must worry about. They had to find a junior high school for Safir. The last child Kasafuloh had to stay in third grade for another year. He had skipped school so often when the series of attacks happened it affected his grade. The attacks left a permanent scar on Kasafuloh. He became a stutter. He became a slow learner. Khaerudin's son Hafidz also didn't pass first grade. Another victim to the traumatizing attacks.

But the couple's biggest concern was their granddaughter Yuni. She was old enough for school. But her father Suhaidi was far away in Jakarta. 'Too busy to find work ' Suhaidi said over the phone to his wife Sri when she asked for money to send Yuni to school. It was impossible for Sri to work. Sri had another baby girl Hijwana, still breastfeeding to her mother.

For a while it looked like Yuni had to delay starting her education. Fortunately there were donations from distant relatives and old family friends. The Marwans. Faizah's mother-in-law, Ahmadis from Jakarta, charity groups.

Nasipudin thought about Suhaidi often. How can someone so distant be so caring and someone so close so ignorant?

'Have I failed as a father? Have I done what I shouldn't?' he must have asked himself and the heavens. 'Will I be able to right his wrong? Will I be able to save him from Your wrath? Help him God. Show him mercy. Forgive him. Keep him safe in Your arms. Keep him from going astray.'

CHAPTER 26

The English tutor came three times a week. Khaerudin and
Kamarudin were making very little progress. They never mastered
past 'Hello,' 'How are you?' 'Fine, thank you,' and a few other basic
greetings. Suhaidi faired better, having actual interest in learning the
foreign language. He asked questions. He spoke up and practiced
new words and phrases every chance he got. The others were
scratching their heads when asked to simulate simple conversations,
let alone learning the tenses.

They studied at a hall under a flight of stairs, down at the
basement of an Ahmadiyya mosque in Kebayoran, South Jakarta.
They studied at night so that during the day, they could accompany
their leaders to meet politicians, activists and embassy officials. Or
at least that was the original intention. The three had spent almost
four months in Jakarta during their third visit and the leaders came
less and less frequent.

Khaerudin and Kamarudin filled their time by finding work as
construction workers for wealthy Ahmadi families and bosses. The
two went to see senior clerics they would otherwise never see back
in Mataram. They went to see senior Ahmadi officials and leaders.
They were taking life as congregation members seriously.

Suhaidi was less interested. He found no amusement in
discussing religion or Ahmadiyya organizational affairs. He spent
more time with new found friends he met in Kebayoran. There were
people of Pakistani descent whom he could practice his English
with. He asked questions about the country of their ancestors. About
what life was like in a land he dreamed of setting foot on. He asked
if they had been to other countries and what they were like.

The wealthy man came from time to time to check on their
progress. Four months had passed and this time it was Suhaidi's turn
to ask about progress of another kind.

'Have you heard anything from the leaders?'

The wealthy man said nothing, prompting Suhaidi to quiz him again.

'C'mon, you must have heard something.'

The wealthy man seemed reluctant to divulge anything. He explained that it was best to let the three heard the truth from the leaders themselves.

Suhaidi sensed there was something wrong. Had the leaders given up? Had they reconsidered the plan for seeking asylum? It seemed their dreams, or at least Suhaidi's, were shattered. Time wasted. Efforts and works down the drain. All that waiting, all those meetings, all those talks, all those places meant nothing.

'So that's it? All this? Worthless?' Suhaidi must have told the wealthy man picking up the worksheet for his English lessons.

Suhaidi was devastated. He was angry. He felt used. He should have known that he was used when the leaders summoned the three of them only when there was another attack to another Ahmadiyya community somewhere. He was made an icon. A symbol to attract sympathy. Perhaps he was made an example for perseverance and patience. A real life poster boy for other Ahmadiyya communities suffering lesser pain and more minor attacks to see.

Other than the time when they needed them the leaders were impossible to see. Suhaidi did not intend on becoming a role model. He never wanted to. What he wanted was a chance to live in peace. Free from pain and hardship. Perhaps a chance to escape poverty. He was desperate for them.

He must have thought about the things he had given up coming to Jakarta. A marriage to his second wife. His son born without a father. His first wife without a husband, struggling to get by. His daughter barely got her first taste of formal education. His relationship with her sister ruined. With his father shattered.

He dreamt of the future in sacrifice of the present and past. He was infuriated. He was devastated. They all were. But the difference was Suhaidi kept finding excuses to blame his anguish on others but himself.

'Is there another way?' Suhaidi said.

The wealthy man, who so passionately believed in their asylum attempt, joked that perhaps they should try making their way to Australia illegally by boat.

'I'm up for that.'

'No… no… no… I was only joking. Those trips are dangerous. You know how slim your chances of making the journey alive?'

'I've had been driven away from my hometown. I've rebuilt my life from scratch. I've seen my home pillaged and burned. I've seen my sister got harassed. My every possession stolen,' he said. 'I've been spat at, yelled at, attacked, and now in Jakarta ignored. I could go home, get attacked again and be dead next week. So I don't know what my chances are of making it to Australia alive… but I'll take it.'

The wealthy man was stunned. He stared emptily at the floor they were sitting, thinking about what Suhaidi said. Chances were slim. But should he make it, even if he perished at sea, there would surely be a wave of international condemnation and the ignorant Indonesian government would have to right what was wrong.

'The leaders would never agree. They would never agree to such a dangerous act,' he said smiling and shaking his head.

'The leaders don't have to know,' Suhaidi said.

For the first time since he came, the wealthy man turned his attention to the other two.

'What do you guys think of all this? Going to Australia by boat?'

Khaerudin shook his head. 'I have two sons and a wife waiting for me. I can't… I can't do it… I can't risk my life.'

Kamarudin said the same thing.

'Well looks like it's getting late,' the wealthy man said.

Suhaidi must have taken a deep breath from all that heavy talk. He was close to signing his own death warrant.

The wealthy man got up. Shaking their hands gently. He too was breathing deeply. Had the conversation continued he would have been responsible for sending a man to his watery grave.

***

The leaders came the following day. Disembarking from their SUVs to be greeted by everyone inside the mosque. The men had their hands shaken, the children their cheeks brushed and heads patted. Leading the pack was a skinny man with thin moustache and thin beard at the tip of his chin. He had a milder shade of brown for a skin and a pair of small eyes hiding behind thin-rimmed glasses. A black velvet cap perfectly snuggled his head, concealing his graying hair. It was the national Emir. A man named Abdul Basith.

The three also greeted their Emir, Suhaidi as well. But not the usual luster in his face. The presence of his Emir used to mean hope, new people to meet, new places to go. This time, Suhaidi knew that their Emir came only to tell the truth that there was never any hope. Hope was only a cruel excuse to keep going.

The Emir asked the three to join him at the mosque's main prayer hall. The Emir was first to be seated, in front of a podium where sermons were delivered each Friday. The three and the lesser leaders sat beside him, together forming a circle.

As predicted, the Emir was there to tell the truth but not the whole story. It was sugar coated with lengthy discussion of how it all began. How the plan to send some young men to seek for asylum was conceived. The Emir divulged that there was a huge argument but eventually it was decided that the outcome outweighed the risk.

The Emir explained that although inside the Ahmadiyya congregation everyone was committed to the plan, when the plan was discussed with their lawyers and activist friends, it was met with huge criticism. Only a handful supported the plan.

The Emir went on saying that the congregation decided to try nonetheless without the knowledge, let alone the support of anyone else outside the organization. But eventually the plan was exposed. From the top, the government pressured other countries not to grant them asylum. From the grass root the move found more criticisms.

'We tried to ignore them at first. But over time, after much discussion with our friends outside [Ahmadiyya], we felt maybe it was best to show that Ahmadiyya is very much a part of this country. We have been in Indonesia long before there was even a country named Indonesia. We want our rights as Indonesians. I think that would be the better strategy. And continuing to seek asylum doesn't fit this strategy. And so, after giving it much thought, after much discussion and deliberation, I think we should stop our efforts to seek asylum.'

And so it ended. With a pat on their backs and a leader thanking them for their hard work. It was work without reward. Twenty two months of waiting wasted. Their new found English skills rendered irrelevant.

Suhaidi perhaps just sat with his head down. Hiding his disappointment and perhaps teary eyes. He probably clenched a fist. Pressing his nails against the palm of his hand. Blood was clogging inside his fingers, making them numb. His palm felt like it was on fire from the sting. He was suppressing his anger. Trying to stop the tears from falling. Turning his attention away from his racing heart. The butterflies in his stomach. The memories flashing in his head. The weight of the world was crushing his dream.

He must have felt like running. But the Emir was not done with his lecture. Suhaidi wished not to offend the great leader but his urge to escape was also strong. So he lashed his emotions out by tightening his fist. Like rage was a thing in his palm needed to be crushed.

The leader had made up his mind. Suhaidi and his brother and uncle were to return back to Lombok. Their days in Jakarta were over.

***

The disappointment and rage traveled with Suhaidi as he returned to Transito. If it was up to him he would skip the hugging, the chit chat, the small talks and the pretend smile and just be alone. Privacy was a luxury in a complex filled with nearly two hundred refugees. Impossibility in a hall with no doors and locks. So he wandered. Riding his motorcycle aimlessly. Stopping at a secluded corner of a busy street. Resting underneath a tree at an intersection. Ordering a cup of coffee which he drank slowly, sometimes hours.

He probably chatted with strangers and told lies. Making up imaginary histories of himself. In one tale to strangers he was a migrant worker returning home from a faraway land. In another make-believe scenario he was a student on holiday to visit a relative. It was his way of not dealing with reality. A broken man with no job or future.

He was miserable for weeks. Venting his anger at his friends and families. People avoided him. They tried to cheer him up to no avail. The older folks tried to preach, how his misfortunes were the works of his own neglect. Refusal to take responsibility for his family. Inability to formulate a back up plan, a safety net. The disillusion of his own selfish dreams.

'This is your own fault. Our leaders did all they could,' Suhaidi was told. Then came the unavoidable comparison to his brother. 'Khaerudin this... Khaerudin that...'

That made Suhaidi more frustrated, more desperate, more outraged. 'What do you know? You weren't there in Jakarta with me were you?'

Then came the call. On the other side was the wealthy man, speaking to him over the phone from Jakarta.

'How are you Suhaidi?'

'I'm good sir.'

'So what's your plan?'

'I don't know sir. I honestly don't know.'

'You still dream about going to Australia aren't you?'

Suhaidi smiled. It was like talking to the only person in the world who understood his dreams, hopes and fears.

'You know back in Jakarta we talked about going to Australia by boat.'

'I remember.'

'You told me that you were up for it. Is that still the case?'

'Yes sir. I'm ready to do anything.'

'Good... good... good...'

'What do you have in mind sir? If you don't mind me asking. Have you figured out a way for me to do that?'

'No... no... no... But I am curious. I'm just thinking. This is just a thought...'

'I'm listening.'

'Would it hurt you to go to... let's say Kupang. And while you're there maybe you can ask around the locals there... I just want to know... What would it take to make it all the way to Australia?'

The wealthy man was referring to a city in West Timor, East Nusa Tenggara province. It is a city so close to Northern Australia it is infamous for being a hub for people traffickers and smugglers and asylum seekers looking to make a dangerous voyage across the treacherous Indian Ocean.

'I will wire you some money, enough for you to get to Kupang. Afterwards you call me OK?'

'OK sir. That's wonderful. That is a great plan. I'll do it.'

'Listen… the leaders can't know. No one can. No one can also know I'm behind all this. I mean, you can talk to your family and all that since this is dangerous and this might be the last time you get to talk to them. But that's it. That's it.'

'Don't worry sir.'

It didn't take long before Suhaidi went to his family explaining his intention to head south to Australia. He made a long speech of how he thought the journey was important, the reward outweighed the risk. At one point he asked his brother Khaerudin to join. He declined. He thought the plan was suicidal. Many people have perished in the Indian Ocean. Even seasoned seamen. How did Suhaidi thought a peasant like him, with no experience at sea, dreamed of making it alive?

Nasipudin was more concerned about his wife becoming a widow, his daughters without a father. He was also concerned about doing something out of the Emir's knowledge and consent. Zubaidah couldn't bare the thought of her flesh and blood lost at sea. Nurul and Faizah just stayed quiet. What Suhaidi was about to do was something way beyond their wildest imagination. But everyone in the family knew there was no stopping Suhaidi. No words, no matter how well composed, how cleverly presented, could change his minds.

And so Nasipudin spoke. Neither agreeing nor dismissing. 'May God protect you, my son.'

CHAPTER 27

The beautiful beaches and crystal clear water gave a false impression of paradise, drawing visitors to its rows of coconut leaves waving along a strong, dry, salt water infested wind. But water is scarce and nothing grows in this barren land, not even the number of houses and cars. A few footsteps inland were jagged cliffs and rocky hills pinning down on people's homes as their front lawns were being encroached slowly by the sea.

The locals retold stories of how the island of Timor was once a giant crocodile with the western part serving as its more rugged back. Kupang was on the mythical beast's teeth. The terrain viciously unforgiving.

The only source of life was at sea. The sea provides bountiful catch with Kupang standing at a crossroad for some fish species' migratory route. It was a natural port. Where ships shelter behind the islands of Semao to the west and Rote to the south from the incoming waves and currents from the open Indian Ocean. The first stop after a perilous journey from the North, the final stop before an even more hazardous journey south.

It was the first week of 2008 and Suhaidi was among the handful of people arriving in Kupang. The rest rushed themselves to get away. Embarking on ships and airplanes ferrying them to much more fertile ground once they were done spending Christmas and New Year with their families.

Greeting Suhaidi at the seaport where faces he had once or twice seen at Ahmadiyya gatherings and some he had never met before. They accompanied him to the Ahmadiyya mosque in Kupang. Traversing through this strange new town only ten kilometers from one edge to the next. He looked around. Every corner seemed to be filled with the same thing, four story buildings mushrooming haphazardly with no apparent guidelines, each with different facade and style unrelated to one another. On the streets were colorful public minivans, intricately decorated to entice customers.

Just minutes later he found himself at Kupang's Ahmadiyya mosque complete with pictures bearing the image of his Messiah. After introducing himself he was immediately welcomed. Ahmadis were a tight-knit community. Everyone was a brother and a sister. Handshakes were warm as if to a lifelong friend. Any requests were immediately met as if made by a close kin.

He asked if he could stay at the mosque and was promptly shown an empty room for him to use. What followed were small talks and white lies as a sign of politeness. In Indonesia, the polite way was for the host to explain the guest how modest the room was. The host must then pretend to be embarrassed that he could not provide a more comfortable accommodation. The guest was supposed to say that the host was being generous, arguing to him that he expected no more than what was being offered. There was to be flattery about how his offer was more than adequate. A cherry on top was to show how grateful you are. Perhaps indebted for life for his kindness. An offer to repay perhaps. The host was supposed to refuse. The guest was supposed to do so anyway.

It didn't take long before he met the entire Ahmadi community in Kupang. Suhaidi met everyone, introducing who he was and where he was from. The Ahmadis in Kupang instantly asked him to explain what happened in Lombok. They have heard about the attacks from clerics and leaders and television reports and were dying to hear about the persecution straight for the one who lived it. Suhaidi happily obliged.

Suhaidi had a thing about speaking. Had a thing about story telling. He was able to take the listeners into the narrative, enticing their imagination. He wasn't able to grab people's attention in Lombok. There, he was perceived as a loud mouth fraud. A trouble maker who abandoned his family. A dreamer who ignored his real duties. In Jakarta, people were beginning to feel the same way about him. But here in Kupang, where everyone didn't know the real him, he was worthy of admiration and awe.

'So what brings you here to Kupang?' an Ahmadi asked.

'I'm looking for work.'

Perhaps there were people who found his excuse strange. Why come to a barren, small town where even the locals struggle to land a job? Why go to where everyone was so desperate to leave? Why not find work in Jakarta, a place he had been for almost two years? Why did a man with experience in construction and farming look for work in a town where the only source of work is out at sea?

But it wouldn't be polite. Passing suspicion to a man persecuted. Putting further scrutiny to a man who had lost his home. To a brother in faith. Many were not satisfied with Suhaidi's answer but only one dared to know more. It was a man named Bob Akbar.

Bob was a seasoned sailor. A first mate for the Indonesian state-owned ferry operator ASDP. Suhaidi felt if anyone could help with his attempt to reach Australia it would be Bob. And so he decided to reveal the truth to Bob while carefully observing his reaction.

First he needed to know whether he could trust Bob. Needed to know if he could keep secrets. Words spread easily inside the Ahmadiyya and the leaders might find out and tried to stop him. He could be expelled from the mosque and no longer be welcomed. He could put the wealthy man sponsoring him at risk too.

And so Suhaidi started to ask questions to find out more about Bob. He asked if Bob was actively involved in the organization. How much Bob knew about the Ahmadis in Lombok. He started asking questions about what he does for a living. Make him explain what his role was in a ship and how long had he known the sea. He asked if he could learn doing what he did and how long it would take.

'Why? Do you want to be a sailor?' Bob replied with a few questions of his own.

Suhaidi smiled. 'I want to go to Australia.'

'What? By boat? You mean illegally? With a fishing boat?' Bob lowered his voice to a whisper.

Suhaidi stayed quiet, but a faint smile betrayed all the answers.

'So that's why you want to learn to be a sailor?'

'Can you help me?'

Bob stared straight into Suhaidi's eyes with his mouth gagging, instinctively blinking rapidly and excessively. He broke his stare to look over his shoulder. It was at this point Suhaidi felt comfortable knowing his secrets were safe. Bob's moves suggested he wanted no one else to hear what he had to say next.

'I'm leaving for another trip out to sea in a few days.' Bob's whisper grew softer, so much that Suhaidi had to bend over to hear what he said. 'You can come if you like. I'll teach you everything.'

***

The crew's quarter was located next to the ship's wheelhouse connected to the passengers' cabin by a tight alleyway. A circular porthole provided a view of the ocean and an open deck below. Bob introduced Suhaidi as his brother tagging along for the ride to learn about life at sea. The captain couldn't care less, asking him to stay away from trouble. Reminding him not to bother the seamen there to do their job. He was given a broom and told that it shall be his true companion during the entire trip. Suhaidi nodded.

A crew member showed him where he would be sleeping, a spot on the plastic mat covered floor surrounded by metal walls fast corroding from seawater. The rust was simply covered over with heavy coats of paint making the surface wavy and uneven. On the walls were calendars bearing the images of half-naked women. A mirror framed in neon colored plastic rim. Three plastic ropes running from one wall to the next to dry their clothes.

The plastic mat covered floor was full of cigarette burns and coffee stains. There were cockroaches feasting on what was left of people's food: peanut shells, bread crumbs, rice. Suhaidi was no stranger to living in dirty rooms and quarters having lived as refugees for years. He was no stranger to sharing a small space with others. Just like the police headquarters back in Pancor, he thought.

But not the smell. The stink of urine mixed with seawater mixed with leftover food mixed with the smell of sweat from bodies unwashed for days. The nauseating fume from diesel engine permeated to every corner of the ship. But he was there to learn. So he endured.

The entire voyage took 26 days. During that time the crew worked hard, making sure that the ship ferried passengers from one East Nusa Tenggara island to the next. They covered vast distances and made sure they make the trip in one piece.

The ship first set sail from Kupang to Alor. Scouring the western coast of the Crocodile before venturing north by northeast to the placid Sawu Sea. When the Crocodile is but a tiny spec on the horizon, when they encounter land mass up ahead they were an hour away from landing. It took the small ship sixteen hour to make their first trip.

After unloading, reloading and refueling, the ship set sail for Larantuka on the eastern tip of a big island named Flores. The ship sailed north before coming to the vast Banda Sea. Then the ship headed westward, past a chain of small islands accompanying them port side throughout this leg of the journey. The first was a big island named Pantar. Next came the tiny islands of Lapang and Batang. Another big island named Lembata was next, followed by Adonara where they decreased speed and ready to make land. That leg of the journey took twelve hours.

They scoured the southern part of Flores. Making their ways to another town called Aimere. An eight hour journey. From Aimere they sailed southwest. To another big island named Sumba. Specifically its biggest town Waingapu. It took them six hours. From Waingapu they traveled back the same route, stopping in the same towns, passing the same islands, crossing the same straits and seas.

Most of the time Suhaidi just stayed in the crew's quarters while the others were busy at the wheelhouse or at the engine room. During the night, when the First Mate Bob was at the helm, when the captain and the majority of the crew were fast asleep, his lessons began.

He learned that one of the most important things to surviving at sea was to understand how the sea and his ship worked. The sea, Bob said, may be level at plain sight but beneath the surface are rugged cliffs and hills and mountains and shelves and plains.

Bob trained Suhaidi's eye to distinguish shallow and deep water by the different shades of blue. He was taught how to avoid water shallower than what his ship allowed. He taught Suhaidi at which particular point at sea a wave would break. Suhaidi learned about the high and low tides and which time of day they occurred. How the movement of the moon affected the sea level. Which day of the month was the tide highest. And which was lowest.

He learned what each instrument inside the wheelhouse did. He learned how to tie ropes and the functions of different knots. He learned that a ship almost never sailed on a straight line, saying that there are forces of nature at work influencing its movement. He learned that navigation is key to the survival of his ship. How one wrong turn could mean the difference between life and death.

Bob introduced Suhaidi to navigation charts and almanacs of celestial bodies, his holy books at sea. He taught Suhaidi the different symbols and lines on the charts and what they meant to the success of his journey. He taught how to use the compass, explaining how he should peep through the hole in the compass to get accurate readings of a bearing or reference point. He explained the need to be as accurate as possible, saying that a degree off could overtime mean being off course for miles from where he needed to be.

He taught Suhaidi how to figure out where he was by using two terrestrial reference points. He explained the importance of keeping track where he was over certain time intervals to calculate his speed and to check whether he was on course. Suhaidi learned how to navigate using celestial bodies when there was no island he could use as reference. Or if he was sailing at night.

He learned the ancient knowledge of forecasting weather through observation. Weather lore. A thin white wavy cloud high above signals the later arrival of rain. Red sky in the afternoon means dry weather the following morning. Red sky in the morning forewarns of a wet day. The absence of seagulls in the air means the weather would be so violent it is best to stay on land. A cloudless day, a still air and a dark line above the horizon means a strong wind is approaching. A still air on a dark sky signals the coming of a storm.

The amount of knowledge he gained was so overwhelming it took a second voyage where he would put things to practice. Rope skills, navigation, steering, weather forecasting. Bob was contend seeing how well Suhaidi progressed. Suhaidi was confident with the skills he had. He was ready for a voyage on his own.

There was one surprise that Bob wouldn't divulge until he was sure Suhaidi was prepared with the necessary skills to survive at sea alone. A fishing boat was up for sale. Bob learned about this from a friend while he spent a week in Kupang before their second voyage.

'It's small but she might fit your budget. I think she's as good as it gets. I think it's enough to get you to Australia,' Bob said on his last night at sea.

'Thank you. I will check it out. '

Bob must have grabbed Suhaidi's wrist.

'You be careful. This is a big ship with all the modern equipment.'

Suhaidi nodded while Bob stared deeply into his eyes.

'This here is Sawu Sea. What you will be sailing is the Timor Sea. It'll be different. It'll be much more hazardous. You hear?'

Suhaidi nodded once more.

'The waves will be bigger. Your boat will be smaller. Much smaller than this. Much more unstable. Much more likely to capsize under the pounding waves. You will have no modern equipment to help you navigate.'

A silence followed.

'Are you ready? Don't be foolish and say that you are when you're not. It's OK to be afraid. I'll understand if you don't do it. So are you ready?'

'I'm ready.'

'Are you sure?'

'Yes... I'm ready.'

Bob hugged Suhaidi. Tightly. He was about to send a friend away on a perilous trip. A trip, he confessed to Suhaidi, which he himself was too afraid to take. It could well be their last farewell.

CHAPTER 28

First thing in the morning Suhaidi went to a local fish market by the harbor. He was searching for a particular fisherman. The man who would sell Suhaidi his boat.

Days earlier Bob introduced Suhaidi to him. Suhaidi had inspected the boat on offer. She was a small wooden fishing boat, two meters wide and nine meters long. She had a makeshift cabin to shade from the sun. An open hull. A 40 horse power diesel motor was attached to her stern. Suhaidi asked him how much he was asking. The man replied 25 million rupiah, the price of three brand new motorcycles. He consulted Bob if he taught it was a fair price. Bob went for a closer inspection and told him she was worth it. She was in fact a bargain. The fisherman was desperate for money. He needed to raise funds to send his son to college.

Suhaidi told the fisherman that he would think about it and shook his hand. He was making an excuse to buy time. He needed to report back to his financier, the wealthy man from Jakarta. A man whose identity was a well kept secret even from Bob his mentor and closest of friends. Suhaidi told the wealthy man about the boat and how much she cost. He told the man he would also need money for gasoline and food supply.

The wealthy man had agreed to provide all the money necessary almost instantly. Suhaidi gave the man his bank details and promised the wealthy man to return his money if the plan soured.

The day was February 27, 2008. That morning he met the boat owner for the second time. This time he was on his own. Bob had already left Kupang for another voyage.

'Before I buy this boat... Is it possible for me to have a go?'

'What do you mean?' the boat owner asked. He was starting to doubt if Suhaidi was a serious buyer.

'I mean a test run... I've never sailed a fishing boat like this before. I want to know if the boat is right for me.'

'A test run? You're telling me... you're... not a sailor?'

'Yes... I want to try it first... Just take it for a spin... A day... a full day...'

The fisherman looked puzzled. Suspicious perhaps.

'You want to sail out here in Kupang Bay for a few hours?'

'No... a full day... Out in the open sea... I'll... I'll pay... ' Suhaidi was so nervous he stuttered.

'The open sea? Why do you want to have a test run out on the open sea?'

Suhaidi got so frustrated trying to convince the fisherman he finally laid everything out in the open.

'I want to know if your boat would make it all the way to Australia.'

The fisherman smiled. Exhaling so heavily he could have sworn it was making him feel lighter. It was an answer he had heard so many times here in Kupang, a place ridden with people smugglers and those desperate to cross to Australia illegally.

'Australia... Yeah... she'll make it to Australia... I've sailed to Australia and back on a smaller boat.' His smile grew wider revealing a set of cigarette stained teeth. 'I can ferry you to Australia myself if I'm younger, if I don't have a son who needs money to go to college.'

Suhaidi froze, not saying a word, waiting for what the fisherman will say next.

'You want to see if she'll make it out on the open sea? And you'll pay? For the test run and the boat?'

'If I'm happy with the boat I'll pay you the full asking price... If not... just think of me renting your boat for the whole day.'

'Do you have money for fuel?'

'Sure'

'For food and supply?'

'Yup'

'Great... Come again tonight... We'll sail very early in the morning, between midnight and sunrise when the sea is calmer.'

Suhaidi withdrew enough money to buy food and gasoline and soon head out further into the market. Suhaidi initially thought about bringing enough just for the test run but the boat owner told him to pack more because the sea could be unpredictable.

So he bought seven jerry cans instead of three, each with 30 liters of diesel fuel. The fuel alone cost him 980,000 rupiah, more than what he would earn in a month as a market laborer or a motorcycle taxi driver. He bought enough food to feed two people for a week. Even if he didn't end up using all, he would still need it for the trip to Australia, the fisherman told him.

Unexpectedly Suhaidi got a call on his mobile phone from a number he did not recognize.

'This is your Emir, ' a man spoke on the other side

'Emir who? '

'Your National Emir, Abdul Basith. '

Suhaidi was stunned. He couldn't believe his Emir would call him personally. He was not sure how, but his plan had been exposed.

'What do you think you're doing? You think I wouldn't find out about what you're doing? This plan of yours it's ludicrous. It's madness. Call it off! Go back to Mataram now! Do you hear me? Go home!'

The leader had spoken. But it was too late to change his mind. Money had been spent. Preparations had been made.

And so that night Suhaidi and the fisherman set sail. Pushing the boat to sea and let the current took them further into deeper water where the fisherman was sure his engine's propeller would not hit the bottom of the rocky sea bed.

He fired up his engine and soon they were off, heading first west by northwest to get out of the Kupang bay. The boat soon scoured along the mouth of the Crocodile and into a tight channel separating Timor and the tiny island of Semao. The boat headed south, decreasing speed to carefully navigate around the shallow water and jagged reef along the channel.

Suhaidi just watched the fisherman as he skillfully adjusted his speed and bearing. He didn't bother to consult any charts or keeping logs as Bob had taught Suhaidi to do. The seasoned fisherman was relying on his long honed sailor's instinct, years of experience at sea, the stories and myths and oral histories learned from other fishermen and naked eye observations to guide him.

At the bottom tip of the Crocodile's jaw, when the island of Rote came to view, they continued east by southeast into the edge of the treacherous Timor Sea. Gentle waves began to form, a sign that they were heading for open water. A sea which connects the volatile Indian Ocean and the massive Pacific Ocean. The fisherman offered Suhaidi the helm, teaching him how to control the engine. The steer, the throttle, the angle of the propeller. The fisherman told him which direction he should be heading. Which way was Darwin, North Australia.

Suhaidi would take the steer for the next few hours venturing further into the unknown. The big open sea. After throwing out the splashing seawater trapped inside the open hull, the fisherman rested on a plank of wood keeping him away from the wet floor below.

Then Suhaidi saw it. A red sky with the rising sun casting a halo as it shone through the moist air sitting below a cluster of thunderous clouds, black as smoke. The clouds had blanketed the sky above them, making the day as dark as night. The air was still. The sea unusually placid. It was the calm before the storm.

***

By night, the sea was raging with waves pounding harder and harder. Suhaidi had given up the helm to the more experienced fisherman. The headlamp failed to provide a clear view of where they were or where they were going. Only droplets of rain being swept sideways by the gushing wind. Only walls of waves four meters tall closing in. The fisherman pointed the boat's bowl to the waves coming in from east by northeast to charge them head on. He hit the accelerator hard as they climbed up the wave and releasing the throttle once they dipped.

Suhaidi held on tight to the edge of the boat, struggling hard not to vomit. For the first few minutes there was exhilaration. He never felt so alive, facing the biggest danger in his life. He felt like being on a giant thrill ride. But afterwards he was begging for the waves to stop. He was feeling nauseous like his gut was being churned. He lost sense of direction. One moment he could see nothing but the black sky. Seconds later he was staring at the bottom of the wave, bracing himself for a powerful impact.

There was a crashing sound when the boat plummeted to the bottom of the wave and the hull slammed into the water. Followed by a hiss when the splattering water rejoined the sea. During the climb was the deep sound of the engine struggling. At the apex the sound of the engine screaming in high note as the propellers hit nothing but air.

It went on for hours with waves coming at less than a forty second interval. With each pounding wave Suhaidi's hope of reaching Australia dimmed. He wiped the seawater from his face. Spat the salty taste of the sea. He was cold. His body started to tremble. His arms were starting to feel numb. But he kept holding on to the boat for dear life. He wished that it was all a bad dream. He thought about those he left behind. In a desperate time he must have sent a prayer.

'Please God. Help us…. Please God…. Save us. Save us please. '

He then made an offering to God. A bribe in exchange for his life.

'I know I haven't been good. I let a lot of people down. I promise… I promise I'll be good… Save us please… '

He thought about the things he had done. The people he had disappointed. It turned into a confession.

'I should have listened to my father. I should have listened to my mother. I should have head back to Kupang when I saw that the storm was coming. I should have stayed. I should never have come to Kupang in the first place.'

Finally, when all hopes seemed lost, an acceptance of God's plan.

'If this is my time… Forgive me… Forgive my sins… '

***

The boat had been in rough seas for eight straight hours and finally the storm died down. The fisherman was finally letting his engine some rest. Himself and Suhaidi as well. Suhaidi was panting heavily, lying lifeless on the boat. The fisherman sat, fatigued, unable to think, let alone say a word. He was drowsy. They both were. They had been up all night. They haven't had anything to drink or eat. Too preoccupied with staying alive. Keeping the boat afloat.

The boat still rocked from side to side. Compared to the ones which they had been fighting before, the waves seemed like mere ripples. Like the swaying of a baby's cradle. Like the rocking of an old man's chair.

The fisherman looked up into the sky searching for stars to provide clues to where they were. But the heavens were still shrouded by thick blanket of clouds. There was nothing to do but be thankful for the life they still had. To drink a sip or two of water. And to have a good night sleep, far long overdue.

***

It was way past noon when Suhaidi woke up. The fisherman must have been up for hours, studying the sun's movement, carving out the angles of the shadows it cast on the wooden floor of the rickety boat. He wasn't sure where they were, but he could tell that the sun's path was further north than it would have been when observed from Kupang. Way north. It was clear that they had been pushed south by the pounding waves but with no island he could use as reference the fisherman didn't know for how far.

The only thing they could do was eat. Suhaidi checked their supply to see if they were still intact. Only the canned sardines had not been spoiled by salt water. They had enough water to last for six days. Only one out of seven jerry cans of fuel had been exhausted. But with no clue to where they were and how long they would be out at sea or whether another storm would be on their path, the name of the game was conservation.

The sky was clear blue with a cluster of small snow white clouds close to the ground. It was a sign that the sky will be clear throughout the day. It was a sign that later that night he could consult the constellations.

The first star appeared in the East and perhaps immediately the fisherman tracked its position. He would have gazed at the star, one eyes closed while his right hand was holding a string attached to a flag pole. He kept his hand closed to his opened eye, making sure it was level, parallel to the horizon. He arranged his own position so that the star appeared just behind the flag pole. With the use of his left thumb he measured the star's height and scratched a mark on the pole with his nail.

More stars appeared. The North Star was but a spec on the horizon. The Southern Cross was high in the sky. He consulted the star directly above his head. Based on oral histories he learned over the years, in his mind he was able to draw a constellation chart and knew where every star needed to be.

He consulted other markings on the pole, made during other voyages. Some marking stood out, painted with a black marker. That marking was made while he was home, in Kupang. He compared the fresh scratch with other markings, measuring the distances between them. He would have cared little about using rulers, relying on the width and depth of his thumb.

He knew the width of every knuckle of his fingers, index to pinky. The width and length of his palm. The distance from the tip of his thumb to the tip of his pinky outstretched. In fact he was using all of his body as measuring instruments. The length from his finger tips to his elbow. The width of his shoulders. The length of his lower legs, toes to knees.

Suhaidi was probably startled. He had learned navigation using sextants, compasses, charts, calculators and complex equations. But the fisherman relied on the simplest of things. A scratch on a wooden pole, the measurements of his body, the strength of his memory. Suhaidi was curious to learn what he was doing but the fisherman was concentrating so much it looked like he was in a trance.

From the scratching on the pole he was able to figure out their latitude. Kupang was eleven degrees south and they were at least 240 nautical miles further south. He noticed that the waves were traveling from the northeast so they must have been swept southwest. Judging from the size and interval of the waves and how long they had been pushed southwestward he was able to estimate that they must have been parallel to Timor Island.

The fisherman told Suhaidi the good news, he roughly knew where they were. They must keep following the North Star where the clusters of islands of East Nusa Tenggara lie. It was the safer option than to proceed east to the less familiar Australian waters. Then there was the bad news. It would take six days to get home and he wasn't sure if they had enough fuel.

And so they set sail once more, trying to push their luck. Suhaidi could only pray they'd make it. They took turn steering the boat. They rationed their meal very carefully, their water more so. During the day, the fisherman was able to determine that they were approaching land mass. It was still hiding beneath the earth's curvature but he could see its faint reflection on the clouds. When the sun started to disappear they stopped, allowing the fisherman to make another celestial navigation to make sure they stayed on course.

Sometimes it rained. Sometimes there were small waves they had to navigate through. Days went by and they were down to their last jerry can of fuel. Down to their last drop of water. Down to their last tin of sardine.

But then they saw that the sea was alive with fishing boats and cargo ships. The sea also started to reveal tiny patches of land. They were close to shore. There was a sense of relieve from Suhaidi.

'No more, ' he said to himself.

'No more, ' he told his financier.

'No more, ' he said to his father, asking him for forgiveness.

CHAPTER 29

Suhaidi returned to Transito like a man defeated. It seemed that he was never destined for greatness. Never go to places he could only view on television. Never get to do amazing feat. Accomplish amazing things. It seemed that he must accept his fate. Become a common, humble, boring poor worker like his father and the father before him. Like his brother Khaerudin, footsteps and deeds of whom, people said he should follow and emulate. It seemed he was meant to do what people told him to and not what he wanted.

But once he got to Transito, he felt like a hero returning from a war won. The welcome was warm with nothing but smiles on people's faces. 'You made it back,' 'We were worried,' 'I thought you were lost at sea,' were the words spoken to him.

He soon told tales people had never heard before. How he spent weeks preparing for the voyage. How he battled the raging sea. How the thought of people back in Transito was the thing that kept him going. That kept him living. How he was pushed into the open sea by the waves. How he managed to find his way back to Kupang.

What he didn't say was how much the fisherman was responsible for his own safety. How he begged to God for protection, for delaying his death. How he selfishly put everything on the line. His family. What he didn't say was that even if he made it to Australia, it would make little impact to the lives of the Ahmadis in Transito. He would have been likely detained and put into a processing center. He might have been extradited back to Indonesia and caused even more pressure on the Ahmadis.

Nevertheless he was glad that he tried. The elders resented the move, shaking their heads thinking it was madness. Khaerudin was acting older than he should, taking side with the elders he so dearly respected and trusted.

But the young treated Suhaidi with respect, having made an adventure others could only dream of. There was pat on his back. Thumbs up. They couldn't get enough of Suhaidi's stories. Grinning widely at his exploits. The loved how he defied the great leader of Ahmadiyya in Indonesia. A feat which took great courage many Ahmadis wished they had.

Before he knew it, the pledge for change, to do good, to obey. Promises Suhaidi made while he was on the verge of doom out at sea, was forgotten. Sidelined. There was only pride. There was only vanity.

Back was his mischievous ways. He landed a job at the market and made money. But he didn't spend it to feed and clothe his wife and children. Instead he spent it on trendy clothes for himself. On night outs with his friends. Sweet talking to girls he met. Lying about being single. Making girls fall helplessly in love. The girls went crazy over Suhaidi they gave everything. Money, jewelries, clothes, cellphones. Once Suhaidi was done with them he dumped them. Like empty food wrappers deprived of its content. Like toys he no longer play with. Like garbage. Forgotten. Abandoned.

These girls would feel so betrayed they sought Suhaidi with a vengeance. Sometimes they called. But once or twice they would come to Transito, sometimes bringing a male friend or family member, demanding to see Suhaidi. Demanding that he returned what he had taken. Suhaidi didn't steal anything of course. They were so blindly in love they gave every rupiah and every possession willingly. What Suhaidi robbed them of was their trust, their pride, their heart.

Suhaidi was never around though. No one ever knew exactly where he was. With their parents spending most of the day at the market, with Khaerudin becoming more and more involved in congregational affairs, with Nurul living in Ketapang, Faizah was left to clean up his mess. Serving as a buffer between her brother and the people who went after him.

Faizah could only grumbled. Scolding Suhaidi whenever she saw him, threatening to tell their father of his misdeeds. Sweet talking Suhaidi always came up with an excuse. 'I don't know her... I swear...' he would say. 'I never did such a thing... I swear...' And when he ran out of excuses, he did another thing he was great at, disappearing.

Young men too were drawn to Suhaidi. They loved being in his company. Loved hearing his marvelous stories. Tall, marble-clad buildings of Jakarta. Beautiful foreign tourists of Denpasar, Bali. His adventures at sea. Among the youths mesmerized by the stories was Suhaidi's brother Safir. He was early in his teens. Still searching for the things which identify him. Still discovering what love is.

Life in Transito offered nothing but boredom for Safir. People around him were too busy reciting the Koran. Too busy praying. Too busy preparing for the after life they forgot to live. His father constantly tried to lead Safir into the lives of the faithful. The ways of the devotees. Safir joined him on communal prayers, Ahmadiyya gatherings and events. But out of respect for his father. Out of fear of letting his family down. Not of devotion. Not out of passion. It felt like chores to him. Like work. Like something he must do.

What he wanted was to be with Suhaidi. His idol. Suhaidi took Safir everywhere. On Saturday nights he stayed up late hanging out with Suhaidi's friends, people twice his age. Suhaidi too loved taking Safir places. Safir made him feel like he wasn't the bad seed in the family after all. Safir made him fell he was normal. He was human, with human needs and human wants. Not just the disobedient child destined for damnation.

Safir also acted as Suhaidi's eyes and ears. Suhaidi often asked him what his father had been doing. Everyone's favorite son Khaerudin. The independent Nurul. The motherly Faizah. The devoted congregation of Transito. Suhaidi and Safir probably gossiped about them. Laughing and exposing their dirty secrets behind their backs.

Some nights he went to the city center, chatting and laughing while staring at the traffic passing the brightly lit, colorful stores and restaurants. Other nights Suhaidi took him to where Mataram kids go to race their motorbikes. It was the only place in the whole of Lombok which offered excitement, free entertainment. They saw kids making wheelies. Burning rubbers. Making donuts.

It was a chance for Safir to meet girls his age. He wasn't interested in Ahmadi girls. To him they were boring. All they cared about was praying, studying the Koran at the missionary's house. His father would have wanted Safir to marry an Ahmadi girl someday. But the girls in Transito were more like sisters. They knew each other since kids. They have grown up together. The girls in Transito were nice. But not the ones he felt he could fall in love with.

In time perhaps, Safir often thought, he would have to choose a girl of the same faith. With so much resentment against his religion there was no way he was to have a lasting relationship with a non-Ahmadi girl. His father would have been furious. His mother cry for days. But right then and there, he was only looking for someone to share a good time.

'Go on, talk to her,' Suhaidi would say to Safir. Suhaidi noticed that his brother's eyes were fixed to one girl in particular. Suhaidi also noticed that the girl occasionally looked back at Safir. The girl was out with her girlfriends. Probably she was looking for someone too. Perhaps that person was his brother.

'Go on, talk to her,' Suhaidi said once more. Safir's heart must be racing. He wanted to take a shot and talk to her. Find out more about the beautiful stranger. At least a name. Find out where she lived. Where she went to school. Maybe a phone number.

'Go on. Ask her out. What's the worst that could happen?'

'Me making a complete ass out of myself.'

'If she doesn't like you. Then find another one.'

Safir giggled.

'Go on… Don't make me go down there and talk her into coming here for you!'

'OK… OK… I'm going.'

***

Nasipudin felt like his family was tearing apart. It was like losing a son. He tried to reach out to Safir but somehow he couldn't. He did things he would never do as a child. He had secrets. He went out and never said where. Nasipudin didn't know who he was with. Safir never told him. He was dying to know how he was doing at school. Safir just said 'fine' and never elaborated. He wanted to know what he did on Saturdays. He wanted to know what his passion was. His interest. His hobby and perhaps he could play a part in that. Nasipudin felt like Safir was distancing himself from his family.

But Safir must have gone through what every teenager go through, Nasipudin thought. A gradual transformation from a child to an independent man. Safir needed to know his place in the world. To show and express himself more and more.

Nasipudin just hoped Safir chose the right path. It didn't matter that his children have success, fortune and power. He simply wanted his children to have a better life than he ever had. He wanted his sons to be better fathers than he would ever be. But most of all, he wanted them to be good Ahmadis. He wanted no more than a chance to be reunited with his family in the next life.

How he wished Safir would not end up like Suhaidi. Suhaidi showed the same signs as a teenager. In his head, he thought that perhaps he should have reached out to Suhaidi with love instead of disciplining him. It was obvious to him that he had been hard on Suhaidi as a boy. His wife pointed this out to him. His other children too. He thought that perhaps this was the reason Suhaidi distanced himself from his family.

He was not going to make the same mistake with Safir. He was going to guide him. Let him know that it was for his own good. He would make sure that Safir knew his family loved him. He was going to show Safir how to tell right from wrong. And gave him freedom.

He longed for the unity twice forged by hardships. They were together when assailants ransacked the first house he called home. When they were driven from the land of their ancestors. Cast away by the people they thought they knew and loved. They were together when they rebuilt their lives in a new place. Together when they were attacked again. Made homeless. Lose everything they had fought to gain. Perhaps only pain could bring them together.

Nasipudin should have kept his head from such thought for the heavens were listening.

***

The intolerants were banding. This time they plotted ways for total disbandment of Ahmadiyya. Across the country were more attacks. Demonstrations on the streets. They lobbied the Attorney General's Office saying that the Ahmadiyya had been violating the antiquated Blasphemy Law. They called for the revocation of the government decree recognizing the Indonesian Ahmadiyya Congregation as a legitimate organization. They sought for all Ahmadiyya properties to be sealed shut and taken over by the government. They planned for occupation of Ahmadiyya assets. Allowing only clerics affiliated with the hard-liners to preach on seized mosques.

The Attorney General's Office made a public statement, pledging to investigate blasphemy charges against the congregation. They sent letters to the Ministry of Religious Affairs and the Ministry of Home Affairs.

The Attorney General's Office needed other state institutions to share the criticisms and condemnations from international communities and local NGOs. Together they sent 'researchers' to Ahmadiyya communities across the country. They arrived with pre-conceived notion that Ahmadiyya was guilty of blasphemy. The 'research' was a sham. A confirmation to a widely hold belief.

The 'researchers' came to Transito, unannounced, in the morning, when all the men were out to work. They expected the women to give out what they wanted to hear. They wanted no intervention from the Ahmadi clerics which could provide arguments and dismissals.

'Just say that your holy book is Tazkirah' one researcher told Faizah.

'Tazkirah? What is Tazkirah? I never saw one in my life. If you want you can search every room in this shelter for Tazkirah.'

'Who is your prophet?'

'My prophet is Muhammad.'

'C'mon, just say your prophet is Mirza Ghulam Ahmad.'

The move created a stir. The Ahmadi leaders immediately sought help from the Alliance for Religious Freedom, an enemy of the enemy. The group they went to for help in times of trouble and secretly loathed behind their back.

All religious groups in the alliance had a cause they wanted to pursue. The illegal foreclosure of churches, the government's refusal to acknowledge indigenous religions, the criminalization of unorthodox interpretations of existing religions.

The alliance agreed that they must do something and do it together. The country was on the verge of losing its status as a model for religious tolerance. They all agreed that everyone was at risk of becoming the victim. The Sunnis could accuse the Shiites of blasphemy and use it as pretext for attack. The Catholics could put a Mormon to prison saying that their interpretation of the Bible offended them. Those observing minority religions could be forced to leave their faith and adopt an officially recognized religion. Before long everyone would be at war with each other.

They all agreed that the old Blasphemy Law must be repealed. So too must the decree which complicated the building of houses of worship. And so they set a date, June 1, 2008. The anniversary of Indonesia's national symbol Pancasila. The motto 'Unity in Diversity'. They planned on rallying on Pancasila Day. They would gather at the National Monument complex in Jakarta and paraded their way to the Presidential State Palace a few hundred meters away.

Only a handful of Ahmadis showed up to participate in the rally, mostly common congregation goers who stayed on the sideline. The Ahmadi leaders opted out, saying that rallies were against their creed of obeying the government. They simply assigned several people to show up just so that other alliance members saw that they supported the rally in spirit. The alliance was broken. Some religious groups couldn't believe the Ahmadiyya leaders deserted them.

It was the Ahmadis who pay the heftiest of price for abandoning their peers. An anti-Ahmadiyya group attacked the rally. Their allies were hurt. Police arrested the attackers. But to appease the hard-liners, they handed down lenient sentences. A slap on the wrist. At the same time, they issued a decree on June 9, 2008 banning Ahmadiyya from proselytizing their religion.

Although the decree also specifically barred anti-Ahmadiyya groups from attacking Ahmadis, it paved the way for numerous attacks on the community. A gathering of a few Ahmadis could be seen as proselytizing. A refurbishment of an Ahmadiyya mosque seen as provocations. The hard-liners interpreted the decree however they see fit. Using it as a pretext for attack. Police did nothing, laying all the blame on the Ahmadis and let the attackers walked free. Before long there would be more harassment.

The attackers were emboldened by police's permissiveness. It would be time before it came to Lombok once more.

CHAPTER 30

The government officials came one morning carrying a folder filled with letters and documents, pointing their fingers to various corners of Transito's yard.

Nasipudin could only watch as the officials argued amongst themselves as they flipped through the pages of the documents they were carrying. Nasipudin tried to make sense what they were talking about. Eventually he discovered that the men were from the provincial office of the General Elections Committee. By the look of things, they were going to set up a ballot right there in Transito's front yard.

These facts must have made Nasipudin even more confused. He tried to comprehend what was happening but it just didn't make sense to him. The West Nusa Tenggara gubernatorial election was coming up and the government wanted to build a ballot in Transito. The government wanted the Ahmadis to vote and at the same time disallowed them to build a home. Banned them from worshiping in public. The government wanted the Ahmadis to exercise their right to vote but not their right to religious freedom.

From their comfortable homes far away, the Ahmadi leaders came. As soon as their cars stop, the leaders greeted the officials. There were introduction and there were hand shakes. There were chit chats and there were smiles. There were jokes and there were laughs. There were pats in the back. There were thumbs held up shoulder height pointing upwards.

The leaders explained the officials about the refugees' condition. Acting like the leaders themselves were spending cold nights and hot days, choking asbestos in the decaying Transito. The leaders explained the refugees' mental state as if their houses were also burned and looted. The leaders told of the refugees' health as if they spent hours and days talking to people from various agencies while their family members lied sick and dying just for a piece of letter stating they were too poor to pay the medical bills.

It had been years since the refugees lived in limbo and the leaders could have at least asked the officials before them, what was to become of those still living in Transito. Whether their votes would guarantee the fulfillment of their other rights. The right to live from fear. The right to practice their faith. The right for education. Access to health.

The leaders said nothing but a welcome for the officials to build a ballot in Transito's yard. The leaders promised that their followers would gladly support the election and participate. They explained that one of the Ahmadiyya's main creeds was obedience to the government. To obey means to follow, means to do what is told without resistance or so much as a question.

Soon the campaign pamphlets were put up on the walls. Bearing faces of the candidates who wouldn't set foot to Transito and meet them, let alone ask them their hopes and wishes should they be elected.

One was a lawmaker, Zainul Majdi, the grandson of the most revered cleric in the whole of Lombok. The grandson of the founder of Lombok's biggest Muslim organization, Nahdlatul Wathan. A young and handsome man with a conservative view, looking to preserve his grandfather's anti-Ahmadiyya rhetoric. His rival was Zainy Arony, a businessman with equally harsh anti-Ahmadiyya stance.

Soon the campaign T-shirts were handed out. The voters' cards distributed. The banners erected. The ballot boxes transported. The tent set up. The tables and chairs were arranged. The refugees' names were called. The ballot paper punctured, folded, inserted to the ballot box and finally tallied.

A new governor had been elected: Zainul Majdi, the grandson of the great cleric looking to set a name for himself. Those spreading hateful message against Ahmadiyya. Those instilling fear and hatred. Those provoking people to commit violence. To drive their own neighbors and kin away from their homes. Had an ally in the province's top post.

A year later, there was another election. The president whose administration issued an anti-Ahmadiyya decree. The president who made it more difficult for religious minority groups to build houses of worship. The president who looked the other way when the Ahmadis were attacked. The president who was too scared to prosecute the attackers and ensure justice to the victims. The president who called the hardliners and the intolerants 'partners of the state.' Got reelected. A sign that nothing would change.

***

It was their fourth year in Transito. Eight years had passed since they were driven from their land in East Lombok. The number of refugees ballooned and deflated. Sulaeman, the man from North Sumatra. The man who was married to the daughter of one of Pancor's wealthiest Ahmadis, Mahmuludin. The man whose wife's aunty was married to Nasipudin's uncle. The man who had the biggest shop in Pancor's main market, lost a daughter. Not by death. But by leaving her religion.

The daughter asked her father's permission to marry the man she loved, just days after finishing high school. A non-Ahmadi boy, who said that he had landed work in Bali and planned to take Sulaeman's daughter with him and start a family together.

Sulaeman was heart broken. As if he had failed as a father. He tried to dissuade his daughter not to leave Ahmadiyya. He tried talking to the boy, explaining Ahmadiyya, the signs of impending Armageddon, the promise of salvation for the followers of the Messiah. To no avail. The boy was not interested. In fact showing his contempt towards Sulaeman's explanation of his religion.

Was it because they were poor, Sulaeman must have asked his daughter. Was it because they could not afford to leave Transito? Was it because they once had a normal life? Was it because he was too old to work? Was it because he couldn't buy the things she needed to have? Were Ahmadi men not good enough for her?

Sulaeman's questions went unanswered. So he quizzed her again.

Was it because she was tired of living in Transito? Was it because she was tired of being an Ahmadi? Being persecuted? Being discriminated against? Being taunted at school? Does fitting in more important than God? Does a house worth more than salvation? Does love more important than family?

No response was garnered. So he expressed his feelings.

'I am sad. I am sad we will not be together in heaven.'

No one knew what they later said. The words spoken were too painful for Sulaeman to remember. But everyone recalled what happened next. A daughter kissed her father goodbye. Sulaeman was too devastated to attend his daughter's own wedding. Sulaeman was never his cheerful, vivacious self. Spending days and weeks and months weeping.

Like all his friends, Nasipudin tried to cheer him up. Talking about other things. Distracting him from the pain. But no word or deed could offer Sulaeman comfort. Nasipudin, as sincere as his intention may be, could never understand what Sulaeman felt. Nasipudin was starting to sound like their leaders. Telling Sulaeman to be patient.

Nasipudin's words of empathy must have felt like insults to his wounds. Indeed Sulaeman was jealous of Nasipudin. Nine children and not a single one abandoned their faith. Sulaeman had four and now only three shared the same religion.

What was Nasipudin's secret, Sulaeman probably wondered. Khaerudin married an Ahmadi woman. Nurul twice married Ahmadi men. Faizah successfully made Guntur converted and devoted his live to Ahmadiyya. Even the womanizing Suhaidi managed to stay an Ahmadi.

Why can't his daughter be like Masitah, Sulaeman must have thought? Nasipudin's fifth child was also desperate to get out of Transito but she asked the clerics to find an Ahmadi man for her.

And now, Masitah and her husband Muhtarom returned from Kalimantan, this time with a two year old child. She couldn't stand living in a village in the middle of nowhere, surrounded with thick forests and wildlife. She missed her family and her family missed her.

But there were worries where the family would sleep. Transito was not getting any bigger but children were being born and matured and starting families of their own. The only solution was for those who could afford not to live in Transito to move out.

Faizah volunteered. Her sister Nurul had been living in Ketapang for more than three years, without hassle or intimidation. Nurul had paved the way for more families to fix their homes and moved. First two and then five.

Faizah thought that maybe she too should move to Ketapang. In Transito she had been calling an old storage barely two meters wide and two and a half meter long her home. The room barely fit her, her husband and their seven-year-old and three-year-old sons. They couldn't afford to buy furniture because there was no room to store them.

She had to keep all their clothes in an old suitcase. Overtime the suitcase was starting to decay. Wetted from the dripping rains leaking through the roof. Holed from roaches and bugs. Her kapok mattress too was starting to worn off. Slowly crumbling from the cold, dirty, humid floor on which it laid. The air in the room was becoming more and more suffocating. Inside was where she kept their wet laundries, their plates and dishes, their cooking utensils, her son's school uniforms and books.

It was almost impossible for Masitah to stay with their parents too. Their makeshift room was only three by four meter, divided into three sections, one for Nasipudin, Zubaidah and their disabled daughter Nisa. On the opposite side of the room were Safir and Kasafuloh. They were getting bigger and needed more space of their own. Safir was in the ninth grade and was on his way to become a tall and handsome man. Kasafuloh was in the sixth grade and was tall for his age too.

Masitah and her husband slept in the living room. Storing their mattress in the morning to make room from praying and people's access before unstoring it again at night.

'Be patient, Tah,' said Faizah to her sister Masitah. 'I'm moving out soon. Then you can have my room.'

Faizah said that their leaders had given permission for more families to refurbish their homes in Ketapang. She told Masitah that Suhaidi had sold what was left of his property to Nurul, in exchange for absolving the debt Suhaidi owed to Nurul long ago. It took Suhaidi six years to repay his debt. The money he borrowed from Nurul by telling her he needed cash to find work in Malaysia. The money that was instead used by Suhaidi to buy himself a motorbike. The money Nurul earned by working so hard she had to lose her pregnancy.

Faizah had no money to pay Nurul. But Nurul was so happy that her sister was going to live next door to her. Nurul was so happy that it was the more trustworthy and hardworking Faizah that owed her money instead of the unreliable Suhaidi.

Faizah came to Ketapang as often as she could. Uprooting the weed which had encroached the entire floor. By noon, Guntur came from a half day renting his motorcycle to customers at the market. He came carrying tools, shovels, crowbars, brushes, brooms. Sometimes pick up trucks hauling cement, new wood beams, window frames and corrugated metal roof came with him.

A roof was erected. The missing tiles were proved to be hard to match. Replaced with the ones a shade off in color from ones that were still intact. They brought buckets of paint. She painted the entire wall pink, her favorite color. They bought faux-leather couches. It was also pink. She planted pink roses on the front lawn. She bought pink mattresses and pink carpet. It was unique. It was small. It was lovely. It was the house of her dream.

It was August 2010 and Masitah was pregnant with her second child. She was happy that she would have a child of her own. And Faizah divulged another reason for Masitah to celebrate. She was moving out and Masitah and her family would have a room of their own.

CHAPTER 31

Malik couldn't stop staring at his own reflection. He looked good in his security guard uniform. He was taller in his thick-soled, black boots. He strapped the boots tightly, snuggled perfectly on his lower legs, right down to his ankles. Toes reinforced with quarter domes of metal.

Above the boots were loose fitting trousers made of cotton with oversized pockets. The top half of his uniform made him look sturdier with its cut complementing his broad shoulder. The uniform was in dark blue adorned with badges which provided some colors. A brass pin sat on top of his front left pocket.

He looked sharp. He looked like someone of authority, particularly when he put on his cotton cap, hiding his droopy eyes in the shadows. Occasionally he smiled at his own reflection. A set of white pearly teeth were sitting behind his thick lips.

At 19 years of age, he felt like this was where he belonged. His place in the world. Doing something which he felt he was good at. The pay was lousy and the hours were long. But he liked being a security guard. He even enjoyed the one month training filled with intense physical regime. Enjoyed having his trainers barking at him.

He may have even forgotten his initial dream of becoming an Ahmadiyya cleric. The Mubarak campus, where Ahmadiyya clerics were rigorously trained, was not accepting fresh intakes for at least another year. So when he graduated from high school in July 2010, he came to Jakarta in look for work.

He followed a friend which he met while he was at an Ahmadiyya boarding school in Tasikmalaya. The friend was from Tangerang, a city on the fringes of Jakarta, a city where his sister Nurul used to work. The friend also dreamed of becoming an Ahmadi cleric and with Malik not wanting to be a burden for his family back home in Mataram, he asked if he could tag along.

And so he called his parents asking permission to go straight to Jakarta the day he graduated from high school. It cost next to nothing to get from Tasikmalaya to Jakarta compared to going back to Lombok. So his parents gave permission.

Once in Tangerang he and his friend enrolled at a security company. Only Malik got accepted. His trainers were impressed with him. He had the right physique. He had the right psychological profile. Malik was good at following orders. He had initiatives. He was a natural fit.

After the one month training his company assigned him to a shopping mall in the northern part of Jakarta called Mangga Dua, Indonesia's own electronic Mecca. It was filled with the latest gadgets and gizmos fresh from container ships harboring at Jakarta bay just a few kilometers away.

Mangga Dua was where retailers got their merchandise. It was where everyday users came to buy computers, phones, televisions at a bargain. It was where thousands of people flocked everyday. It was where billions of rupiah changed hands. It was the kind of place which attracted tricksters and pickpocketers.

Malik immediately made an impression with his boss in Mangga Dua. He was never late. Never called in sick. Never complained. He was responsive. He delivered all the tasks his boss set him out to do. He was able to be friendly to the customers. Helping them navigate through the maze of shops and blocks and floors. But he was also able to be firm to those looking for trouble. Stop contrabands from entering the building. Stop customers from parking at the wrong spot. Stop quarrels between store clerks and owners. Stop thieves, shoplifters and pickpocketers.

Three months into his job, Malik became the most promising guard in his batch. His boss loved him and thought highly of him, believing he would rise up the ranks and maybe someday take over and become a security boss on his own.

It was until his boss spotted a keychain hooked to Malik's bag. It had the image of fourteen stars circling an Arabic alphabet saying 'There is no God but Allah.' Fourteen stars was an Ahmadiyya symbol. Signifying the Messiah's revelation which occurred fourteen lunar centuries after the birth of Islam.

'Malik…Is this yours?'

'Yes sir. Anything wrong?'

'This is an Ahmadiyya symbol.'

'Yes.'

'So you're an Ahmadiyya?'

'Yes'

Malik could have lied and that would free him from the hassles at work. He could say that he was a mainstream Muslim and secretly practice the teachings of the Messiah, secretly obeying his caliph, his emir, his leaders.

But what was there to be ashamed of? He was indeed an Ahmadi. And he was proud of it. The follower of the promised Imam Mahdi. He was prepared for the consequences here on Earth for he believed greater rewards shall come to him in the afterlife. He had nothing to hide for he believed his religion teaches nothing but kindness. Despite what anyone else might say.

Malik's boss was stunned. Looking down on his most favorite pupil like he was not human. The blasphemer was upon him. A follower of the man who claimed to have received a direct revelation from God. Revelation was reserved for the prophets. And the last of God's messenger was Muhammad. Before him was a man whose religion was deemed deviant. Deserving of attack. Deserving to be treated as filth.

Malik could see the changes in his boss's expression. He understood why his boss reacted the way he did. He knew nothing of Ahmadiyya than what the hateful clerics had told him. Years of indoctrination made that notion went unchallenged. He was trained that what the Ahmadis said about their religion were lies. And so eyes no longer see. Ears no longer hear. Heads no longer think.

Irrational thing, faith is. Governed only by one's conviction. But what is man compared to the wonders of the universe? The glory of God's creation? What is man to define God? What is man to defy His will?

At 19 years of age, Malik could empathize what his boss was feeling. If someone had come to him and said that his Messiah was a fraud, he would be offended too. If someone had told him that everything that his father, his mother, his brothers and sisters, his clerics had taught was false, he would be outraged.

But what separated the 19-year-old from his boss, who was at least twice his age, was what they did next. Malik reminded himself to be patient. To be professional. Never to let his emotions, or the differences he had with his boss distracted him from his duties. From time to time he prayed for acceptance. For God to open the hearts and minds of his boss and his colleagues.

The boss reacted differently. Determined to kick Malik out. But with no professional excuse to fire him, he made Malik's days at the shopping mall more difficult. Malik would get the least desirable of work. He forced him to take shifts no one else wanted. Man the floors no one else touched.

It was Ramadan. The Muslim fasting month. Malik had not had a sip of water since dawn. It was two hours passed since he was supposed to end his shift did his colleague finally came and relieved him of his duties. Two hours since he was supposed to break his fast. This happened everyday during Ramadan.

Finally he quitted. He didn't mind the hassles. He didn't mind the discrimination. He had been getting them since he was a kid. But Malik felt sorry that people around him felt so uneasy with his presence he thought it was best to back away and find a more welcoming workplace.

At an Ahmadiyya mosque in West Jakarta, he gave his mother a call, explaining what had happened. A son was on his way back home to Mataram. To be with his family.

***

It was like the hardliners were competing with each other to see who could carry out the most number of attacks against Ahmadiyya. The local governments too were competing as to which province, which district, which city could be the first to enforce the anti-Ahmadiyya decree, passed a little over two years ago.

The decree stipulated that Ahmadiyya must not teach interpretations of Islam which are not accepted by the mainstream. It was an instruction which the Ahmadis felt they have always obeyed. Nothing than what was inscribed in the Koran and what was taught by Prophet Muhammad was being propagated by the Ahmadis to his followers, the congregation argued, something which non-Ahmadis greatly disputed.

Another article banned Ahmadiyya from proselytizing their teachings. It was as things unraveled, a pretext to further violence. A Pandora box had been opened sending chaos across the country. Everyone had their own interpretation of the decree. A mass prayer could be seen as an act of proselytization. So did the refurbishing of a mosque. So did the sending of Ahmadi children to an Ahmadiyya boarding school. So did a handful of Ahmadis banding together to discuss religion.

The Ahmadis tried to keep a low profile. But the hard-liners always find an excuse to attack them. In August 2010, an Ahmadiyya mosque in Manis Lor, West Java was told to seize all activities with local officials ready to seal the mosque shut. The officials were aided by a group of hard-liners standing just a few meters away. An instruction had come from the Ahmadi leaders in Jakarta, to resist the foreclosure but avoid bloodshed at all cost. A clash ensued. But with the threat of violence lurking they decided to back down.

Two months later, Cisalada, a West Java village where 600 Ahmadis lived was attacked. Their homes were torched and looted while their mosque was burned to the ground. A few weeks after the boarding school in Tasikmalaya were shut down with the students locked inside.

30 Ahmadiyya mosques were closed that year. 50 Ahmadi communities were attacked. And across the country there were more than 200 religiously charged attacks, victimizing all kinds of religious minority groups.

The government did nothing, too afraid to stand up against the hard-liners. Too scared to ensure justice for the victims who were instead jailed for provoking violence by doing nothing but demanding their right to practice their religion in peace. To build houses of God.

It attracted pressure from the international community. But the indecisive president chose to do nothing to stop the hardliners from getting what they wanted.

The hard-liners were banding with retired military generals. Generals who were demanding for seats in the government. The hard-liners wanted a full ban on Ahmadiyya. They wanted to stop churches from being built. They wanted no other form of Islam to flourish in Indonesia aside from their orthodox Sunni views. The generals meanwhile sought power. To topple the president or at least have him hand them out several strategic posts.

To break these subversive, dangerous bonds the government quickly sided with the hard-liners. Giving them what they wanted. Across the country decrees after decrees were being issued. The religious affairs office was told not to recognize Ahmadi weddings. Civil servants told not to list Ahmadis as Muslims on their identification cards. Bodies of dead Ahmadis were being unearthed from Muslim burial grounds. Ahmadi children were being barred from participating in their schools' Islamic classes and festivities.

In West Lombok, a decree was enacted. Ahmadiyya was a banned religion. Spurred by a recent event, the wave of Ahmadis returning to Ketapang. The demand of some 14 Ahmadis for the Lingsar subdistrict government to issue them identification cards.

There were secret meetings. There were hate speeches made in sermons. There were rumors of attacks. Ketapang was about to become the scene of another violence.

CHAPTER 32

The day was November 26, 2010 and the leaders came telling the Ahmadis to leave Ketapang except for ten Ahmadi men tasked to guard the complex. A rumor of a likely attack had been circulating for days. Faizah immediately went with her husband and children to Transito, seeking refuge. Her brave sister Nurul however refused to leave.

'It is not safe,' one of the leaders said.

'No, I want to stay.'

'Are you defying the words of your leaders?'

Nurul stared deep at the leaders' eyes. This was her home. A house she had painstakingly built with her two hands. A house that was destroyed in 2006. A house she had restored little by little. A house she had been living for the last four years without any incident. She was not ready to part with her home. She was not ready to watch her dream went up in flames once more. She would give up everything not to let that happen. Even her own life.

The ten men came from Transito while the leaders fled to the safety of their homes. Among those tasked to guarding Ketapang were Khaerudin, Suhaidi and Masitah's husband Muhtarom. Khaerudin asked her little sister to retreat to a safer place promising that she would be allowed to stay.

'Suhaidi and Basir will stay here. The rest of us will stay and watch in the distance over there. That way we'll get greater vantage point to monitor what is going on.' Khaerudin said pointing to a hill less than a kilometer away.

Before they parted Suhaidi must have grabbed Khaerudin by the arm. 'Don't let Malik know about this.'

Khaerudin promised not to. He promised to lie and tell Malik nothing happened in case Malik called and asked if he should come to Ketapang and help them fight. In fact, Suhaidi told all of his family back in Transito to downplay the attack in front of Malik.

Malik was a smart boy. Suhaidi thought he was the family's best hope for a decent life. The family member who was likely to succeed in life. Suhaidi cared so much for his little brother he vowed to keep him safe from harm, no matter how keen he was to help.

Suhaidi knew that had Malik known another attack was about to happen, Malik would come to Ketapang in a heartbeat. Abandoning his work as a fritters vendor in downtown Mataram. It happened last time. The instant news reached to him of a planned attack he quickly closed his stall, asked permission from his boss and rushed to Ketapang.

This time no one told Malik anything. Suhaidi lied and told Malik that this attack was just rumors no one should take seriously.

The men escorted Nurul up to their hiding spot. They traveled down the slope into a small creek next to the last house in the entire Ahmadiyya neighborhood. They jumped over the stream and picked themselves up to the slope and onto a slippery, small dirt path which led to the other side of the village. Near the main road. Near the holiday homes of the rich. Shaded by tall trees and thick shrubs, they waited. They have reached their spot.

Suhaidi and Basir hid inside Faizah's pink house. The house was about center in the neighborhood allowing them good access to anticipate attacks from either side of the complex. They shut the door and kept the house dark, creating the impression that the whole complex was deserted. Their only eyes and ears were their friends waiting from afar.

From the distance the men could see that police were not coming despite plea for them to guard Ketapang. There was no police truck filled with heavily armed officers like in 2006. In fact there was only one police car spotted, stopping in front of the village's mosque. It seemed like people were gathering inside the mosque. There were people in public servants' safaris attending the meeting too.

***

The clouds hung close to the ground, overshadowing the entire neighborhood making the colors mute. If it were in the summer their wait would be unbearable. Their bodies drenched in sweat. They could be dehydrating. But still, at the start of the wet season they sweated. The agony uncertainty brings took its toll on their bodies' metabolism.

Alas some movement. The men got up from their seats to take a better look. A car was seen driving out of the mosque and headed to the main road. It looked like the car the government officials were using, passing by the neighborhood and quickly escaped from view.

Immediately the men sent a text message to Suhaidi. The government officials had left.

'Well that's good news isn't it?' Basir said. 'The car left so maybe today nothing will happen.'

Basir and Suhaidi felt somewhat at ease. Chatting and joking but cautious not to attract attention.

***

Half an hour later there was another text message in Suhaidi's phone. Before he got a chance to read it, Khaerudin called.

'There's smoke coming out from somewhere and there are a lot people.'

Suhaidi immediately got out of Faizah's house and saw that the old man Mahmuludin's house was on fire. There were around 80 people descending upon the neighborhood and at least 20 people were inside Mahmuludin's house poking the roof and smashing everything they could with bamboo poles, sticks and rocks. The rest were starting to attack other houses.

Suhaidi immediately ran towards Mahmuludin's home, armed with a plank of wood and a loud roar. It must have been confusion. The attackers must have been teenagers out looking to do some vandalism for the sake of fun. But they ran at the sight of the wood-wielding Suhaidi fast approaching them. Furiously roaring like a man possessed and deranged.

For a second, Nurul watched some attackers pelting rocks at her house and became hysterical. She was angry and wanted to chase down the teenagers herself. The men struggled to keep her at bay.

Suhaidi chased down the attackers. Inside Mahmuludin's house the youth immediately dropped whatever they were doing and ran for their lives. Suhaidi immediately turned his attention to the ones attacking the rest of the neighborhood from the rear. They too ran with all their might like being chased by a mighty beast of prey.

They had every reason to be afraid. Suhaidi was brave and most of all he was desperate and had nothing to lose. Even alone he was no less deadly. Who knew what would happen if Suhaidi caught just one of them? Perhaps he would do something violent. Perhaps the kid could break a leg or two or even worse die.

Suhaidi, it seemed, didn't care. He didn't care if he died in the process. It would only make him a martyr, he must have thought. A glorious death deserving of praises and admiration. Something he had sought for so long. An act which would erase all sins and grant him immediate access to heaven. Even as the attackers ran away, Suhaidi continued to chase them. Like a man thirsty for blood.

'Stop,' Basir yelled at Suhaidi. 'Enough,' he said as he struggled to keep up with Suhaidi.

Basir was only interested in keep Suhaidi on a leash. Never pointing the wooden plank in his hand towards the attackers. Never ran to chase down them either. He didn't share the same bloodlust as his friend. No adrenaline to boost his running.

'We have to do something about the fire.'

Suhaidi stopped but couldn't keep his eyes away from the fleeing teenagers, like a lion watching its prey slipped between its claws. He gathered his composure letting his head taking over from the emotions running inside.

'C'mon… The fire,' Basir yelled again.

Suhaidi ran towards Basir and together they took out the burning tires from inside the house. Suhaidi went to the well to fetch water but the line has been cut and the bucket was floating at the bottom, 13 meters deep.

'Keep your eyes open,' Suhaidi told Basir as he scaled down the slippery walls of the well, passing down water to Basir who was waiting above. The fire had not raged beyond the point where it was out of control. The thick smoke was coming from the burning tires instead of the house. Before long the fire died. The second it did, Suhaidi thought of chasing down the attackers again.

'No, it's too dangerous. What for anyway?' Basir said.

***

By the time the rest of the Ahmadi men came the attackers were regrouping in the distance. Some rearmed themselves with rocks, readying themselves to strike again.

Two cars came and the teenagers in the distance cheered. The cars were driving slowly at walking speed. Behind them was a mob perhaps of 400 strong. The teenagers joined the group of machete and pole-wielding crowd.

Khaerudin gave an instruction to pull back. Violence was imminent. If they had stayed blood would spill. Their houses were beyond saving. Retreated they did. Nurul was struggling and struggling as the men pulled her to safety. Pulled her away from what was certain to be the scene of another attack.

As the mob were meters away from the Ahmadiyya neighborhood, the cars stopped and the crowd began to swarm into the complex. Burning, hitting, smashing and pelting rocks at every inch of people's home.

They saw the crowd poking at people's roofs. Swaying them back and forth until the roofs collapsed. There were loud cheers each time they succeeded. Overtime the mob grew larger. Perhaps close to one thousand. From a distance they could see a woman with a child on one arm and a rock in the other running barefoot just to smash their windows.

Nurul cried, begging the attack to stop. Shouting uncontrollably as if the attackers were to listen let alone obey. Khaerudin grabbed his sister. A few more did the same. Trying hard to stop Nurul from running to the scene and get herself killed.

Faizah's home was swarmed. Its bright pink color made the house stood out, making it the more likely target for people to lash out their inner beasts.

Soon it was Nurul's house's turn. The muscles on Nurul's legs seemed to lose their strength. She tumbled to the ground with her mouth gasping for air. She was confused, unable to comprehend what she ever did to those ransacking her house. Eyes fixated on the bricks she had tirelessly built one by one.

***

'Everything is gone,' so Faizah was told by everyone around her. The ransacking on Ketapang continued for days. From time to time, there would be a group of people coming to the neighborhood to put more holes on the walls or to steal whatever they could lay their hands on.

'Even the door hinges, clothe hangers, cheap plastic clocks,' people continued. There were police guarding the scene of attack but they were there to stop the Ahmadis from coming back and not to prevent more looting. 'Even they took the plants, the vegetables and fruits that we have grown.'

'I have to see it,' Faizah told her husband. 'I have to see our house.'

Faizah and Guntur borrowed a motorbike from a friend and rode all the way from Transito to Ketapang. Racing in her mind was all kinds of thoughts. 'Why?' she asked herself. 'What did we do to deserve this?'

It was the first house they ever owned. She remembered how sweat ran on her forehead when she patched up the holes on the walls. How sweat soaked her clothes when she replaced the missing tiles, taking out the wild grasses and weeds encroaching the floor. She remembered coloring it pink, her favorite color. She remembered they needed to hire labor to finish the roof. Her husband selling off their motorbike just to raise enough money to complete the house.

She remembered she was so happy she invited everyone. Everyone in Ketapang came. Ahmadis and non-Ahmadis sitting under one roof, hers. She remembered how they feasted on the food she had prepared. Eating from her plates. From her spoons and forks.

'Why?' she thought. 'Why?'

The second they got to Ketapang four officers guarding the scene immediately approached her.

'I want to see my house,' Faizah said as one of the officers tried to stop her.

'I want to see my house,' she said once more. Her voice grew louder. From a distance she could see her pink house was reduced to rubbles. Her entire roof had been toppled outwards to the back of the house.

'Let me go! I want to see my house,' Faizah screamed. Tears started rolling from her eyes.

The officer tried to push her back using his arm resting on her chest. 'I'm a woman. Don't push me.'

The officer was ashamed at what he had just done. Faizah was right. She was a woman. A woman who had lost everything.

'But it is not safe.'

'This is my house. The house that I built from nothing. The house you vowed to protect.'

Finally the three other police officers came and agreed to escort Faizah to take a quick glimpse at her home. She got her wish and it made her even sadder inside. Sad to learn that there was nothing left of her house. Just pink rubbles of her dreams and memories.

The attackers had taken her furniture. Her cupboard full of clothes. Her television set. Her mattress where her boys used to sleep and play and studied and did their homework. Her sons' favorite toys. Even her garden lied in ruins. Her flowers uprooted and stomped. Her chicken were stolen. Her Koran being defecated.

She got what she came to do in Ketapang. A confirmation to the news she had heard back in Transito. With a broken heart she returned to Transito. Masitah was kind enough to lend her room. But Faizah refused her offer. Masitah had another baby boy born just four days before the attack. It was supposed to be a time for joy.

***

That night Faizah and Guntur had a private talk. They had no money. Guntur had no job. They had no house.

'What if we build our own home again? I mean we can gather enough money....'

Before Faizah could finish her sentence Guntur interrupted.

'If there is no security from the government, what for?'

'Then what do we do? I can go back to the market.'

'No. We were driven away from the market. You said it was too painful for you to go there.'

'I can try. I mean my parents are working there. It can't be that bad.'

'I'll find a way. I'll ask my family if there's work. Maybe my uncle. He sends construction workers to Malaysia.'

'But you hate construction work. And... Malaysia? We won't be seeing each other.'

'They paid well in Malaysia. This way I can raise money fast. Before you even miss me I'll be back.'

And so Guntur went. Faizah was left to care for her boys on her own. She kept herself busy by taking Azmi to school along with her three-year-old son Barahin. But at night, when her boys were fast asleep, she wept. Longing for the man she loved. The man who had been beside her three attacks in a row.

She wondered how he coped with the hard life of a laborer. In a foreign land far away from home. Out on his own with no one to care for him if he got sick.

Nurul too could not accept her fate. 'Why?' she must have wondered. All this time in Ketapang she was nothing but nice to her neighbors. But they were the ones who robbed her of her home. Forcing her into life as a refugee once more.

***

With Ketapang families suddenly returning back to Transito, everyone was fighting for space, Nurul and Faizah were no exception. Faizah had to share a room with her mother. Nurul had to convert an extra bathroom in Transito into a room for his elderly husband and their adopted child Sultan. On the tiled floor and tiled walls she laid a piece of plywood to stop the cold. Lying on top of it was a plastic mat. The final layer was a kapok mattress where everyone would sleep. She covered the toilet with more plywood, converting the section into a cupboard. The water container normally used for people to bathe themselves was used as storage.

Nasipudin could probably feel his daughters' anguish. Their angers at those attacking them. So he called them. Asked the sisters to meet him at Transito's front yard after dark where they could talk in private.

'A lot has happened to this family. Don't you think?' Nasipudin must have asked her daughters.

The sisters were quiet. Their father usually called family members for a private talk if they were in trouble. But not this time.

'You remember Pancor don't you? Do you remember before we built our house? Do you remember the small wooden shed out in the middle of a rice field?' Nasipudin would've likely continued. 'Nurul must have remembered this. You were old enough to remember weren't you?'

'I remember dad,' Faizah said. 'I was old enough to remember too.'

'You know that permanent home in Pancor. I never asked for it. Our family… we were just peasants. We never owned a property. I never dreamed of it. How could I? I just worked hard, stay honest, did what I think was right, avoid what our religion says is wrong. And through some grace from God… God showed me a way. Beyond my wildest dream, my distant uncle gave me a plot of land. Beyond my expectation we met a nice couple, the Marwans.'

Nurul and Faizah just listened, unsure what their father was trying to say.

'When our homes in Pancor got destroyed, you know what I said? I said 'so be it. This home was never mine. God was gracious enough to bless me with one and He could easily take it all away. God has reclaimed what had always been His.' Our real homes are in the afterlife. Be it in heaven, in hell, it all depends on our deeds here on Earth. What good do grudges bring? Resentment? Desperation? Vengeance? Do our homes here on Earth mean more than the ones in the afterlife? Does being together here on Earth matter more than being together in heaven?'

Nurul and Faizah smiled as if ill thoughts and feelings never nestled in their hearts and minds. The three hugged. Telling each other how much they loved them.

CHAPTER 33

The leaders came to Transito armed with a laptop computer. Inside was a video file of the most heinous of attack on the Ahmadiyya community in Indonesia. The content was graphic, but the leaders felt it was important that every adult in Transito should see it. The leaders' intention of showing the footage was unclear but not its impact on the refugees. It made them feel like they were more fortunate despite living like outcasts for five years.

The footage was of Cikeusik, a small village in a remote part of Banten, the westernmost province in the island of Java. It was taken on February 6, 2011. The day three Ahmadi youths were brutally killed. A mob of 1,000 strong was descending upon an Ahmadiyya missionary home guarded by a dozen Ahmadiyya youths from Jakarta and elsewhere.

The footage was taken by two Ahmadis posing as television journalists. They were careful not to reveal their identities. Careful not to betray any emotion as their friends were being butchered. Their friends were beaten to death. A man was bludgeoned in the head with a huge rock the size of a helmet while he was lying flat on his stomach helplessly on the ground.

Some refugees in Transito couldn't bear to keep watching. They only watched it because their leaders told them too.

The leaders must have thought that the gruesome attack could further embolden their followers to persevere and be patient. To the outside world they thought they had enough to build an argument for the government to repeal their anti-Ahmadiyya decree.

But what happened was the opposite. Politicians spun the event's significance for their own agendas and argued the need to push for a full ban on Ahmadiyya. Provinces and districts began enacting their own decrees. The military volunteered to assist the new decrees' implementation and launched 'operation prayer mat' to take over Ahmadiyya assets and create enough pressures and harassments that Ahmadis left their religion. Several wealthy donors pledged a huge sum for each Ahmadi willing to convert to 'the right form of Islam'.

Back in Lombok the government began formulating 'a final solution to the Ahmadiyya problem'. The West Lombok government suggested that the entire Ahmadiyya population in Lombok should be forced to relocate to an island, far off of Lombok's westernmost tip Sekotong. The governor thought it was a brilliant idea but halted its actual implementation because of logistics concern.

The wave of intolerance, the Lombok's government 'final solution' was enough for Muhtarom to feel that he and his wife Masitah and their two children should return to Kalimantan.

'Here we have no future,' he said. There were no hard-line groups in Kalimantan. The 50 Ahmadi men, women and children in Pangko lived so remotely there was little chance they would be attacked.

Muhtarom was a loud and fiery man. He spoke out everything what was inside his head. He didn't care that he would offend those who chose to stay in Transito.

'Sure it's remote. Sure it's in the middle of a jungle. But at least we will be safe. At least we have an oil palm field from which we can make money. Do you want to live as a refugee for the rest of your life?'

Before long Muhtarom and Masitah were on their way back to Central Kalimantan.

There was to be another goodbye. Malik had finally landed a scholarship from Mubarak campus just south of Jakarta. His dream of becoming an Ahmadiyya cleric was one step closer.

A family was separated once more. Its impetus was the same, another violent attack. Its incentive too was the same, the quest for a better life.

***

Separation did not sorrow Nasipudin. For Masitah and Malik called almost everyday, asking how their families were doing back in Mataram, catching up every single event which shaped their lives, no matter how miniscule. Sharing grievances no matter how trivial.

How he wished Safir would do the same. Safir was with him in Mataram but Nasipudin barely knew him. Safir was always busy doing things he would not say what, going out with friends he would not say who, to places he would not say where.

'Safir was just being a teenager,' Nasipudin must have hoped. Safir was in his first year of vocational school, still discovering what he wanted to do and who he wanted to be. For Nasipudin, he only wanted Safir to be a good Ahmadi like his older brothers Khaerudin and Malik. Finish his education, get a decent job, ask his clerics to have a prearranged marriage with an Ahmadi girl and have children.

But Safir had other ideas. 'Why can't I have some fun first?' he thought. 'Why can't I be an Ahmadi but still like music and art and girls?'

He didn't want to be like Suhaidi. As much as he looked up to his older brother, he didn't want to be 29 and married with three kids and still flirting with girls. He didn't want to live a carefree life with no steady job and no steady income. He didn't want to marry at 16 to his brother's sister-in-law like Suhaidi. He didn't want to be in the front line chasing after attackers. He didn't want to risk his life chasing a far fetch dream of living in a foreign land. Safir was 16 and he wanted to have some fun while he was young.

***

Safir caught the eyes of the prettiest girl in school. Her name was Fitri and she was very popular. All the boys at school had at one point tried to win her love. All except for Safir and this made Fitri curious.

'He's a player,' Fitri was told by girls closest to her. 'He will break your heart.'

Indeed, Safir had turned into a player who liked to break young girls' hearts. He once dated a girl who called him by mistake. The girl dialed the wrong number but ended up chatting with Safir. He was polite, his voice had a certain confidence which made girls felt comfortable, his words made you think he was to be trusted, his tone made you fall in love. The girl asked Safir to meet face to face and Safir gladly complied. She had two best friends which went along with the pair everywhere they went. Safir went out with the girl but cheated on her by dating her two best friends in secret. The three girls were best friends no more.

Safir's notoriety spread from one girl to the next from high school to high school. Before time it reached Fitri's ears. But this only made Fitri more curious. Thinking she could tame this bad boy.

Fitri was majoring in textile design and rarely shared the same classes as Safir who took graphic design. Fitri only knew Safir by name and by reputation and was never formally introduced. The prettiest girl in school was feeling insecure that Safir never even tried approaching her or at least introduce himself. So when they did share the same class together, Fitri made the first move.

'You're Safir aren't you?'

Safir just shook her hand without saying much.

'I heard you like to hang out in Udayana (a Mataram area). You know I go there often too. Maybe we'll meet and hang out together.'

The prettiest girl in school was asking for his number. His friends must have been jealous or perhaps even proud of Safir. Many have tried and failed to get the girl's number and now Fitri was asking for Safir's.

Safir only thought lightly of it. 'What does she want with me?' he thought. With a round face sitting on a boney posture he was not the best looking. He was poor and living in a refugee complex. He was a religious minority people hated. Safir never thought much about Fitri before and he thought 'why start now'.

But cruel is the teenagers' version of the game of love. Fitri never called. Safir went to Udayana almost every night and Fitri was never there. At school, Fitri never seemed to approach him again. She acted like they were strangers. Like she never asked Safir for his phone number. This made Safir couldn't stop thinking about Fitri. It drove him mad. Fitri had outwitted Safir. The player had just got played.

'Hey you never called me?' Safir got so tired of waiting he decided one morning to confront her.

'I'm sorry. I lost your number when I reset my phone. Here let me give you mine.'

It might have been what Fitri had always wanted. It was Safir's turn to chase after her.

The two began dating. Fitri was madly in love. Gladly staying hours after class just to wait for him. She let Safir ride her motorbike for he didn't have his own. In the morning, Safir would walk for a few hundred meters from Transito where Fitri would wait. They would ride together to school.

Safir was careful that his father did not know that he was seeing Fitri. His father would be furious if he knew Safir was dating a non-Ahmadi. He would even be furious if Safir dated at all. Ahmadis don't date, particularly those in the more conservative rural areas. 'A step away from adultery,' the Ahmadis would say. 'A step away from the big sin.'

Fitri was originally from East Java. Her father sent her to Mataram to live with her aunty so she could expand the family's business to Lombok. Fitri's family was in the cellular phone retail business. She would use the latest gadget before anyone else when she was in school.

Her family was wealthy and she often showered Safir with gifts. A cellular phone no member of his family could ever afford. No one in Transito perhaps. She texted. She sent pictures of herself holding up a piece of paper with the words 'Crazy over Safir' boldly written with markers.

After school, Fitri would tend the family's shop in Mataram's biggest shopping mall. When she graduated in 2013 she tended the shop full time.

With no money for college, Safir also worked. Landing a job at one of Mataram's biggest printing houses just before he graduated. He worked from 8 a.m. until 4 in the afternoon. Afterwards he would go to the mall and hung around at Fitri's shop waiting for her shift to be over.

They went everywhere together. The motorbike must have taken the young pair for thousands of kilometer over the years. Fitri never liked being home. 'My aunty wouldn't let me breathe,' she would often tell Safir. 'Take me with you. Anywhere… as long as I'm with you.'

Safir told his friends that it was never serious. Telling them what they wanted to hear when his friends warned him that they could never be together. Safir was an Ahmadi and Fitri was not. A union that was frown upon by both families.

'It was better than being alone,' he told his friends.

'Well… you found hell of a girl not to be alone with,' his friends told him. 'At least you got nice gifts. Oh… I see… Is that why you date her? Because she owns a cellphone shop? Brilliant.'

Safir just smiled and told them to stop when they suggested he should manipulate her into getting cellphones for the rest of them

But Safir was lying. He cared for Fitri. Staying by her side, semester after semester, even after they graduated from school. Not once had he flirted with another girl. They knew it was impossible for them to be together forever but the relationship somehow lasted. The two were inseparable. Fitri was too deeply in love with Safir. Before long Safir was starting to see no future without Fitri by his side.

CHAPTER 34

Nasipudin couldn't remember the last time he felt so happy. For the first time, his daughter Nurul gave birth to a baby girl. She was 36-years-old and she had been trying to get pregnant for the last 16 years of her life. It was like the weight of the world had been lifted off her chest. Finally the chatters behind her back could stop. Finally, she felt secure that her second marriage was not destined to doom like her first. A child was born. One that was coming out her own womb. She named her Nuril. Perhaps subconsciously she wanted a name that resembles her own. Her legacy to the world.

Nasipudin would most likely be overwhelmed with joy. He was seeing how the agony of not being able to produce a child was stressing Nurul out, consuming her health and sanity and happiness. He was worried about his daughter. And now he felt worry no more.

He played with Nuril as often as he could. He must have been teasing her by puffing his cheek and crossing his eyes. He carried her everywhere, like she was his most prized possession which needed to be flaunted to the world. He watched his baby granddaughter as she slept. Inspecting her every curve, her tiny fingers and toes, her fragile body, her deformed nose.

Nasipudin was obsessed with his granddaughter. The last piece of comfort God had blessed his family. It was the kind of comfort he wished would last. The kind of comfort which he hoped would accompany his family long after he was gone.

All this time he was worried about Nurul. About the weight of the world crushing her joy or worse her faith in God.

He was worried about Suhaidi. What would become of him if Nasipudin could no longer be with his family? For years, neighbors and friends had been bringing ill news about Suhaidi and his misadventure. 'Suhaidi had another wife,' they would say to him. 'He ran away, eloped with a young girl and abandoned her,' came some other news.

Suhaidi had also left a trail of debts. People would come to Transito looking to collect. Suhaidi chose to run away. He said he had found a job in Bayan, a town three hours drive north from Mataram. Nasipudin suspected Suhaidi was only hiding. Hiding from his responsibilities, from the people chasing after him.

He worried about Yuni, Suhaidi's eldest daughter. News of her father had started to take its toll on the young girl. She was 13. She had just entered junior high school a few months back. Her father was never there. Never fed her or clothed her. Never called to ask how she was doing. Or just to say how much he loved her.

Nasipudin thought about one day sending Yuni to college. She must be successful. Perhaps to reward her mother who was often cheated, who had patiently stood by her side. For her sister Hijwana.

But Suhaidi was always there when his family desperately needed him, Nasipudin must have thought. Suhaidi was always on the frontline. Nasipudin watched him courageously fending off attackers and protecting his friends and family. Nasipudin watched how Suhaidi passionately keeping Malik out of trouble. How he took care of the sick and accompanied them to the hospital, taking care of mountains of paper works because they couldn't afford to pay.

He thought about Safir. How he preferred to go out with his friends instead of being in Transito with his family. He was growing up. Like a baby bird learning to fly and ready to leave his nest, he must have thought. But at least Safir still made the time to pray together alongside his family. He only hoped he didn't wander far and continued to care for his younger brother Kasafuloh.

Kasafuloh was struggling at school but he was persistent. He studied hard despite his shortcomings. He had been a slow learner ever since the attack on Ketapang seven years ago. But success doesn't come to the smartest but to the most determined, he must have thought. Nasipudin was sure his last child would grow up to be a good man. A good Ahmadi.

'Seven years…' he would probably ask himself. 'Has it really been that long?'

He remembered the attack like it was yesterday. He remembered the first time he was told to live in Transito temporarily. He never thought he had to live there for seven years.

He remembered building his house from scratch. He remembered when it was still an empty plot of land. He remembered he had to sell his property back in Pancor, the home he last seen eleven years ago.

'Eleven years… My God.'

It has been eleven years since he was driven from the land of his birth. Eleven years since he had to live in limbo, struggling to get by. He thought about Pancor more and more. About his older brother Sarapudin. The only close kin who still called Pancor home.

Inside Nasipudin's mind were probably memories of how Sarapudin was kind enough to shelter his family while they were being attacked. Even though he was not an Ahmadi. Even though they might have had their differences. He missed him. He thought about their childhood. How they played together on the rice fields. Catching fireflies and playing hide and seek.

He thought about Sarapudin's children, Nasipudin's nieces and nephews whom he hardly saw. Would they still recognize him after all these years? They were not Ahmadis just like their father. But would they feel about Ahmadis the same way as their hard-line peers and firebrand clerics? Would his brother's children spill the blood of his children? Spill the blood of their cousins? Denounce their Ahmadi kin? Desecrate the grave of their Ahmadi grandfather?

'Father.' Nasipudin would probably call his deceased father, Nafsiah. He remembered the day his father died. He remembered his father's prophecy.

'In three days there will be chaos,' Nasipudin probably recounted the prophecy in his head. His father was right all along. Indeed, three days after the prophecy their lives were never the same. They were banished. Systematically persecuted. Driven from their land. Their every possession gone. Marginalized.

He must have wondered why. Who has to gain from all this bloodshed? Somebody has to. Otherwise why did they orchestrate such an elaborate ploy to oust them? With the exception of a few elites, everyone's lives were as miserable, perhaps worse than before.

The Ahmadis certainly didn't benefit. They lost everything. The weapon-wielding kids who attacked their houses... have they had their faith strengthened? Are they closer to heaven just like their clerics promised? Then why had God not blessed them with peace and joy here on Earth? Why had the mosques remained empty? Why do people have to stage communal Friday prayers at different mosques every week because there were fewer and fewer attendees?

The clerics seemed to profit from the attacks. They were feared more and more. Their houses got bigger and bigger from all the donations flowing from their devoted followers or some oil money flowing from the Middle East. They became more powerful. Their organizations grew rapidly and exponentially. In a rate they themselves could never had imagined. But then as they get bigger along came greed. Power struggles. Schisms. Their days were no longer filled with prayers. With propagation of God's words. Only the preservation of power. Of wealth.

The president who issued the anti-Ahmadiyya decree got reelected. The governors and district heads who implemented them got to sustain their power. The security officers who ignored the Ahmadis got promoted. At what cost? Religious tensions grew. Houses of worship were being destroyed. People were being driven from their homes. Christians weren't able to build churches in Muslim-majority communities without resistance and Muslims couldn't build mosques in Christian areas without objections.

The hard-liners the government desperately tried to please, managed to get what they wanted and soon asked for more. The Pentecostal Church who wouldn't wholeheartedly support the Batak Christian Church when their houses of worship were sealed had their churches sealed as well. The Buddhists who wouldn't speak up for the Christians' rights to practice their religion also had their temples attacked.

The Ahmadiyya Lahore Congregation who was quiet when their Ahmadiyya Qadian brothers were attacked was also banned by the government from proselytizing their version of Ahmadiyya. The Shiites who long joined the chorus of condemnation towards the Ahmadis also had a taste of what it was like to be outlawed and persecuted.

The political parties who claimed to be guarding people's moral code when they sought to ban Ahmadiyya turned out to be corrupt to the core. Siphoning taxpayers' hard earn money so they can control beef import, forest concession, land conversion. Awarding gold, copper and coal mining concessions to their cronies. After the military regime ended, they thought they could use politics to advance religious values. In the end, it was the other way around. It was religion which had been used to advance personal political ambitions.

And who had the right to say what the correct form of Islam is? Who said that Ahmadis and non-Ahmadis cannot live in peace? He had been working at the Bertais market and nothing happened. How weak did the clerics think their followers' faith was for them to say that Ahmadiyya had offended their religious interpretation of Islam? Or was it all a charade? Was there another agenda hidden behind layers and layers of excuses?

Nasipudin had entrusted his fate in the hands of God. He was thankful. The attacks had strengthened the bonds inside Nasipudin's family. They changed them. He thought about Khaerudin. He was a shy boy back in Pancor but eleven years later, he was an able leader. A caretaker for his family and his siblings. The cleric had even asked Khaerudin to live with him in his missionary home.

Amidst the attack, Faizah had found the love of her life. Malik was inspired to become a cleric. Masitah, as far away as she was, always remembered to call. She always took the time to ask about her sister Nisa whose muscular dystrophy had become so severe she may not have much to live. Masitah always took the time to chat with Kasafuloh, exciting his mind.

And now Nurul had her own child. Nasipudin couldn't be more delighted. More relieved. He was feeling like he had done all which he could do as a father. Like his tasks fulfilled.

He had been thinking about Pancor. Thinking about his old neighborhood Montong Gamang. Thinking about all of his relatives who were still there. It was days away from the holy month of Ramadan and he thought he should go there. He would visit everyone he knew. He wanted to know how they were doing. He wanted to spread a message of peace. A gesture to bridge whatever differences that they might had. An offering to erase the past and create a clean slate. A Koran for each mosque in the whole of Montong Gamang, whatever the creed, the group, the interpretation of Islam.

He asked Khaerudin to one day accompany him to Montong Gamang to ensure that such gesture was passed on from one generation to the next. Ramadan was around the corner. A time to erase all sins, rekindle old ties. Asking and offering forgiveness.

All sorts of things were running in Nasipudin's head, his children thought. He was acting strange. Strange things were coming out of his mouth. He wandered off, thinking, muttering words no one understood. He made funny faces and teased his grandchildren like he was a child himself. But there were nights when he got all serious, summoning everyone in his family for a sit down. Khaerudin, Nurul, Faizah and their mother Zubaidah.

'You know your grandaunty Nafsilah? Your grandfather's little sister? She's old now. Her children are all grown up. She's the only one who stays in Transito. No one cares for her. You guys are all the family she's got. So don't abandon her.'

The siblings just looked at each other. Wondering what they did to their grandaunty so that their father felt it was important to stress the fact that she's family.

'Just promise me.'

'OK father.'

***

The month was July 2013. Soon Transito would welcome guests. Ahmadiyya men aged 40 and up coming from all parts of West Nusa Tenggara, East Nusa Tenggara and Bali. There were getting together for Ijtima Anshar, a yearly gathering of Ahmadiyya elders for three days of religious discussions and games and sports. 2013 was Transito's turn to host the event.

For some reason, Nasipudin thought Transito was not yet fitting for the gathering. He felt that it was not clean enough. So he bought new carpets for the praying room to make sure his guests were nice and comfortable. He took out the damp, old carpet and dried it in the sun. He asked no favor from others. This was something he must do on his own he thought. Nurul saw this and went out to help her father dusting off the old carpet. She helped him dragged the carpet to Transito's front yard and hung it over the complex's main metal fence.

She thought her father was done with cleaning but he was just getting started, cleaning the bathrooms inside and out. He scrubbed the tile floor and toilet bowl and water containing tub. He swept the hallways and porches. He swept the motorway and the front yard.

He felt that the prayer room needed more sandals so people can take wudlu (cleaning oneself before praying) in the bathroom. He found mismatching sandals in the market and brought it home. He found broken pairs and fixed them.

Transito had never been cleaner. The complex was ready for the guests who would arrive the following day. Nasipudin's family couldn't help but wonder why he spent all day doing this. Particularly without asking anybody's help. Cleaning Transito's every corner from morning until late in the afternoon.

Nasipudin didn't have answers for these questions. He felt like it was something he had to do to welcome old friends from faraway. He wanted to make some contribution to the event, some contribution to the congregation. In the only way he can.

***

The guests arrived and Nasipudin welcomed them each with a hug and a kiss like that to an old friend. He was warmer than usual. Holding his friends in the upper arm and hugging them in the shoulder.

The event started and Nasipudin must have felt something very familiar, a feeling he had years ago. It was probably like dejavu. It must have been like reliving an old memory. He was taken back to a time of peace and joy. And then it hit him. He had been in this situation before. Eleven years ago to be exact. He went through the same event with the same exact faces.

The only two exceptions were that this one was held in Transito instead of Pancor. The second was that his father was not there for he passed away on the last day of Ijtima Anshar eleven years ago.

This familiar feeling must have disturbed him throughout the first two days. He would probably thought about his father more and more. This time the memory of his father was likely to be so vivid he could swear his father was there somewhere amongst the crowd.

He questioned what was left for him in this world. He had a wonderful life. He had a wonderful wife. They had wonderful children together. He did what he thought he needed to do. He felt like his duty was over. Like a soldier who had finished his tour of duty and was about to be called back to his homeland. It felt like his whole life drawing to a close. The end of his long journey. Like his time here on Earth was over.

'Do you remember your grandfather? Do you remember he died during an Ijtima Anshar like this one.' Nasipudin told each family member he ran into that day.

'Yes father I remember. What's wrong?' they each told him.

'No… I'm just asking if you remember.'

Suhaidi had also come to Transito for the event, traveling all the way from Bayan where he worked tending someone's field. He was not an elder but he wanted to catch up with some friends. The Ahmadis from Bali who used to accompany him going from one consulate to the next back in Denpasar. The Ahmadis from East Nusa Tenggara which he met during his time training for his failed attempt to reach Australia.

Nasipudin's mood changed at the sight of Suhaidi. He was disappointed that he went straight to meet his friends instead of saying hello to his wife and daughters. Nasipudin could only close his eyes. He felt his time was over and he could no longer tell Suhaidi what to do.

There was a loud roar. People were clapping jubilantly. The next morning they would all spend the final day of Ijtima Anshar at one of Lombok's famous beaches. They chose one beach in particular, Krandangan III just north of Mataram.

CHAPTER 35

Three cars had gathered in front of Transito that morning, ready to transport the elders to Krandangan III beach. As his friends boarded the cars, Nasipudin went in search for his sons.

'Are you going?' he told Khaerudin.

'Dad, I'm not feeling too well. I'm planning to go to Java tomorrow so I think I'll stay and rest for the rest of the day.'

Nasipudin met Suhaidi and asked him the same question.

'Are you coming with us to the beach? There's some spot left in one of the cars.'

'I don't know. I have to meet my boss later this morning. Maybe later I'll join you.'

'Good… good…'

'I'll call you, OK? I just have to meet my boss real quick.'

The last offer went to Safir.

'Are you coming with us to the beach? Your friends are going.'

'Yes dad. I'll join you.'

'There's still room in that car.'

'I'll meet you there dad. Don't worry.'

'Well… then…How will you get there?'

'I'm borrowing a friend's motorbike. I'll see you there.'

'Well OK. Now you be careful.'

Safir wanted to spend some time with Fitri. He also wanted to spend time with his father and friends. So he thought he could go with Fitri to the same area and then join the group briefly, carefully hiding Fitri's presence from the Ahmadi elders and his father.

He called Fitri asking her to pick him up at 'the usual place' just a short walk from Transito. He didn't want his mother to see he was with a girl. Fitri asked where they were going. 'To the beach,' he replied. Without asking many questions she was on her way to meet her boyfriend. She needed to be away from her iron fisted aunty. She just wanted to be with Safir.

Throughout the ride Fitri must have hugged Safir tight, pressing her body to his back, resting her helmet on his shoulder. She wanted to hold Safir and never let go.

They settled for a spot on the top of a hill, overlooking a steep cliff and sharp rocks below. The sea was crashing down on the rocks sending huge splashes. There were two couples sitting at the edge of the cliff, holding hands while watching the Bali Sea. Bali's mountainous terrain appeared as a faint silhouette. He could see a group of people on the beach below. They must have been the Ahmadis. He couldn't see their faces but he recognized some of the bright colorful T-shirts his friends were wearing.

Safir and Fitri sat shaded under a huge tree. They must have locked hands. Fitri would probably rest her head on Safir's shoulder.

'Do you love me?' Fitri said.

'Of course I do.'

'Then let's marry. Let's be together. We'll run away. No more all this silly religious stuff about you being an Ahmadi and I'm being a non-Ahmadi. It's silly don't you think?'

'Oh yeah. I agree with you.'

'It's ridiculous right? I mean the other day I asked my aunty what she thinks about Ahmadiyya. And she was like... oh they are bad people and they will go to hell and they don't practice Islam the right way and all that. I mean... who gets to decide? You don't decide who goes to heaven and who doesn't.'

'Do you think I'm all what your aunty says I am?'

'I think you're sweet. How about yours? What will your family think about me?'

Safir smiled. 'They'd probably be furious I'm dating a non-Ahmadiyya.'

'You see that's crazy right? You can't chose who you love.'

Safir smiled again.

'Let's marry. Let's run away from our family. Let's just be together. Forget about Ahmadiyya or non-Ahmadiyya and all these nonsense,' Fitri said.

'Marry? I can't even keep my vocational school diploma because I still owe the school money.'

***

Safir saw the two couples at the edge of the cliff standing up. They were screaming and pointing to a speck on the water. 'Help… help…'

Safir instinctively got up and walked towards them to know what had happened and get a closer look. There was hardly any other person on the beach. He thought if someone was to be drowning it was likely some Ahmadi he knew.

'What happened?' he asked the screaming couples.

'Someone got swept by the undercurrent. I think he's drowning.'

Safir saw the man but couldn't make out who he was. The beach was notorious for having strong currents and dozens have died. He could see the man was heading towards the rocks. There were boats which tried to reach him but didn't dare to come closer and risk being slammed into the rocks by the pounding waves.

He immediately ran along the edge of the cliff so he could climb down to the beach below, leaving Fitri behind all on her own. Safir was in fact ignored her altogether. He was dying to know who the man was, he had completely forgotten that she was even there.

Safir descended, carefully scaling down the rocks to get to the beach. He ran with all his might across the beach towards some familiar faces. Teenagers his age from Transito. But as he got close, his cousins and friends grabbed his shirt and pushed his chest and telling him to stop.

'What are you doing?' Safir asked. He was puzzled by his friends' reaction. 'Let go of me. Who is that in the water? Someone we know?'

'Don't tell him,' one of his friends told the others.

'Tell me what? Who is that? Tell me!'

'It's your father.'

Safir went hysterical and immediately pushed the hands that grabbed him and ran away from his friend. He headed towards the water, instinctively trying to save his father. Seven friends chased him down but Safir outrun them all. It was when he hit the water, the pounding waves slowed him down, did his friends managed to catch up with him.

Safir cried, his face covered in tears. He could see his father's hands as if waving goodbye. He yelled out 'dad.' Seconds later his father's hands were visible no more. Nasipudin was but a spot in the water floating adrift by the waves. His friends kept saying that it was dangerous for Safir to go after his father. Had he continued they would burry two people that day.

They kept telling him to be patient. Safir heard but didn't listen. His eyes fixated on the few boats trying to reach his father. Nasipudin seemed lifeless. A small portion of his father's back was all that seemed to be floating above the water's surface. His hair was waving in the water washed by the movements of the sea. One of the elders tried to soothe him and asked him to step away from the shoreline.

'Until my father is found, I'm not moving an inch. I'll stay until dawn if I have to.' Safir replied.

Eventually a surfer managed to reach Nasipudin. Nasipudin was dead when the surfer retrieved him from the sea.

Safir couldn't believe his father had drowned. He regretted not spending more time with him. He regretted not joining him this morning. He regretted he was more interested in spending time with his girlfriend Fitri. He realized that his family was more important to him than Fitri. The whole time he realized his father was drowning not once did he check on his girlfriend. Fitri could see that she meant nothing to Safir compared to his father. She watched Safir from the distance, watched him went hysterical for such a tragic lost. She went home without saying goodbye.

The elders hauled Nasipudin's body into one of the minivans transporting the group to the beach. They rushed to the nearest hospital. Nasipudin's body was cold and had turned blue. They all could swear that he was smiling. As if he was happy to finally meeting his maker.

***

Words spread about Nasipudin's untimely death. Zubaidah was at the market and abruptly told by a close friend that she must head back to Transito. 'There's been an accident,' the friend told Zubaidah. She was lost for words. Confused.

Khaerudin immediately went to the beach to discover that everyone had left for the hospital. Faizah was in so much shock to hear the news she fainted. Nurul was stronger but was so overwhelmed she was unable to do anything. Kasafuloh locked himself in his room.

They tried repeatedly to call Suhaidi but he didn't answer. His boss had asked him to take his car to Bayan. Suhaidi saw a speeding car which nearly hit him. It was later that he realized that the car was hauling his father's lifeless body. As if Nasipudin wanted to say goodbye to Suhaidi one last time.

***

Masitah was in Kalimantan. She couldn't believe that her father had died she repeatedly asked if the news bearer was sure that it was her father that drowned. 'Are you sure it was my father Nasipudin? It can't be... It must be someone else.' Her legs buckled and she collapsed to the floor. Wishing badly that she had enough money for the plane ride home.

Malik also didn't answer his phone. He was in his class studying hard to become a cleric. Everyone tried calling another future cleric from Lombok who was also studying at the Ahmadiyya campus. Malik learned of his father's death from a friend.

***

Zubaidah was even more confused when she got to Transito. She saw Faizah fainted and thought that something bad must have happened to her.

'Has she been poisoned or something?' Zubaidah asked as she tended her unconscious daughter.

But her people told her that Faizah was not why they asked Zubaidah to head back to Transito. Her husband had drowned. Faizah fainted from hearing the news. Like a woman disoriented, Zubaidah got even more confused. She couldn't picture her farmer husband drowning at sea.

'Drowned? In Mataram?'

'No at sea. They were on the beach.'

Zubaidah shook her head. She just wouldn't believe any word. Wouldn't believe that her husband was dead.

***

Word spread from one friend to the next, one family member to another. It reached Nasipudin's friends at the market. It reached his extended family in Pancor's Montong Gamang. His wife's family in Sawing and Montong Golong. It reached old friends at Pancor's market. It reached his former neighbors in Ketapang. It reached the leaders' ears in Sweta. The kind, honest and hardworking Nasipudin was dead.

There must have been two hundred motorcycles parked at Transito and dozens of cars some hailing from faraway East Lombok. Everyone wanted to see Nasipudin one last time before he was buried. The hallways were full of people, Ahmadis and non-Ahmadis, chanting prayers for his safe passage into the afterlife.

There were people that once tried to torch his home in Pancor. There were people who were once less welcoming when he tried to rebuild his life at Mataram's market. There were people from Ketapang who didn't stand up against the attackers and protected the Ahmadis' homes from getting ransacked.

There were Ijtima Anshar participants who met Khaerudin and Suhaidi when they traveled from one foreign consulate to the next applying for asylum. There were elders from Kupang where Suhaidi tried to embark on a failed attempt to reach Australia.

The old man Mahmuludin told the guests how he was the one who saw Nasipudin last. They were burying themselves in the sands as a cure for rheumatism. Nasipudin told him that 'this must be what it's like to be buried.' Minutes later he felt like washing himself in the water. Getting rid of the sands covering his body, like they were earthly filth he wanted to leave behind before his journey to the afterlife.

Parmono said he was sitting next to Nasipudin throughout the journey to the beach. He remembered Nasipudin saying he was worried about Suhaidi and his daughter Yuni. 'Will you care for Yuni? Will you see to it that she goes to college? Will you keep reminding Suhaidi to be good?'

Nasipudin's body came to Transito with an ambulance. Here Ahmadis and non-Ahmadis got together and paid their last respect to Nasipudin before he would be buried at Karang Medana cemetery. They shared stories of this amazing person named Nasipudin. How kind he was. How hardworking. How honest. How loving.

***

It was the first Ramadan the family had to celebrate without Nasipudin. But somehow his presence was felt. With the mismatching sandals their father had found they cleansed themselves before praying. The carpet their father had bought they prayed together.

Khaerudin was wearing their father's old batik shirt. They were about the same height. They shared the same face. Khaerudin must have looked like the ghost of a younger Nasipudin sending Zubaidah into a hysterical cry.

The family all chipped in to buy 30 copies of the Koran. One of their father's final wishes was to rekindle old ties. To spread the message of good by donating copies of the Koran to every mosque in their old neighborhood Montong Gamang. Whatever the creed. Whatever the sect.

Their father's gesture inspired Faizah to go back to Pancor. A place she hadn't set foot in a long time. A place where she once thought was too painful to revisit. She promised herself to go to the houses of everyone she once knew. The Marwans. Her uncle Sarapudin. Her aunty Ramlah. Her childhood friends.

***

For Zubaidah, sleeping alone in her room with no husband by her side was too painful. She covered her face with a tubular sarong and sobbed. Reliving the memories of their past. The first time Nasipudin laid eyes on her. The first time his uncle came to her family's house asking for her hands in marriage. Their first house in Montong Gamang. Their nine children. She was silently crying, silently calling out to her late husband, silently screaming how much she missed him and how she thought she couldn't go on without him.

Then she felt a warm touch on her shoulder. It was her crippled daughter Nisa slowly moving her fragile arm. It felt like her late husband Nasipudin telling her that she must go on with her life for her children's sake.

***

Nurul had many recurring dreams since her father's passing. She dreamt of a very big house painted in glossy white. The house was perched on the top of a grassy hill surrounded with colorful flowers and small creeks running to a clear blue pond. The house cast a bright white glow. It was massive. Bigger than any house she had ever seen her entire life. It surpassed even the marble-clad homes of the rich she saw in Jakarta. 'This must be heaven,' she thought.

From inside the house, exited a man in white garb. His presence created a warm feeling all around her. Like that of a loving embrace in time of sorrow. She was drawn closer to the man and details began to emerge. It was her father. Much younger than she last saw him in real life.

He didn't say a word just gazing at Nurul with a smile. She could feel his love. She could feel that he was the owner of the big house. How she wished she could stay. How she wished she could be by her father's side for a little longer. But it was not her time.

Nasipudin was in heaven, living in a home he built with every prayers, patience, deed and love.

The home that he would spend all eternity in.

The one true home that had always been his own.

THE END

ACKNOWLEDGEMENTS

This book would not have been possible without those who have from time to time opened their doors and minds for discussions, often for hours and days, and as a result inspired, compelled and pushed me to move forward and exceed my own expectations.

To Philip Jacobson and Daniel Powell, who introduced me to the book "New New Journalism", which really opened my eyes to areas of journalism that I thought never existed. That gesture, insignificant maybe to both of you, ignited a passion inside me that I thought long lost and motivated me to really start writing my first book.

To Okky Madasari, an author and former fellow reporter whom I really respect. Thank you for the discussions and for believing in me. My thanks also go to Andreas Harsono, Bonar Tigor Naipospos, Taufik Basari and Usman Hamid for helping me realize that I should tell the story of the persecuted. Huge thanks also go to Chika Noya, one of the first people to become excited about the project even before there was a project.

To my colleague and smoking buddy Katrin Figge, thank you for providing me with the impetus to finally plunge myself into this project. Thank you also for being a constant discussion partner. You really provided me with the courage and strength to keep going.

To the people of Transito. I can't thank you enough for opening your doors and welcoming me into your lives. Thank you for sharing with me your most intimate thoughts, hopes and fears. For patiently taking the time and helping me complete this book. For taking a leap of faith and allowing me to write the things closest to your heart. Particularly Pak Sayidin for letting me stay at an unused room, making me breakfast, lunch and dinner. Pak Sulaeman for staying up late just so we could share stories and some good laughs. To Khaerudin, thank you for taking me to East Lombok and showing me the places that shaped your family's past and present. To Suhaidi, for your boldness and kindness. All of you are true inspirations.

Thank you to Imam Shofwan and the people at Pantau Foundation for helping me with the research for this book. Also to Fitri Rachmawati and her husband Latief, for being such wonderful hosts in Lombok. And most of all for being such brilliant, courageous and uncompromising journalists. To Hayat Indriyatno for lending me a fresh pair of eyes.

To my father and my mother, thank you for being among the first people to recognize that I had a story worth retelling. Your nod of approval means so much to me.

But my biggest thanks go to my wife, Wiwiek Astuti. For trusting in me even when I didn't trust myself. For believing in me when no one else would. Thank you for your patience and sacrifices. For understanding that I must do this project. For reminding me that I must eat, sleep and rest as I typed on our old computer at the living room sofa.. Most of all, thank you for your undying love.

www.ingramcontent.com/pod-product-compliance
Lightning Source LLC
Chambersburg PA
CBHW070633290526
45790CB00001B/82